chocolate *passion*

chocolate*passion*

Recipes and Inspiration from the Kitchens of *Chocolatier* Magazine

Tish Boyle and Timothy Moriarty

Photography by John Uher

Food Styling by Liz Duffy

JOHN WILEY & SONS, INC.

New York • Chichester • Weinheim • Brisbane • Singapore • Toronto

Illustration on page 6 (pot of foaming chocolate placed before Mayan King)
© Justin Kerr
Illustration on page 10 (man and woman in seventeenth-century France drinking chocolate, a social affair) © Collection Viollet
Photos on pages 35, 37, and 39, products courtesy of J. B. Prince Co., New York

This book is printed on acid-free paper.

Boyle, Tish.
    Chocolate passion/by Tish Boyle and Timothy Moriarty: photography by John Uher.
        p. cm.
        Includes bibliographical references and index.
        ISBN 0-471-29317-2 (cloth: alk. paper)
        1. Cookery (Chocolate). 2. Desserts. I. Moriarty, Timothy, 1951– II. Title.
TX767.C5B68   1999
641.6'374—dc21   98-41505

Printed in the United States of America.

10 9 8 7 6 5 4 3 2 1

Acknowledgments

"You have the greatest job in the world!" some people have told me over the years. Yes, I do taste gourmet chocolates and desserts for a living, but I'm even more fortunate than that. Many fine people helped propel this project along and aided in the preparation of the manuscript. Michael Schneider, editor-in-chief and publisher of *Chocolatier* and *Pastry Art & Design,* supervised the shoots and watched the deadline. Liz Duffy did a superb job styling the food. Mark Kammerer is the straw that stirs the drink. Michelle Edwards is the cream in our coffee. Mary Goodbody and Janice Henderson are generous with their support. Lisa Lahey was the heart of the equipment section. Tracey Ceurvels helped assemble the equipment source and chocolate company lists. Stephanie Banyas is our good luck charm, with charm to spare. Judy Prince, of J. B. Prince in New York, was gracious, as always, in supplying equipment. Pam, Andrea, and Stacey at John Wiley & Sons, Inc., managed to be both delightful and professional. The Chocolate Manufacturers Association was forthcoming with statistics. The Walnut Board provided product. Kate Jackson supplied some invaluable research. Geri, Ryan, and Evan put up with me; free chocolate hardly compensates.

T M

My thanks to the talented culinary professionals (and good friends) who developed recipes for this book: Melissa Clark, Carole Harlam, Mary Schaaf Mulard, Tracey Seaman, Trish Shoemaker, Nicole Rees Smith, Lisa Yockelson, and Adrienne Welch. Thanks also to Liz Duffy, whose impeccable food styling always exceeds my expectations and whose patience and good humor always amaze me. To John Uher, dessert photographer extraordinaire, who takes a good-looking piece of cake and turns it into poetry. To our editor, Pam Chirls, for her guidance, support, and flexibility. To Judy Prince, Rennis Garner, and Fran Shinagel at J. B. Prince for their expert advice on equipment. And finally, to my adorable husband, Dick, who doesn't even like chocolate all that much, for eating lots of stuff and giving me his opinion whenever I asked.

T B

We would like to offer special thanks to Adrienne Welch, the former food editor of *Chocolatier* magazine. An outstanding chocolatier in her own right, Adrienne developed much of the melting and tempering information in this book, and offered invaluable assistance with the manuscript. She is also responsible for creating most of the candy recipes in this book.

T M & T B

Contents

A PASSION FOR Chocolate

Once upon a time a prince went to battle, to defend the borders of his father's kingdom against a hostile tribe. His wife, the princess, was left to guard the kingdom's vast treasure. The invaders were fierce—they defeated the prince's army and advanced on the capital city. Alarmed, the princess hid the treasure. The barbarians took the city, captured the princess, and ransacked the royal keep, seeking the treasure. Not finding it, they tortured the princess. Despite her prolonged suffering, she did not reveal the treasure's hiding place. Enraged, the barbarians killed her. But from her blood sprouted the cacao plant, and ever since that time people have known that there is treasure hidden in its seeds, as rich and strong as love itself, but as bitter as love torn asunder.

*T*his is one of the Aztec legends concerning the origin of the cacao tree. The more common legend, the story that predates the apex of the Aztec culture, involves the man-god Quetzalcoatl, who was led into paradise, the realm of the sun god. On his return to the world of men, Quetzalcoatl brought cacao seeds with him.

Both of these legends speak to the reverence that the peoples of Central and South America hold for cacao. They call it "the food of the gods." What else but chocolate could live up to the name?

Chocolate is the world's favorite flavor. There is a mystery, excitement, and wickedness associated with chocolate you'll find in no other food. Chocolate desire is expressed with a sense of mischief; more than sneaking a few potato chips or a second order of nachos, indulgence in chocolate—indeed, the very mention of the word chocolate—evokes wanton giggles and stabs of guilt. Chocolate passion is akin to its sexual counterpart in so many ways. Consider the gleam in a person's eye when the subject of chocolate is raised, the anticipation when it is near, the rapture when it is enjoyed.

For the past 15 years, we at *Chocolatier* magazine have experienced America's passion for chocolate firsthand. We've seen a steady growth in Americans' chocolate consumption, as well as an increase in the quality of chocolate and the sophistication of consumers. Americans have begun to appreciate the simple, unadorned chocolates fashioned by hands-on craftsmen: truffles or pralines—delicate, balanced confections that melt perfectly and impart a quiet silken wave of chocolate flavor. They are willing to pay a little more for quality. They can appreciate the subtle, European-style filled chocolates, and are developing a taste for dark chocolate. But Americans will never lose their love for chocolate bars studded with nuts, peanut butter, caramel, nougat, or coconut.

At our restaurants and hotels, pastry chefs fashion chocolate desserts into towers, stoves, pianos, cones, and pyramids. And that's

Crunching the Numbers

- •→• The average American consumes 12.1 pounds of chocolate per year. Americans have, on average, increased their chocolate consumption by 2 pounds over a 13-year span.

- •→• 3.1 billion pounds of chocolate are purchased per year in the United States.

- •→• The manufacturer value of that 3.1 billion pounds of chocolate is $7.6 billion.

- •→• $11.7 billion is spent by Americans on chocolate products every year. Approximately $600 million of that amount is spent in February, for Valentine's Day.

- •→• The percentage of Americans who expressed a preference for milk over dark and white chocolates: 73%.

- •→• The people of Switzerland consume more chocolate than the citizens of any other country in the world: 20.7 pounds per person per year. Switzerland is followed by Austria (19.6 pounds), Germany (18.6), Belgium/Luxembourg (18.4), Norway (17.4), United Kingdom (16.8), Denmark (16.0), United States (12.1), Sweden (11.2), Ireland (11.0), France (10), Netherlands (9.6), Finland (7.2), Italy (5.4), and Spain (3.3).

Sources: U.S. Department of Commerce (1996, 1997), CAOBISCO Secretariat, Brussels (1997), and Chocolate Manufacturers Association of America.

just the beginning. People want their chocolate in the form of an Easter egg or bunny, a Santa, a pumpkin or a valentine, a lion, a tiger or a bear, a car, truck or plane, a baseball, golf ball or puck, a champagne bottle or hatbox (filled with truffles), a chocolate videotape, a company plaque or business card, a chocolate photo (see yourself in chocolate!), a flower, leaf or rock, or a body part molded in chocolate—and we do mean any body part. Chocolate is formed into regional maps, state parks, and mountain ranges. Chocolate pizza features drizzles of white chocolate to represent the mozzarella. Chocolate serves as the canvas for re-creations of Monet paintings in edible paint. Chocolate enrobes potato chips, pretzels, and insects. It is combined with liqueurs, fruits, and jalapeño peppers. Adventurous chefs create all-chocolate meals featuring chocolate pasta, shrimp swimming in a chocolate sauce, and, of course, chicken in a mole sauce. We have known people who take a bite of every piece in a variety box and leave the bitten pieces for the next person, without apology. Some people who claim to eat a pound every day say that it is the secret of their health and longevity. We have seen women with their bodies entirely dipped in chocolate (not as pretty a sight as you would imagine). We have sampled chocolate body paint and its rival product, chocolate body frosting. Chocolate inspires toys: we've seen a Choco-holic Relief Spray, a Chocolate Deprivation Survival Kit, and a chocolate "patch" to help relieve chocoholics of their craving. The intoxicating scent of chocolate is the basis for a chocolate body wash and cocoa-scented soaps. We've sampled chocolate cologne. Chocolate beer. Just when we think we've seen it all, someone devises another chocolate something. And we are kids again.

Why does chocolate arouse such passion? Like any passion, there are reasons, but no final answers. Like any passion, it is best not to analyze it too much, or the mystery is ruined. Here are some obvious reasons why chocolate is the world's favorite treat.

THE MOUTHFEEL   Cocoa butter, the fat in chocolate, melts at almost exact body temperature. Other foods melt, of course, but there is that moment in chocolate in which it is neither solid nor liquid, both and neither. All the while it is sending sparks of that flavor, vibrating deliriously from the mouth to the extremities. Or as a scientist would explain, heat is absorbed from the lining of the mouth, which creates a most pleasurable sensation.

PLEASANT MEMORIES   We associate chocolate with comfort, good times, and special occasions of childhood. When we enjoy chocolate, we evoke these memories.

CRAVINGS   Food chemists point to chocolate's combination of fat, sweet and carbohydrate ingredients; the survival mechanisms in our brain are naturally attracted to this cocktail. Some have theorized that chocolate releases opiates in the brain; cravings may be linked to this desire on the part of the brain for chemicals such as serotonin.

PRIMAL INSTINCT   Giving sweets to loved ones is primal behavior—primates really do it. While a taste for hot and bitter foods is acquired, we were all born with a love of sweets.

FLAVOR   The primary reason we love chocolate is for its rich flavor, mouthfeel, and aroma all working as one.

Composition of Chocolate

Chocolate is a complex food, and this may account, at least in part, for its marvelous flavor. So far, scientists have identified some 400 compounds in the cacao bean, twice as many as the closest other food. They think there may be as many as 1200.

Over half of a chocolate nib (the shelled bean) is fat. Ten percent is protein and starch. The rest is composed of these 400 (and counting) biochemical and pharmacological components. They include polyphenols, which are flavonoids; amino acids, which contribute bitter and sweet tastes; organic and phenolic acids, whose influence on flavor is unknown; carbohydrates, including glucose, fructose, and sucrose; pectins, cellulose, crude fiber, mucilage, and gums; and ash, tannins, and magnesium. There is serotonin, a mood-enhancing hormone also found in the brain, and phenylethylamine. There are the alkaloids: tyramine, caffeine, and theobromine, which are stimulants.

To date, chemists have not been able to understand the nature of chocolate flavor, which is the sum of hundreds of these substances. There have been attempts to manufacture a synthetic chocolate, based on the known compounds. They have failed, and many tests with human subjects to satisfy cravings with similar foods or components of chocolate in combination also fail. The international craving for chocolate appears to be more than can be explained by brain chemistry, sensory pleasure, or childhood memory.

A History of Chocolate

Chocolate passion may not be hardwired into the human brain, but men and women *have* enjoyed it in one form or another for thousands of years.

The genus *Theobrama* dates back millions of years. It evolved, for the most part, on the eastern slopes of the Andes in South America. There are some 22 species of *Theobrama*. The species *Theobrama cacao*—the only species that produces beans that will create chocolate—probably first appeared ten to fifteen thousand years ago. This is roughly the same time that the human species began to populate that region of the world.

In that primeval jungle, under the canopy of trees, in the oppressive heat and humidity, cacao beans waited. They sat in a milky pulp, enclosed in a pod, on a slender tree. The first to discover the beans were animals—monkeys, squirrels, rats, and bats probably chewed on the pods to get to the pulp, or they would wait for the pods to burst and then feed. At first, the primitive mountain people mimicked the animals and fed on the pulp. They ignored the seeds, which were bitter. These discarded seeds then had a chance to sprout into new cacao trees.

At some point, these cultures discovered that the beans tasted interesting, or at least different, if they fell on the ground and were exposed to the sun—if they fermented, in other words. Once washed, they would have been ready to be pulverized, perhaps by members of the next generation. Roasting? Primitive peoples were always throwing things in fire, and quickly learned its alchemical properties.

The cacao that first appeared in the northern and western portions of the Upper Amazon Basin is the antecedent to the form forastero. The type that eventually came to be known as criollo originated in pre-Conquest Mesoamerica (the highly cultured areas of southern Mexico, Belize, Guatemala, and corners of El Salvador and Honduras).

THE DEMISE OF QUETZALCOATL

We know some specifics of the cultures that first domesticated cacao. The civilization of the Olmecs flourished in the rich lands of the Mexican Gulf coast, peaking around 1500 B.C. and beginning to dwindle about 400 B.C. It is believed that a word similar to cacao was in their vocabulary.

The Mayan civilization reached its apex around 250 A.D. The Mayans established the first known cacao plantations. Legends point to King Hunahpu, the third Mayan king, as the one who encouraged this cultivation. It is through Mayan writings that the word cacao (*u kakaw*) first appears. Archeologists have unearthed elaborate and substantial pots, tools, and other containers that clearly indicate chocolate use, and its importance in their culture. Between 800 and 900 A.D., in what historians call the Collapse, the Mayans suddenly abandoned their magnificent cities. Possible reasons are the decay of their environment due to humidity and heat, the aggressive growth of surrounding jungles, and overpopulation.

The Toltecs moved into the territory abandoned by the Mayans. The culture of the Toltecs thrived between the decline of the Mayans and the true ascent of the Aztecs. They also knew of cacao beans; they called them "sun beans."

It is from this powerful, cultured people that the myth of the man-god Quetzalcoatl springs.

Chocolate by Any Other Name . . .

*W*here do the words "cacao" and "chocolate" come from?

Though there is no written record, historical linguists have traced a word roughly pronounced "kakawa" back to the Olmecs (1500 B.C.). The word was passed down to the Mayans; the word "ka-ka-w" first appears in their writings (250 A.D.), and it was probably their word for the tree and the beans.

The Mayans also formed a word for the substance extracted from the bean and the beverages made from it: xocolatl. This word is most probably a combination of the native words xoco (bitter) and otl (water). But easily the most appealing theory for the origin of the word comes from Thomas Gage, in a 1648 essay entitled "New Survey of the West

Indies." Gage expresses the belief that the word is a combination of the Indian words atta (water) and choco, from the sound made when cacao paste and water are stirred with a molinet: choco, choco, choco.

The Aztecs (1400 A.D.) inherited both the word for the tree (cacahuatl) and the word for chocolate (xocolatl) from the Mayans. Europeans adapted the pronunciation and spelling of the word, to give us chocolate.

Today, we use the word cacao (ka-KOW) to refer to the tree, the pods, and the unfermented beans. Once the beans have fermented, they are referred to as cocoa beans. And cocoa, is, of course, the word we use for the powder used for drinking, food manufacture, and dessert-making.

Over the centuries, the story of this simple man and his exile was passed from the Toltecs, to become a part of Aztec mythology. It is a unique example in history, many historians feel, in which myth and reality collide—a circumstance that perhaps accounts for the Aztecs' maddening passivity and generosity toward the plundering Spanish some 600 years later.

Quetzalcoatl was the political leader of the Toltec nation in the tenth century; though he was a wise and popular leader, plots from within his palace forced Quetzalcoatl to flee his capital in northern Mexico. He finally settled in a small town, Tollan, in what is now the Yucatán. It is here that legend replaces history: there are stories of a lavish treasure stored in Tollan—gold, silver, gems, and cacao trees of many colors. But three evil sorcerers trick Quetzalcoatl into drinking a beverage that drives him insane. Setting sail on a raft of snakes Quetzalcoatl is disguised, or transformed, into a serpent god. As a hint of the treasures to come, Quetzalcoatl gives mankind cacao. He promises to return, and he is specific: According to the Aztec calendar, he will return in a year falling under the sign of *Ce-acatl* ("one reed") to the same place (the eastern coast of Mexico), bringing with him an entire palace bulging with a treasure of the gods.

AZTEC NATION

The ascent of the migrating Aztecs coincided with the decline of the Toltec culture. The two warred in 1325, and the conquering Aztecs settled in the Valley of Mexico. They set about vanquishing neighboring city-states. By 1375, they had a king, an army, a government, and a culture in place. They

established as their capital Tenochtitlán, and constructed dazzling, imposing palaces, public buildings, temples and common areas. The Aztecs' was a sophisticated culture, with an estimated 10 to 11 million people, 200,000 of them living in the capital.

Although human sacrifice was a part of their culture, the scale and barbarity were probably exaggerated in accounts by the disapproving Europeans (particularly the priests), and these accounts have been passed down and reinforced through the ages.

Cacao was an important part of the economy and culture of these peoples, so how barbaric could they be? They believed that cacao conferred a sort of cosmic wisdom that would continue in the afterlife.

For the most part, the Aztecs and Mayans consumed their chocolate in liquid form. After fermentation, they dried the seeds in an earthen pot over a fire. Then they broke the seeds with stones and ground them into a "flour"; they transferred the flour to gourds and moistened it gradually with water, adding "long pepper" (chili) and perhaps maize and other spices as they went. Often they would beat the liquid or pour it from vessel to vessel; this was to give the drink a frothy, foamy crest, which was very highly prized. This procedure might have also allowed the fat to rise to the surface so that they could skim it off. Once it was sufficiently foamy, they drank it. This was the basic chocolate recipe of the Mesoamerican peoples and, to contemporary palates, it would have been a bitter drink indeed.

Both the Mayans and the Aztecs developed several additional "recipes" for chocolate. These recipes probably evolved as these cultures matured, and they would have been employed only to honor a personage of high status. These chocolate recipes included porridges, powders, possibly solids, and drinks that were flavored in a variety of ways and perhaps colored red or green. It is documented that Montezuma ordered retainers to obtain snow from mountaintops and pour it over his xocolatl, to make a sort of bitter chocolate snow cone.

The Aztecs were known to flavor their chocolate with chili peppers (a very pleasant burn to the drink), fruits, vanilla (which was native and familiar to them), honey, allspice, and pita juice. The drink was served either hot or cold, but in general the Aztecs preferred their chocolate drink cold, while the Mayans drank it hot.

Sometimes, perhaps for storage or transportation purposes, the chocolate paste, rather than being immersed immediately in water, was shaped into loaves (about the size of an adult fist) by wrapping it in leaves of maize and binding it with grass stalks. To make xocolatl, the loaves were unwrapped, grated, and melted in a lightly salted corn mush. Another way of treating the loaves was to heat the chocolate to the point at which the cocoa butter melted; it was then molded and cooled. In other words, the Aztecs were familiar with many of the basics of chocolate manufacture. It is thought that early Spanish missionaries to the New World in Mexico had a flourishing side business creating solid chocolate sweets and selling them.

Xocolatl was for the elite of Aztec society. It was preferred over the other exotic drink, *octli,* which was a sort of wine. Intoxication was frowned upon in their culture, so xocolatl gained prominence among the military, religious, and merchant classes. It was drunk primarily by the royals, lords and nobility, the elite warriors, and important merchants. The drink was customarily served from fine gourds at the end of a meal, with the smoking of tobacco. The only commoners who received it as a matter of course were soldiers on the march. Ordinary people did not drink it, except perhaps for those who lived near the cacao trees.

An historian of Cortés's time, Diaz del Castillo, makes reference to xocolatl's aphrodisiacal properties (a report that in no small part would account for its ready acceptance in Europe). It is not known whether the Aztecs prized it for that, but it was known as a stimulant and as a carrier of medicines.

The beans were also used as a form of currency. A rabbit cost ten beans, and the services of a courtesan could be purchased for twelve. One bean would buy you a tomato or a tamale. One hundred beans purchased a slave. Tribes conquered by the Aztecs had to pay tribute in beans. The Spanish were surprised to discover that the Aztecs prized the beans over gold.

The peoples of South America were cultivating cacao for some 1,000 years before the arrival of the Europeans. It was an important facet of their religious rituals and social fabric. But the Aztec culture, like its predecessors, was fated to decline.

IN THE TIME OF CORTÉS

In 1502, Christopher Columbus, on his fourth voyage to the New World, came to the island of Guanaja, 30 miles north of what is now Honduras. He and his men encountered natives piloting one of the distinctive, 25-man "canoes." Onboard, native nobles were resplendent in their elaborate, feathered headdresses. The boats were tied off, and there were trades offered. During the encounter, some cacao beans spilled and the natives gathered them up with great eagerness and care. The Europeans noted how closely the natives prized these "almonds" (according to an account by Columbus's son, Ferdinand); they traded for some. Columbus himself apparently never tasted chocolate. He was the first to bring cacao beans back to Europe (1504), which he offered as an example of New World currency.

In 1519, Hernán Cortés of Spain led a fleet of 11 vessels to the coast of Tabasco, west of the Yucatán peninsula. With him was an army of some 700 men, armored, carrying cannon and primitive firing weapons called harquebuses. They began to march inland; many contingents of Aztec nobles dispatched by Montezuma met them, among them Montezuma's brother, Atauchi. From the nature of the gifts offered him and the lavish dress of the nobles, Cortés correctly guessed the riches of this country and resolved to march to its capital, Tenochtitlán. He ordered his ships to be burned to prevent desertions and set off for the capital. There were some minor skirmishes with Aztecs along the way, but once he reached the capital, he was greeted warmly by Montezuma.

Montezuma declared to Cortés and his own people that the Spaniard was "home in his native country." Historians have often wondered why he offered this warm greeting to these aggressors. The answer may lie in the legend of Quetzalcoatl's return.

It so happened that 1519 was a *Ce-acatl* year, the year that legends indicated Quetzalcoatl would return. Emperor Montezuma received word of a house on the water (such unimaginably large ships must have impressed him as the serpent-god's promised palace). Further reports were that the people on it shone like treasure (armor) and had plumes like the serpent (plumed helmets). Not only did Montezuma bid Cortés welcome, but he is quoted by reliable historians as offering to return Quetzalcoatl's kingdom to him. This may be why the Aztecs offered no resistance when the Spanish plundered the Aztec palaces and treasure hordes without respite.

All was at Cortés's disposal; this included the fruits of a cacao plantation. Cortés immediately recognized the value the Aztecs placed on the bean; he and his nobles closely observed the cultivation of the plant and the making of the brew. Cortés sent ships laden with New World treasure in 1519 and again, in 1528. He sent novelties like bouncing rubber balls, jaguars, armadillos, actual Indian nobles, gold, and trinkets. It was on the second shipment that he sent cacao beans to Europe as an element of a recipe, which he also provided. "A cup of this precious beverage permits a man to walk an entire day without food," he wrote to the court.

King Charles V of Spain and his queen enjoyed the beverage, and members of the court felt obliged to also enjoy it, though privately they confessed they didn't like it much. History records that an adventurous duchess determined to improve its flavor. She added sugar, and soon this sweeter and smoother beverage soared in popularity at court. Nobles drank it from silver goblets, and ladies-in-waiting competed to see who could further improve the drink's flavor with more spices. Mace and cinnamon are among the spices tried, often in stomach-churning abundance. At times it was served hot.

CHOCOLATE CONQUERS THE WORLD

In 1585, the first official shipment of cacao beans from Veracruz arrived in Seville. The court entrusted the secret of chocolate-making to monks, who managed to keep the recipe secret for nearly a century. In the meantime, Aztec civilization collapsed; this was not due to its own corruption or the superiority (militarily, culturally) of the Europeans, but primarily through alliances of enemies in city-states all around, and through the epidemics of smallpox and measles that the Europeans brought with them.

The Spanish conquistadores settled in for a long stay among the Indians. They did not like the chocolate drink at first; in fact, they rejected all New World foods and crops. But it was offered so often by the Indians that the Europeans gradually began to accept it, particularly the Spanish women. The colonists learned to press the "flour" into the form of a tablet, which could easily be transported and immersed in water. They learned to separate the cocoa butter and use it as a cosmetic, mimicking the Aztec priests, who, on high ceremonies, smeared the chocolate paste on their faces. They occasionally served the chocolate drink hot; this was probably due to the surging popularity of coffee and tea, which was being imported from China and Arabia at the same time. The Spanish are credited with introducing the *molinillo,* a special jug for preparing chocolate. The dried paste or loaf was placed with hot water in a special jug; on the jug was a lid with a hole to accommodate a stick that was spun to beat the chocolate.

But most crucially, in the 1600s the colonists added sugar to the chocolate; so successful was this that the Spanish planted sugar cane in Mexico and what is now Haiti. In this way, chocolate use spread throughout the colonies of the West Indies. Drinking chocolate became an important morning custom; in time *chocolaterías*—appointed public places for the drinking of chocolate—came into being. The Spanish also experimented with flavorings, such as aniseed, cinnamon, almonds, and hazelnuts.

By the early 1600s, chocolate had become so popular among the colonial Spanish, particularly the women, that it sparked a religious controversy. In the village of Chiapa, where villagers were predominately Catholic, the women complained that they could not endure the kneeling and standing of an interminable high mass without some hot chocolate and sweet meats; chocolate was already perceived to have medicinal properties. The bishop, seeing servants rush in and out of church with chocolate

The Poisoner's Guide to Chocolate

"Beware the Chocolate of Chiapa." The unfortunate bishop of Mexican legend was not the first or last to (allegedly) experience death by chocolate. Because of its full flavor, rich texture, and the variety of spices that can be used in it, chocolate has historically been a favorite disguiser of poisons.

In Italy in the eighteenth century, chocolate was the favorite carrier of poisons among the clergy. It was rumored to be the vessel by which Pope Clement XIV was poisoned in 1774, and it was very popular in the 1600s Spanish court of the Hapsburgs for the same reason. It is recorded that Mme D'Aulnoy, a Spanish lady, got revenge on a lover who had spurned her by poisoning his cup of chocolate. When the poison began to take effect, and the man realized he was doomed, it is said that he took the time to advise Madame that next time she might add more sugar to eliminate the bitterness of the poison. With that gallant gesture, he died.

for their ladies during services, forbade them to do so. The women defied him. The bishop called in soldiers to enforce his rule, but townsfolk armed themselves as well, and eventually the bishop relented. But shortly after the incident, he died, and it was rumored he was poisoned by the chocolate-drinking women. (It sparked a phrase that resonates to this day: "Beware the chocolate of Chiapa.")

The story, though true, is deceptive: the members of the clergy were never against chocolate, as they were against tobacco, which was newly discovered and distributed at that time. The bishop of the story, in fact, loved chocolate, which is the reason it is suspected as the vessel of his doom. He simply didn't want it at services.

The story points to the reason that monks, nuns, and priests of the time loved chocolate: it helped fortify them through fasts. This chocolate devotion led to a widespread debate about whether chocolate was a food or not. Most held that it was not, that it was more of a medicine, and that to use it during a fast was acceptable. The controversy would last for more than two centuries. The issue was clouded by the fact that some religious orders were actively involved in the cacao trade.

The Spanish brought the beans to Trinidad, and tried to keep the cultivation procedure a secret because the sweetened drink was gaining popularity in Europe. They kept the secret for 100 years, but eventually the beans were cultivated across the West Indies, the Philippines, South America, and Africa. For the greater part of the seventeenth century, Madrid had been the center of the chocolate world. All cacao flowed from Spain and its colonies. The decline of Spain as a world power coincided with this escape of the secret of chocolate.

Chocolate followed the conventional trade routes of the time. From Spain, it was first known in Portugal. It may have reached Italy as early as 1606, when it was imported by an Italian merchant who had enjoyed it in Spain. It was an instant hit and spread quickly throughout the country, partially because it was a time of ferocious warfare of city-states, and there was busy traffic from court to court. Italian *cioccolatieri* were soon exporting their product to other countries.

The French referred to Spain in a contemptuous manner as "the country without forks," but the French embraced this product of Spain as quickly as other countries. In 1660, Infanta María Teresa of Spain married Louis XIV, King of France. The Infanta's personal maid was

Un Caualier, Et vne Dame beuuant du Chocolat

nicknamed La Molina; it was a critical part of her job to prepare chocolate for her mistress. Historians record that the queen drank six or seven cups of chocolate a day. Within ten years chocolate was popular at Versailles and among aristocrats and the intelligentsia. Marie Antoinette, doomed wife of Louis XVI, employed her own personal chocolatier, who made her preferred mix of chocolate with orange flower water and orchid powder.

The drink soon spread to Holland and neighboring countries. By the 1650s, chocolate caught on in England. From England it traveled to the colonies in North America. In these countries, it was still very much a seventeenth-century luxury item, out of reach of all but the aristocracy. Part of its popularity stemmed from its reputation as a medicine. Scientists of the time analyzed chocolate and attributed all sorts of benefits to it, particularly as a stimulant and for its digestive benefits. It was also said to be good for the breath and voice, a curative for hypochondria and consumption, and as an aphrodisiac.

THE DRINKS OF KINGS

By a quirk of culinary history, Europeans were discovering coffee and tea at the same time as chocolate. Tea was the most expensive beverage of the three, and the most prized. Coffee was the least expensive.

For the most part, chocolate was now offered in paste form, available in quarter-, half- or full-pound quantities. The paste typically consisted of cocoa, vanilla, cloves, cinnamon, and sugar. A typical recipe for a single serving of chocolate at the time called for four ounces of chocolate paste, four cups of boiling water, and four ounces of crushed sugar. When the water boiled, the chocolate and additional sugar were poured in and stirred well. The pot was removed from the heat before it boiled over, and the mixture was beaten with a stick until it frothed. It was then poured into a cup and served.

Hot chocolate was generally drunk in the mornings and during receptions. Tea was the beverage of choice in the afternoon, while coffee was reserved for after meals. The man of the house also might take an hour from work, at around four or five o'clock, to go home and have a cup of chocolate. By and large, chocolate was considered to be the ultimate feminine drink. It was the custom among royalty, nobles, and the leisure class for the lady to take chocolate in bed, upon rising. In general, men preferred coffee.

Chocolate at this time was served in chocolate pots and apportioned in chocolate cups. There is dispute as to whether the French or Spanish invented the *chocolatière,* or chocolate pot. This is a reworking of the molinillo introduced by Spanish colonists. The chocolate pot is a vessel wider at the base than at the top, with a spout and a horizontal wooden handle for serving. In the lid is a hole for the whisk, which stirred the chocolate. Sometimes the pot was mounted on a stand and heated from underneath. Chocolate pots were made of ceramic, tin, copper, or pewter. The pots of the nobles and royalty were fashioned of silver, porcelain, and even gold, with matching sets of cups and saucers. The chocolate pots of the rich and royal were elegantly appointed, and designed to confirm the drink's erotic, sensuous qualities. The wildly baroque Austrian pieces are the most extreme. The most elaborate chocolatière ever fashioned was said to belong to Madame de Pompadour, of the court of Louis XV.

The early eighteenth century saw a very gradual transformation, as chocolate consumption, once reserved for the rich and royal, began to be enjoyed by commoners. Smuggling cacao beans became unnecessary as taxes, particularly in England, fell. Prices fell with it, and the drink that had been perceived first as a medicine, then as a delicacy, began to be enjoyed by all. And the popularity of these consummately social beverages—coffee, tea, and chocolate—gave birth to the coffee and chocolate houses. As rivals, these houses became important centers of social and political life.

Is Chocolate an Aphrodisiac?

Everyone knows that Montezuma consumed 50 goblets of chocolate a day, much of it before entering his harem; the drink was intended to bolster his stamina and desire. The problem is that this story is probably not true; there is no evidence that the Aztecs actually considered chocolate an aphrodisiac. It was sacred, yes, and medicinal, yes, but any talk of aphrodisiacal properties was probably the result of feverish Spanish imagination.

Still, chocolate's reputation in this area followed it to Europe. It positively flourished in the courts of the French kings of the eighteenth century. The art and literature of the time are thick with erotic imagery in connection with chocolate, partially propelled by the of the Marquis de Sade, who mixed the erotic qualities of chocolate with its ability to disguise poisons. Casanova, too, used chocolate (and champagne) as a means of seduction.

In the court of Louis XV, Madame de Pompadour took her chocolate with ambergris to stimulate her desire for the king—it was said that she was cold to him. Madame du Barry was the opposite: she was reputed to be nymphomaniacal and encouraged her lovers to drink chocolate in order to keep up with her.

Chocolate's reputation as an aphrodisiac lasts to this very day. There have been persistent rumors that eating the green M&M's (only the greens) is an aphrodisiac, or at least will summon good luck in love. So pervasive was this story that a woman formed a company to sell only green candy-coated chocolates.

Part of this contemporary re-stimulation of the legend stems from a 1980 study by Columbia University. Researchers observed that a significant number of patients with depression who were hypersensitive to romantic rejection also craved chocolate. The researchers isolated phenylethylamine (PEA).

Phenylethylamine is a stimulant (found in small amounts in some foods, and also found in the brain) that raises blood pressure and heart rate. A miniscule amount of PEA is released by the brain at moments of emotional euphoria.

The Columbia researchers hypothesized that when a person consumes a food containing the substance, romantic feelings were enhanced or the euphoria of being in love was reproduced. (On further study, however, the researchers rejected these conclusions, particularly the chocolate link.)

The problem is that there is no evidence that dietary PEA increases PEA in the brain. PEA in food is quickly broken down by digestive enzymes in the body so that it does not reach the blood or the brain. Other intrepid scientists literally ate pounds of chocolate and then were measured for their PEA levels. There was no change.

Perhaps they were eating the wrong food. Among the foods that contain more PEA than comparable servings of chocolate are cheddar cheese, salami, and pickled herring. A standard serving of smoked salami, for example, contains more than four times the PEA of your average chocolate bar.

History of Chocolate

The history of chocolate, anticipating the Industrial Revolution, began to take the form of giant, industrialist steps:

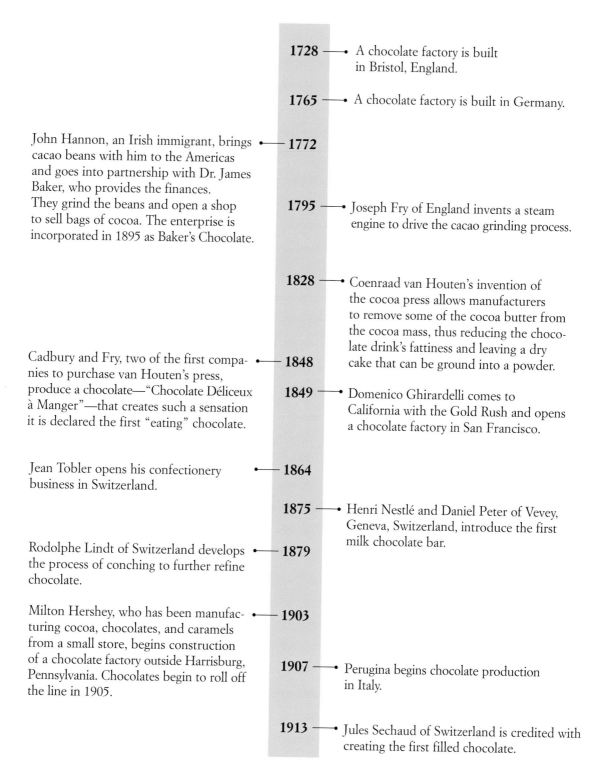

1728 → A chocolate factory is built in Bristol, England.

1765 → A chocolate factory is built in Germany.

1772 — John Hannon, an Irish immigrant, brings cacao beans with him to the Americas and goes into partnership with Dr. James Baker, who provides the finances. They grind the beans and open a shop to sell bags of cocoa. The enterprise is incorporated in 1895 as Baker's Chocolate.

1795 → Joseph Fry of England invents a steam engine to drive the cacao grinding process.

1828 → Coenraad van Houten's invention of the cocoa press allows manufacturers to remove some of the cocoa butter from the cocoa mass, thus reducing the chocolate drink's fattiness and leaving a dry cake that can be ground into a powder.

1848 — Cadbury and Fry, two of the first companies to purchase van Houten's press, produce a chocolate—"Chocolate Déliceux à Manger"—that creates such a sensation it is declared the first "eating" chocolate.

1849 → Domenico Ghirardelli comes to California with the Gold Rush and opens a chocolate factory in San Francisco.

1864 — Jean Tobler opens his confectionery business in Switzerland.

1875 → Henri Nestlé and Daniel Peter of Vevey, Geneva, Switzerland, introduce the first milk chocolate bar.

1879 — Rodolphe Lindt of Switzerland develops the process of conching to further refine chocolate.

1903 — Milton Hershey, who has been manufacturing cocoa, chocolates, and caramels from a small store, begins construction of a chocolate factory outside Harrisburg, Pennsylvania. Chocolates begin to roll off the line in 1905.

1907 → Perugina begins chocolate production in Italy.

1913 → Jules Sechaud of Switzerland is credited with creating the first filled chocolate.

Dates of Birth

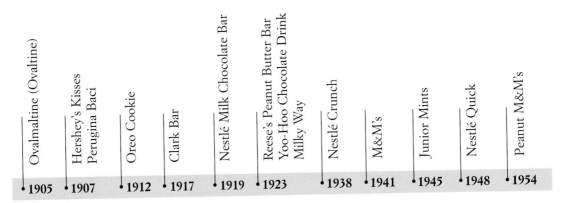

The first English chocolate house opened in 1657. Here, gentlemen would enter, slap a penny on the counter, peruse the newssheets, order a cup of chocolate (which was generally served hot), and sit and swap lies with their neighbors. Sherbets, savory dishes, cider and other drinks were served to patrons, who would spend hours disseminating rumors and news, as well as playing cards or dice. The most fashionable of these houses for hundreds of years was White's. In London and small towns all over England, the chocolate houses became critical to the lives of the people.

Sometime during the Baroque era in Europe (before 1750), solid chocolates took their place alongside other sweets on the banquet tables—candied fruits, sorbets, and sugar candies. Chocolate sticks were sold in English chocolate houses and by the early eighteenth century chocolate was available all over Europe in bars, tablets, and lozenges. It was also served as an ice, and there were drink recipes for chocolate with milk, with wine, and with egg yolk. Drinks were more often flavored with lemon peel and other citrus fruits, jasmine, almond paste, and flowers.

In 1753, the Swedish naturalist Carl von Linné (Linnaeus), who was the inventor of the binomial system of classification of living things, officially named the cacao tree *Theobrama* (from the Greek *theos,* meaning god, and broma, beverage, or "food of the gods") *cacao* (the native term for "the chocolate tree"). It was as though he was conferring a blessing, or firing off a starter's gun.

It is interesting that most of the major inventions involving the manufacture of chocolate were made in the seventeenth and eighteenth centuries. The process has not changed all that much since these first giant steps were taken. And the cultivation and harvesting of cacao has not changed appreciably since the Aztecs.

How Chocolate Is Made

People often ask us: What is the best chocolate? The answer is both subjective and complex. A better question would be: Why is one chocolate better than another? What contributes to quality in a chocolate? There are crucial points in the cultivation and manufacturing processes that can contribute to, or detract from, quality.

CULTIVATION

Chocolate is the product of the cacao bean. The beans are found in pods that grow on trees that thrive only in geographical areas within 20 degrees (roughly 600 miles) north and south of the equator. Only in these regions are there the necessary stable climate of heat (temperatures that never fall below 68°F), humidity, rainfall (between 70 and 90 inches a year), damp soil, and heavy shade the trees require. The smaller cacao trees have slender trunks, with dark green leaves and yellow flowers. In the wild, the flowers, which spring from the bark, are pollinated by midges; on plantations, workers sometimes pollinate them with brushes. Successfully pollinated flowers bear fruit directly on the trunk or on the largest branches. The fruit becomes *cherelles*—long oval green pods much like small footballs, which grow to between six and fourteen inches. Cacao pods are either rounded or pointed at the end, smooth or ridged. Within each is a viscous, pink-white pulp called mucilage, and sitting in the pulp are perhaps fifty almond-sized, pale cacao beans.

Mature trees produce some 6,500 flowers per year, of which only 60 to 120 will become pods. Pods contain 20 to 40 seeds, or cacao beans. On average, a tree yields one to two pounds of dried beans a year (the beans lose half their weight during drying).

There are two basic types of cacao bean, and a third that is a hybrid. The finished chocolate that we enjoy is most often the product of a blend of the following three.

Criollo is a thin-skinned, very aromatic bean with a slightly bitter, yet complex and delicate flavor. The tree is relatively rare and fragile, requiring meticulous care in cultivation. Thus, yields are low—criollos represent only ten percent of the world's crop. Criollos bring balance, acidity, and complexity to fine chocolates. The bean is mainly cultivated in Central and South American countries where cacao originated—Venezuela, Mexico, Nicaragua, Guatemala, and Colombia, plus Trinidad, Grenada, and Jamaica.

Forastero has been thought of as a somewhat one-dimensional bean, lacking in flavor and aroma, requiring relatively intense roasting to bring out its qualities. In recent years, however, cross-breeding has yielded more flavorful forasteros. In most chocolate blends, forasteros give body to the finished chocolate. They are principally grown in African countries, but also in Brazil, the West Indies, Central

---

Name That Candy Bar!

*A*ctual names of candy bars and confections of America's past:

B'Gosh	Alabama Hot Cakes	18th Amendment
Tingle Bar	Idaho Spud	Roasty Toasty
Bool-a Bool-a	Snirkles	Prom Queen
Yacki-Hula	Big Eats	Playboy Bunny Chocolate
Eatmor	It's Spiffy	Abba-Zaba
That's Mine!	Heavenly Hash	Hot-Air
But-a-Kiss	Jolly Papa	Big Hunk
Chicken Bone	Reggie Bar	Baffle Bar

—*Thanks to Ray Broekel*

America, and, increasingly, other countries in South America. This bean represents some 85 percent of the world's production of cocoa beans. It is the mainstay of cocoa bean blends.

The third bean, trinitario, is a hardy cross-breed of forastero and criollo. It represents 10 to 15 percent of the world harvest, and contains a high cocoa butter content. Trinitarios are primarily found in Sri Lanka, Central and South America, and Indonesia, but the highest quality are found on Trinidad, their country of origin and namesake.

Many of the characteristics of these beans depend on their country of origin. Brazilian beans are said to be slightly smoky but robust, Guyaquil beans are sweet, Sumatra beans are acidic, and Indian Ocean cacaos are pungent and sourish but not bitter. Madagascar cacaos are strong in flavor and aroma. Venezuelan cacaos, primarily criollos, are considered by many chocolatiers to be the finest. But these terms can be deceiving; since chocolates are the result of a blend of cacao beans, a slightly acrid bean, such as the variety grown in Trinidad, might be an excellent element in a certain blend.

Cacao in a Nutshell: A Summary of the Chocolate Industry

Chocolate manufacture is a four-tier process. The first tier is the **plantation** where the cacao is grown; cacao beans are cultivated in countries within 20 degrees of the equator. The beans are then acquired by companies primarily in Europe and the United States; this is the second tier—the **plant** where the cacao beans are converted into chocolate. (There are only about ten chocolate manufacturing plants in the United States.) These companies process the beans into chocolate, primarily in the form of 5 and 10 pound tempered bars or pastilles (large chips). These bars and chips are sold in bulk to the third-tier **companies** that make a product with it, often called candy. (There are approximately 760 such companies in the United States.) Candy in the chocolate world is a technical term; it means the confections made by the third-tier producer from chocolate made by a second-tier manufacturer. These third-tier companies generally sell chocolate products to the fourth-tier **shops**, who sell directly to the consumer.

FERMENTATION

The growing season of cacao pods is continuous. The trees are too delicate to be climbed or shaken, so the fruit is cut down by hand, with long-handled knives. The pods are split open with machetes, then the pulp and the beans are scooped out and placed on banana leaves on the ground, and covered with more leaves. Different plantations in different countries vary in the way they place beans for fermentation; in addition to banana leaves, beans can be placed in baskets, buried in pits, or arranged on trays or in crates, but the final step of covering them is universal.

It is the sugar content of the pulpy flesh that ignites fermentation. The pulp turns into acetic acid, which ferments the cocoa (formerly cacao) beans before it evaporates. The seed's embryo is destroyed, preventing germination, but in the process it generates the chemical precursors to the bean's chocolaty aroma. In general, quality beans undergo more rapid fermentation. Criollos need some two days; forasteros and trinitarios take a week or more. But the timing is crucial; the beans must not be allowed to ferment too long, or to be pulled from the pulp too quickly, or the maximum flavor from a cocoa bean will not be evoked.

The seeds, which were bitter, are now sweet, and they have changed color; criollos turn yellow-brown, and forasteros are darker, almost violet.

The fermented beans are next spread out in single layers on raised mats, sometimes in enclosures, and are left out in the open air to dry. Portable roofs may be rolled over the beans to stabilize the conditions. In some areas, the beans are dried in ovens to facilitate the process, but this often results in tainted, malodorous beans. These smoky beans, even in small numbers, can ruin a batch of chocolate, and such beans will not be purchased by quality manufacturers.

Once dried, the beans are packed in 110-pound sacks for inspection and shipment.

INSPECTION, TRADING, AND PURCHASE

Government inspectors visit the plantation and take a large sample from the sacks. They split the beans lengthwise and classify them by grades. Fine grade, second grade, and third grade are determined by the color of the beans. More inspections take place at the plantation, at the port of departure, and before loading.

Generally, cocoa beans are not processed into chocolate in their country of origin, but rather are shipped to Europe and the United States. There are a few manufacturing companies in Venezuela, Brazil, the Ivory Coast, and other countries, but these are exceptions. In general, cocoa beans are purchased in the country of origin by private import-export traders or international brokerages or exchanges; these might purchase all or part of the country's production. These beans are then sold to negotiators, who supply various chocolate manufacturers.

We have seen how the type of bean and the correct fermentation are important indicators of quality. Now it is up to the chocolate manufacturing companies to discern not just quality beans, but beans of various characteristics (and prices) that they believe, once blended, will give them a desirable, and profitable, final product. A few globe-trotting buyers from elite chocolate companies will inspect the growing and harvesting conditions at plantations, and even offer advice on cultivation; they purchase beans at the plantation. These exclusive chocolate companies source the best beans on the best plantations. They then use the best production methods. In general, chocolate companies get what they pay for. Brands of chocolate differ because companies have different budgets for purchasing beans. And as we will see, they also have distinct approaches (and varying budgets) to blending, roasting, grinding, flavoring, and conching.

BLENDING

At the chocolate factory, the beans are checked (for impurities), sorted (for size, toward uniform roasting), and often cleaned of any incidental impurities, such as earth or pests. Now the beans are turned over to the chocolatiers.

The chocolatiers—as few as 1, as many as 20—evaluate the imported beans. At Valrhona, for example, some 20 criteria have been established, including acidity, bitterness, and a spectrum of flavor "notes"—terms like "head notes" (the first flavor) and "heart notes" (the undertones) and the aftertaste, or lingering flavor. Having evaluated the beans, the chocolatiers create various blends. A chocolate is generally the result of a blend of four to seven different bean batches. In creating a blend, the chocolatiers attempt to balance the strength of certain beans with the aromas or acids of others. Chocolatiers generally adjust blends, roasting times, and other factors to create a final product that is consistent with the products made up to that point.

After the beans are analyzed, but before they are physically blended together, each batch of beans to be used in a particular blend is roasted separately.

ROASTING

Qualities the master roaster must take into consideration include a cocoa bean's type, fermentation state, geographical origin, and moisture level. Poor-quality beans are roasted at higher temperatures (as high as 266°F) in an attempt to maximize their few good qualities and conceal their shortcomings. The lower range of temperature, for finer cocoa beans, is in increments below 248°F. Beans may be roasted in the shell, or after the shell has been removed.

Roasting takes anywhere from 10 to 35 minutes. The first phase is little more than a drying; the water content of the beans is reduced to 3 percent and the shells become loosened from the kernel. Afterwards, the actual flavor development begins. Although the roasting process is, by and large, dominated by high-tech, precision equipment with computerized controls and measuring instruments, the best guides remain sight and smell. A bean roasted to perfection has purplish highlights and a strong cocoa aroma. Certain types of cocoa beans are preferred for the manufacture of certain chocolates, of course. For fine milk chocolate, Java beans are chosen for their natural caramel flavor, which blends perfectly with milk. Cocoa beans intended for a milk chocolate recipe are generally roasted lightly.

Next, the beans are winnowed; the now-brittle beans are cracked open and subjected to jets of air to remove their skins. What remains is called the nib. Now, as a nib, it is sent to be blended in the company's "house formula(s)."

THE RECIPE

At this point, the manufacture of cocoa and chocolate diverge. In one process, the ground nibs are hydraulically pressed. The cocoa butter melts, separating from a cocoa powder "cake," which contains some traces of cocoa butter (10 to 20 percent). The cake is pulverized and sifted into cocoa powder.

The separated cocoa butter is eventually reintroduced into the manufacture of chocolate, or is molded into bars and sold separately. (Among the buyers is the cosmetics industry, because cocoa butter's body-temperature melting point makes it ideal as a base for lipsticks and creams.)

Meanwhile, the nibs destined for a chocolate recipe are pulverized in giant rollers. The paste that results is called cocoa mass, or chocolate liquor. This paste is placed in a mixer with precise formulas of sugar, cocoa butter, vanilla (or vanillin), lecithin, and milk products, if they are called for. Obviously, the quality of these additional ingredients and the proportions are crucial to the quality of the finished chocolate. How much cocoa mass remains in the finished product? How much sugar is added? Too much sugar or too little can make all the difference. The aims and budget of the manufacturer come into question here, because sugar costs somewhere between a fifth or a quarter of cocoa beans, and is about a tenth as expensive as pure cocoa butter. Some manufacturers try to disguise inferior beans with overdoses of sugar in order to maximize profits. Likewise, vanilla. Do they use real vanilla, or vanillin? How much cocoa butter is used? Are other fats used, in whole or in part?

Lecithin is a soybean by-product, used here as an emulsifier and stabilizer. It improves the texture and storage qualities of the chocolate, and is part of the formula of virtually all chocolates.

The chocolate mix is still pasty at this point. Now it is refined: the mixer pulverizes it or passes it through refining rollers.

CONCHING

The refined chocolate is then poured into huge vats and subjected to a rolling process called conching; the early paddles resembled conch shells, thus the name. The late stage of conching is a splendid sight, like something out of a chocolate lover's fever dream: huge paddles rolling slowly through great vats of chocolate, smooth and creamy and thick.

Conching develops flavor, eliminating any remaining bitterness by aerating the chocolate and expelling volatile acids; it gives the chocolate a smooth texture by encouraging cocoa butter to coat the sugar and cocoa particles, which reduces grittiness. The paddling is continuous for a period of time. Swiss and Belgian chocolates, known for their smoothness, are conched as much as 96 hours. Some chocolates are not conched at all, or for only 4 to 12 hours. There is an upper limit to conching, however; because contemporary technology allows the chocolate particles to be ground extremely fine, conching times can be reduced.

After conching, the chocolate is tempered; the molecular structure is changed as it is heated, cooled, and heated again. Tempering gives the chocolate a good sheen, smooth texture, and ensures that it will keep well.

Finally, the chocolate is run on conveyor belts through cooling tunnels and molded into blocks (for chocolate companies to use to manufacture chocolate, or for restaurant pastry chefs), pastilles (which are like coins, and also used by manufacturers and restaurateurs), or bars (for smaller manufacturers' use, and sometimes for the consumer). Some companies make their own candy on site, but for the most part, the blocks and bars are wrapped, then stored for shipment.

Chocolate at Home

RECOGNIZING QUALITY

When the container or wrapper is removed, a chocolate should emit a good chocolaty aroma. There should be no hint of chemicals, cloying sweetness or a dusty quality, which indicates poor storage or age. The chocolate should have a smooth, glossy surface. Waxiness, grittiness, or greasy surfaces can indicate inferior ingredients or manufacture.

Color can run the spectrum from the deepest, darkest brown to auburn; many fine chocolates display mahogany highlights. If your white chocolate is white, beware; a quality white chocolate is deep yellow, indicative of high cocoa butter content. A quality chocolate will be smooth and glossy and free of bloom; bloom is caused by a separation of cocoa butter crystals and shows as white splotches. Proper cocoa butter content will determine many of the features of a quality chocolate: it will begin to melt in your hand or between your fingers within a few seconds. If it is a quality chocolate in bar form, it will make a distinct snap when it is broken; the break will be crisp and distinct.

To properly taste chocolate, a small amount should be placed on the tongue and left to melt. It should melt uniformly. The first sensation you should have should not be overwhelming sweetness; flavor notes should sound (as those hundreds of compounds begin to play on the tongue) and there will be a feeling of warmth, as your body heat and the chocolate synergize. There should be no grittiness to the chocolate; that indicates too much sugar was used. There should not be a waxy or greasy texture. It should be balanced between sweet and bitter. The vanilla should be subtle, not striking, and not artificial tasting. The chocolate should have a good, long finish, which is wine-speak for a pleasant aftertaste. There should be no chemical aftertaste.

Quality chocolates do evidence "notes," just as a wine does, and it is fun to refine the palate and reconfigure one's thinking to recognize chocolate notes. Dark chocolate is the Mozart of chocolates, producing a greater number of notes. Among common notes of chocolate you may be able to distinguish are fruitiness, nuttiness, and highlights of vanilla or caramel. Nuances of chocolate flavor are often compared to flower blossoms, to states of nature as in smoke or earth scents, and teas. Good white chocolate should be rich, mellow, not too sweet, and not dominated by vanilla flavorings.

When analyzing the texture of a pure chocolate, you want to find smooth, velvety, creamy. You want to avoid gummy, lumpy, sticky, crumbly, greasy, powdery, sandy, coarse, and waxy.

When enjoying filled chocolates, connoisseurs look for the coating to be thin, and the filling in harmony with, not fighting, the chocolate's flavor.

Did we use the word "connoisseurs?" Ouch. We would hate for this little discussion of flavor notes to turn a simple chocolate lover into one of those insufferable wine people, who bludgeon everyone at a table with their knowledge and narrow proclivities. Chocolate will always be fun, first and foremost. Americans often take a beating for their love of milk chocolate; it is said that truly sophisticated chocolate lovers—like your average European—prefer dark. Yes: Dark chocolate is more

> ### More Descriptive Terms for Chocolate
>
> -•- Other positive terms for chocolate flavor include fudgy, fresh, buttery, rich, intense, clean, consistent.
>
> -•- To describe poor-quality chocolates, words like thin, artificial, medicinal, bitter, odd, soapy, harsh, over-sweet, and watery can apply. The list goes on: sour milk, cheesy, dusty, smoky, musty, chalky, harsh, sour, flat, perfumy, metallic, rubbery, fishy, burnt, and cardboard-like.

nuanced, flavorful and has more character than milk, but milk chocolate offers a buttery smooth, silky, and wonderfully chocolaty experience. And statistics indicate that milk chocolate is a slight favorite over dark for candy consumption in every country except France. The best chocolate is your favorite chocolate, n'est-ce pas?

IS THE BEST THE BEST FOR EVERY OCCASION?

Judging a chocolate for its usefulness in baking and candy-making is a tricky issue. Often, the chocolate that tastes best is not the one that will work best in a recipe. There are subtle differences between chocolates, but such differences are often lost when you blend in quarts of cream or add nuts and zests. Valrhona, for example, is generally considered to be the number one choice for use by professionals when chocolate is the star of the dessert, and for candy-making. Professionals generally value Valrhona for its consistency, smooth texture, and ease of use—quality chocolates with high cocoa butter content are easier to re-temper. And yet Valrhona consistently ranks quite low in simple taste tests when sampled beside less expensive, domestic brands.

In a series for *Cook's Illustrated* magazine, as well as tastings in the *Chocolate Report* (a 1993 supplement to the *Cookbook Review*), milk and dark chocolates and cocoa were tested, and often the results were inconclusive. A chocolate might taste great when sampled by itself but lose flavor when melted or combined with other ingredients. Or it might take on undesirable qualities when joined with certain liquid or solid ingredients.

In general, high-quality chocolates are crucial for candy-making, less crucial in baking. To the extent that this matters to you or your budget, the best solution is to work with one chocolate, and get to know its characteristics: the way it behaves when it is melted, how it reacts to the addition of other ingredients, how its flavor melds with other ingredients, and whether it is consistent from purchase to purchase. In general, the quality chocolates are easier (less frustrating and time-consuming) to work with, with more predictable results; the extra money is well worth it. But that is not to say that quality resides only in imports, or more expensive chocolates; some chocolates react to, and flavor-coordinate better, with different types of contrasting ingredients—nuts, citrus, caramel, and so on. Experiment to find the right chocolate for your desserts, your temperament, your kitchen.

TERMS AND TYPES OF CHOCOLATE

The U.S. Standard of Identity, an arm of the FDA, has established certain requirements that chocolates must meet in order to earn the coveted titles of "white," "dark," "bittersweet," and so on. It's all in the spirit of consumer protection, but sometimes it seems the government can squeeze the fun out of any subject, chocolate included. We will note these requirements when applicable.

CHOCOLATE LIQUOR is composed of cocoa solids and cocoa butter—in other words, pulverized cocoa beans minus the shells and impurities. The cocoa solids contain the flavor; the cocoa butter helps carry it. It is pure chocolate and is inedible. The word liquor is used in the sense of "essence": it contains no alcohol.

COCOA BUTTER, the natural fat of the cocoa bean, helps carry the incomparable taste of the chocolate and is responsible for the mouthfeel. It is also responsible for the finicky and unpredictable nature of chocolate as an ingredient.

UNSWEETENED CHOCOLATE (sometimes called bitter, baking, or plain chocolate) is chocolate liquor. It contains between 50 and 58 percent cocoa butter and the rest pure cocoa solids (plus some flavorings such as vanilla, flavor extracts, salt), the percentages varying from brand to brand. It should not be confused with bittersweet chocolate.

COCOA POWDER is the result of a hydraulic press operation, in which virtually all of the cocoa butter is separated from pure chocolate liquor; the cake that results is ground into powder. There are several types of cocoa powder. Breakfast cocoa contains 22 percent cocoa butter, which is restored at the plant. Dutch-processed cocoa powder is alkalized; that is, an alkali such, as potassium carbonate, is added to the powder during processing in order to neutralize the sour, astringent qualities of the cocoa beans. By also controlling color and flavor, this process creates a darker cocoa with less harshness. Non-alkalized cocoa powder is often lighter in color than alkalized and many brands may convey a more acidic and fruity chocolate flavor. Most European cocoas are alkalized. We do not recommend that you change the cocoa powder called for in a recipe. And, of course, instant cocoa mixes for drinks cannot be substituted for baking cocoa.

BITTERSWEET AND SEMISWEET CHOCOLATE must contain at least 35 percent chocolate liquor. The chocolates in this category are manufactured with such a variety of mixtures of added cocoa butter, sugar, lecithin, and vanilla, that their characteristics differ from brand to brand. If a recipe is tested with one brand, and you choose to use another, you can expect a difference in taste (particularly sweetness) or texture. In general, European companies label this chocolate as bittersweet or dark, while American companies refer to this chocolate as semisweet. There is no standard, technical distinctions between the two chocolates. In general, bittersweet chocolates will carry a stronger chocolate flavor.

EXTRA-BITTER CHOCOLATES (sometimes known as super-dark chocolates) are relatively new. These are chocolates with chocolate liquor content (aka cocoa content) of 53%, 66%, 77%, and more. They are generally available in bulk for professional chefs. A few are being marketed to the consumer in bar form. These chocolates will obviously pack a considerable chocolate wallop, but do not casually substitute them in recipes calling for semisweet or bittersweet chocolate.

MILK CHOCOLATE, American's favorite chocolate delivery system, must contain at least 10 percent chocolate liquor, plus a minimum of 3.7 percent milk fat and 12 percent milk solids. Manufacturers also add sugar, cocoa butter, lecithin, and vanilla or vanillin. European milk chocolates are generally made with condensed milk. American and British chocolates are most often made with a milk and sugar mixture. Milk chocolate is milder and sweeter than dark chocolate, and lacks its subtlety. A good milk chocolate strikes a balance between the milk and cocoa—the milk should not mask the chocolate flavor. It should melt on the mouth without a greasy feel. Because of the milk component, it is intolerant to heat, and is therefore difficult to cook and bake with.

WHITE CHOCOLATE is composed of differing amounts of cocoa butter, butterfat, sugar, milk solids, lecithin, and flavorings. Because this product contains no cocoa solids it is not labeled as "chocolate" in the United States because it does not meet the U.S. Standard of Identity's criteria for "chocolate." Instead, it is sold as "white confectionery bar" or "summer coating." However, the FDA is expected to issue a new standard on white chocolate, determining that a product with a minimum of 20 percent cocoa butter can be labeled as white chocolate. This will be a useful ruling because now the consumer will have a clear way of distinguishing "real" white chocolate (contains cocoa butter) from the "coating" products (made with vegetable fat). Avoid the "coating" products when preparing the recipes in this book, or any other. Read the label to be sure the product you're considering for purchase contains cocoa butter or observe the color of the product: white chocolate is ivory-colored while the vegetable-fat coating is bright white.

White chocolate morsels and chips contain less cocoa butter than any other form of white chocolate; white chocolate in general is very sensitive to heat, so be careful when melting it and storing it.

Cocoa butter has little effect on the chocolate flavor of white chocolate, though it does have an effect on the depth or impact of the flavor. Cocoa butter carries mild chocolate flavor, but also many residual flavors and odors from the earth and climate of its country of origin. Most cocoa butters, in fact, are deodorized as part of the manufacturing process; this is done because chocolates are a result of a blend of different cocoa beans; these blends would be confused with several odors and flavors if the cocoa butter were not deodorized. (One exception is El Rey. Because these chocolates are from a single source [Venezuelan criollos] they have no need to be deodorized.)

White chocolate can be a star in its own right, in desserts or as a treat. But it is most often employed as a back-note, or undertone, in desserts, used to support or contrast the main item in flavor and/or texture.

GIANDUJA (jon-DOO-yuh) is a blending of pulverized hazelnuts and milk chocolate.

GRAND CRU CHOCOLATES are produced from a single cocoa bean, rather than a blend.

SWEET CHOCOLATE is a blend of chocolate liquor (at least 15 percent) and varying proportions of sugar, cocoa butter, lecithin, and flavorings.

COUVERTURE is not a brand or a type of chocolate; there are dark, bittersweet, milk, and white couvertures. Couverture is a term that applies to professional-quality coating chocolate with a high percentage of cocoa butter—from 32 to 39 percent cocoa butter. This extra cocoa butter makes it easier to work with the chocolate in melted form, and it can be used to form a thinner, more delicate shell to enrobe fillings. Though the word 'couverture' translates as 'coating,' this is emphatically not to be confused with confectionery, compound, or summer coating.

CHOCOLATE MORSELS AND CHIPS are formulated especially to retain their shape when used in baking and other desserts—cocoa butter is partially or completely eliminated in favor of vegetable fat so that the chips can tolerate high heat without their flavor or texture being altered; they are the exception to the rules cited in the Melting Chocolate section about chocolate coming in contact with direct heat. They cannot, however, be substituted in a recipe calling for a specific chocolate; semisweet chips will not melt, taste, firm up, or in any manner succeed the way properly chopped semisweet chocolate will if it is called for. A semisweet chocolate, chopped just so, cannot be substituted in a recipe calling for chips.

CONFECTIONERY COATINGS are mixtures of hard vegetable fat, sugar, and milk solids or cocoa powder. Even when made with cocoa, these cannot be labeled as chocolate. Because most confectionery coatings don't need tempering, they are commonly used in bakeries for glazing cakes, cookies, and pastries. Confectionery coatings include compound coatings and summer coatings and are not to be confused with white chocolate. Compound coatings include a small amount of milk solids and cocoa powder. Summer coatings contain milk solids and hard vegetable fat and are sometimes color-tinted.

CHOCOLATE PLASTIC is a mixture of a small amount of chocolate solids with either corn syrup, cottonseed oil, or palm kernel oil in place of cocoa butter. Dull of finish and bereft of chocolate's flavor and snap, chocolate plastic is nonetheless pliable enough to be used as a garnish for desserts—flowers, ribbons, wraps, and much more. It is also known as compound coating or summer coating because even at high temperatures it does not melt.

STORING CHOCOLATE

This section refers only to storing chocolate by itself, not chocolate desserts. Refer to individual recipes for how they can best be preserved.

Chocolate must be stored carefully because it absorbs odors and seems to act as a magnet for moisture. It should be wrapped first in plastic, then in heavy-duty aluminum foil, then (optional, but

Professional Chefs' Chocolate Preference

*W*e asked dozens of professional chefs to express their preferences for types of chocolate and their uses.

FOR MOUSSES and BUTTERCREAMS: baking chocolates (not couverture); their lower cocoa butter content contributes to a lightness in the finished product.

FOR MOLDING, coating, and shells in candy work: high-quality couvertures; their high cocoa butter content contributes fluidity, and them high cocoa solid content heightens chocolate flavor.

FOR GLAZING: couverture, for its ease of handling.

FOR GANACHE: couverture is preferred for its high-impact chocolate flavor as well as its rich, smooth texture.

FOR SAUCES: unsweetened chocolate.

FOR CAKES: a quality chocolate with a high cocoa butter content will help the cakes retain moisture.

FOR FINE CHOCOLATE WORK and decorations: couverture provides strength and fluidity.

a good idea) placed in an airtight container. Ideally, the chocolate will be stored in a cool, dry place with good air circulation, a place with a consistent temperature of around 65°F, and relative humidity of 50 percent. Stored in this way, dark and unsweetened chocolate may keep for as long as several years. Milk chocolate will keep for one year and white chocolate for seven or eight months. Ten degrees warmer and a comparable increase in humidity will not alter this formula significantly, but conditions above that—or wildly inconsistent conditions—will affect the chocolate's quality.

Few of us live in such ideal conditions, so the question becomes: Can chocolate be refrigerated? There is disagreement on this point among chocolatiers, but let's get real: You would do anything to avoid wasting good chocolate, so our advice is to buy only as much as you'll need for a given project, then store any leftover food of the gods as carefully as you can. If the refrigerator is needed, so be it.

Chocolate stored in the refrigerator should be stored in plastic, aluminum foil, and an airtight container; it must not absorb odors or moisture. You must wrap the chocolate with the minimum amount of air. Plastic bags and wrap allow you to force air out before sealing. When wrapped airtight, you can refrigerate or freeze it, extending its life. Baking or couverture chocolates should not be stored in the refrigerator or freezer for any length of time; the humidity may cause sugar bloom, affecting the flavor and texture of the chocolate. When it is time to use the chocolate, do not unwrap it until it thaws; otherwise, condensation may form. (We do not recommend that you freeze chocolate that will be thawed and used for candy-making. It would be better to make the candy first and then freeze.)

White chocolates must be stored away from light because of the milk solids. Light accelerates its oxidation, so that the chocolate can go rancid overnight. Store in a dark place with a dark covering.

Chocolate that is not stored or shipped properly will bloom. There are two kinds of bloom. Sugar bloom results when chocolate has been exposed to too much moisture; as the moisture that has gathered on the surface evaporates, sugar crystals come to the surface, making the surface rough and pitted. The second type, fat bloom, results when chocolate has been exposed to warmer-than-acceptable temperatures; here, stable cocoa butter crystals melt, are destabilized, and then stabilize again, but this time as large crystals on the surface of the chocolate. You will see gray-white streaks and blotches. Chocolate that has bloomed can be re-tempered and used—sugar-bloomed chocolate can be used for cooking and baking, but not candy-making; fat-bloomed chocolate, after tempering, can be used for baking and candy work.

MELTING CHOCOLATE

Melting chocolate should be a simple procedure, but of course it isn't. If you apply too much heat, the chocolate will scorch, lose flavor, and turn coarse and grainy. If there is a drop of moisture in the pan or too much moisture in the air, the dry particles suspended in the cocoa butter in your chocolate will clump together. In other words, your chocolate will seize—it will harden to a grainy, clotted, dull, thick paste and become unworkable; it cannot even be remelted. Add alcohol, and even vanilla, to chocolate during melting, and it can sometimes seize. Add a small amount of a cool liquid to the melted chocolate, and it will seize.

But enough about seizing, scorching, and so on. You can melt chocolate! Here's how:

First, know that chocolate cannot be melted over direct heat. Gentle indirect heat in a meticulously dry environment is required. Milk and white chocolates especially should be stirred often during melting.

Chocolate should be chopped into ½-inch pieces to maximize the melting surface. Use a serrated knife in a rocking motion. Some people prefer to chop their chocolate caveman-style: they cover the chocolate with cloth and go at it with a meat hammer.

To melt chocolate alone, make sure that no moisture comes in contact with it—the bowl must be perfectly dry, as must be the knife used to chop the chocolate, the cutting surface on which it will be chopped, and the spoon used to stir the melting chocolate. Dry, dry, and dry again.

Now select a method. Many people today tend to use the microwave oven in order to completely eliminate the moisture factor of the double boiler. Some people prefer a water bath over a double boiler for melting chocolate, because of the inflexibility—in terms of size—of double boiler components and because most do not allow you to see inside the pot to check the procedure. Again, if the water is kept below a simmer, moisture should not be a factor either way.

IN A MICROWAVE OVEN: Place the coarsely chopped chocolate in a microwave-safe glass container (such as Pyrex) and microwave it at medium (50 percent) power for 1½ to 4 minutes, until the chocolate turns shiny. (You must check often because the chocolate will retain its shape and look solid even though it has liquefied.) Stir milk and white chocolates after about 1½ minutes.

On average, 6 ounces of chopped semisweet chocolate will require 3 minutes to melt at medium power. The higher the cocoa butter content, the faster the chocolate will melt. And believe it or not, chocolate melts faster on medium or low microwave power than it does on high.

IN A DOUBLE BOILER: Place coarsely chopped chocolate in the top of the double boiler over hot (not simmering, not boiling) water. Melt the chocolate, stirring until smooth. Do not cover the bowl of chocolate while it is melting. You risk the possibility of condensation forming under the cover. When the chocolate is melted, remove the top part of the double boiler from the bottom.

- Always melt chocolate uncovered; moisture could condense on the lid, drop onto the chocolate, and cause it to seize.

- The bowl containing the chocolate should be either unlined copper (very responsive to temperature changes), stainless steel, or heatproof glass; enameled cast iron is not appropriate because it retains heat, which will overheat the chocolate.

- Make sure that the bowl is larger than the pot so no steam gets into the bowl. The chocolate container should come in contact with the water. If there is a space between the water and the container, the steam could scorch the chocolate.

- You might remove the chocolate from the heat before it is completely melted; it will continue to melt on its own. Rewarm it if necessary.

SPECIFICS OF MELTING DARK, MILK,
AND WHITE CHOCOLATES: Chocolate
should always be coarsely chopped into small
chunks: ¼ inch for milk and white chocolate;
dark chocolate chunks can be larger, if
desired—but no more than ½-inch thick. Stir
often. When in doubt, stir. Milk and white
chocolates must be stirred frequently, if not
continually, or the milk solids may form lumps.
(This depends partially on the storage of the
chocolate. Milk solids are very sensitive to heat
and humidity.) Stir dark chocolate intermittently.

> ## If the Chocolate Seizes
>
> *P*our 1 teaspoon of vegetable oil per
> ounce of chocolate into the pan and beat
> vigorously. Make sure the liquid is warm
> enough not to compound the problem; it
> should be the same temperature as the
> chocolate. This should revive the chocolate.
>
> An alternative is to save the chocolate
> and store it for a use when liquid must be
> added to it. (Scrape the chocolate onto
> waxed paper, let it harden, and store it safe-
> ly for later use when a recipe calls for it to
> be melted with butter or cream or liquor.)

White and milk chocolates should not
be heated above 110°F, and should be removed
from the heat at 105°F. Dark chocolate should
not be heated above 120°F. This may seem to be very hot, but it is considered warm. Remove dark
chocolate from the heat when it reaches 115°F because the temperature will continue to rise to its
maximum point.

MELTING CHOCOLATE AND LIQUIDS: In general, 2 ounces of chocolate can melt safely with 1
tablespoon of a liquid such as milk, cream, liquor, coffee—even water. Chocolate will seize if it comes
in contact with small amounts of liquid. Follow the recipe and your good sense; again, cocoa butter
content will help to determine this tolerance. (So don't try adding a splash of your favorite liqueur to
melting chocolate; you're only hurting yourself.)

To melt chocolate with a liquid, combine the cut-up chocolate with the liquid (in the proper
proportion), and then warm them together. If you add cold liquid to warm or warming chocolate,
the liquid will harden the chocolate, and it will form gritty particles. (If you add melted chocolate to
cold ingredients, the cocoa butter will harden, and all will be lost.)

Chocolate can be melted with milk or butter directly over low heat, but it must be stirred
frequently and watched very carefully.

TEMPERING BASICS

The subject of tempering strikes terror into the hearts of amateur dessert-makers and chocolatiers
everywhere. The message here is: relax. Chances are, you will never need to temper chocolate. If you
are going to make some or even most of the desserts in this book—or any dessert/baking book—you
will not need to temper. You do not need to temper the melted chocolate you will be using for cookie
doughs, cake batters, buttercreams, frostings, mousses, custards, and ganaches. Even the chocolate for
a glaze does not need to be tempered if the dessert is to be consumed soon after it is made.

Many people do choose to temper the chocolate to be used for curls, ribbons, and leaves. If you are planning to make the candies in this book, or if you plan to learn the discipline of candy-making—for molding and coating and dipping chocolate candies—you will need to temper chocolate. Professional chocolatiers and chefs temper because they want their chocolates and garnishes to look and taste as fabulous as they can be. Properly tempered chocolate is lustrously glossy in appearance, breaks with a pleasing snap, and melts properly on the tongue. Tempered chocolate shrinks slightly as it hardens, and thus will release from molds more easily. Tempered chocolate, if stored properly, will retain its snap and shine for months.

Tempering is the process of heating chocolate to between 110°F and 120°F (in order to melt out stable and unstable cocoa butter crystals) and then cooling it to between 82°F and 84°F (at which temperature-stable crystals can re-form, but unstable ones cannot). This "seeded" chocolate is then heated again to between 84°F and 91°F to give it a workable consistency, and maintained at that temperature while it is being used. The temperatures given here are generalized; specific temperatures apply to different chocolates. These specific temperatures may be included on a package of couverture and should be adhered to. In general, however, the following guidelines apply:

DARK, SEMISWEET, AND BITTERSWEET: 88°F to 91°F

MILK AND WHITE: 84°F to 87°F

All chocolates do not react the same way in the tempering process. And temperature and humidity changes in your kitchen will also drastically affect this process. Do not get cocky if it goes brilliantly the first time; chances are, it will be a time-consuming mess the next.

Remember that chocolates are tempered during the manufacturing process. The solid chocolate bars you buy, of whatever size, should be in proper temper when you purchase them, provided they were properly stored and shipped. They will, however, go out of temper once you melt them.

Also be aware that there are tempering machines on the market. But like any tool, it is best used after you have learned the technique behind it. A short list of tempering machine manufacturers can be found in the back of this book.

TEMPERING METHODS

To successfully temper, you will first need an instant-read thermometer, one with a gauge that runs from 80°F to 130°F in increments of one or two degrees. Fortunately, there are many fine, inexpensive digital thermometers on the market that will do the job. (Remember not to rest the thermometer on the side or bottom of the pan, but do submerge it at least 1 inch into the chocolate.)

There are several methods of tempering chocolate; we will highlight three—the microwave and direct methods, and a simple alternative. Our microwave method is a modified, updated version of the slab method, which has traditionally been the most frequently used tempering method. Our quick-tempering, direct method also involves the microwave.

MICROWAVE METHOD

1. Chop the chocolate into ¼-inch chunks. Put half of the chocolate in a 1½-quart microwave-safe bowl. (Use a 1-quart bowl when tempering 8 ounces of chocolate or less. When tempering more than 2 pounds of chocolate, use a large bowl.) Microwave uncovered on medium (50 percent) power for 1½ to 6 minutes, stirring every 1½ minutes, until the chocolate is completely melted and smooth (A). Stir in the remaining chocolate chunks (B).

2. Microwave uncovered on medium (50 percent) power for 1½ to 5 minutes, stirring every 60 seconds, until the chocolate is almost completely melted. Gently stir the chocolate and when it is completely melted, check the temperature. It should read between 110°F and 120°F (or the temperature recommended by the manufacturer). If necessary, put the chocolate back in the microwave set on low (10 percent) power for 5- to 10-second intervals, until it reaches the correct temperature. (Stir the chocolate for at least 1 minute before checking the temperature.)

3. Transfer the melted chocolate to another 1½-quart (or a smaller or larger bowl, depending on the amount of chocolate being tempered). This will bring the temperature of the chocolate down to approximately 100°F.

4. Wrap a heating pad (normally used for backaches) in plastic to protect it from chocolate stains. Set the control dial to the lowest setting (C).

5. Pour one-third of the melted chocolate onto a clean, dry work surface (such as marble or Formica). Keep the remaining chocolate in the bowl on the heating pad.

6. Using an offset metal cake spatula, spread the chocolate evenly across the work surface into a rectangle (D). Using a pastry scraper, bring the chocolate together, and as you do so, scrape the chocolate off the spatula. Continue this spreading and scraping process until the chocolate cools to 80°F to 82°F for milk and white chocolates and 82°F to 84°F for dark chocolate, loses its shine and forms a thick paste with a dull matte finish. Work quickly so that the chocolate does not lump. This process can take anywhere from 2 to 10 minutes, depending on the amount of chocolate, the type and brand of chocolate, as well as the temperature of the kitchen. The chocolate is now seeded. The professional term for this is "mush."

7. Add the mush to the bowl of 100°F chocolate (E) and using a clean, dry rubber spatula, stir the chocolate gently until smooth. Be careful not to create air bubbles as you stir the chocolate.

A   B   C   D   E

8. Check the temperature of the chocolate. It should register between 86°F and 91°F depending on the type and brand of chocolate. (In general, dark chocolate should register between 86°F to 90°F, and milk and white chocolates should register between 86°F to 89°F.) If necessary, heat the bowl of chocolate in the microwave on low (10 percent) power for 5- to 10-second intervals, to raise the temperature the required number of degrees. (Stir the chocolate for at least 1 minute before checking the temperature. Be very careful not to overheat the chocolate.) The chocolate is now ready to work with. As you work, regularly stir the chocolate and check its temperature. Adjust the temperature and fluidity of the chocolate by turning the heating pad on and off. If for some reason the chocolate becomes too cold, simply reheat it in the microwave oven set on low (10 percent) power for 5- to 10-second intervals. (Stir the chocolate for at least 1 minute before rechecking the temperature.) Never let its temperature exceed 92°F, or the stable cocoa butter crystals will start to melt and the temper will be lost.

DIRECT METHOD (QUICK TEMPERING)

This method breaks the rules of the more traditional methods of manually tempering chocolate. Rather than stabilizing the cocoa butter crystals by melting and reforming the chocolate, this method calls for you to heat the chocolate very slowly just until it melts, and to maintain the chocolate's temperature at 91°F. In other words, even though the chocolate is melted, it is still in temper. It is important that the chocolate you use—preferably couverture chocolate—be in good temper when you open it; it should have even color and smooth grain, and show no evidence of streaking or blotching. You must watch the melting chocolate and monitor its temperature carefully. Always stir the chocolate for at least 1 minute before checking the temperature, as the residual heat in the melting chocolate and the glass bowl will cause the temperature to continue to climb even after the bowl of chocolate has been removed from the microwave.

This method is less messy and very fast, once you have become accustomed to the process. If you should accidentally overheat the chocolate during the melting process 1 or 2 degrees above 91°F, don't panic. Quickly transfer the melted chocolate to another microwave-safe glass bowl (this will help bring down the temperature), and add 1 more ounce of chopped chocolate. Stir gently until melted, then recheck the temperature.

1. Wrap a heating pad (normally used for backaches) in plastic to protect it from chocolate stains. Set the control dial to the lowest setting.

The really simple but not so quick method

1. Melt the chocolate in a manner you are most comfortable with—but make sure that the chocolate reaches a temperature of between 115°F and 120°F.

2. Allow the chocolate to cool by itself (at cool room temperature), stirring occasionally, until it reaches a temperature in the low 80s. (Look for the chocolate to set around the top edge of the bowl.)

3. Raise the temperature of the chocolate to 86°F to 91°F (for dark chocolate) or 86°F to 90°F (for milk and white chocolate). Be careful not to allow the chocolate to go above those maximum temperatures. Maintain that temperature range while working with the chocolate.

2. Chop the chocolate into ¼-inch chunks and put it into a 1½-quart microwave-safe glass bowl. (Use a 1-quart bowl when tempering 12 ounces of chocolate or less. When tempering more than 2 pounds of chocolate, use a large bowl.) Microwave at medium (50 percent power) for 1½ to 5 minutes, stirring a couple of times with a clean, dry rubber spatula, until about one-third of the chopped chocolate has melted.

3. Remove the bowl from the microwave and gently stir the chocolate for 2 to 5 minutes, until it is almost completely melted. (This may seem like a long time, but the residual heat will continue to melt the chocolate.) Using a digital thermometer, with the stem of the thermometer immersed in at least 2 inches of melted chocolate (tilt the bowl if necessary), check the temperature of the chocolate. It should read between 86°F and 91°F depending on the type and brand of chocolate. (In general, dark chocolate should register between 86°F to 91°F, and milk and white chocolates should register between 86°F to 90°F.) If necessary, microwave on low (10 percent power) for 5- to 10-second intervals until it reaches the correct temperature and any remaining bits of chocolate are completely melted.

4. Place the bowl of tempered chocolate on the prepared heating pad. The chocolate is now ready to work with. As you work, regularly stir the chocolate and check its temperature. Adjust the temperature and fluidity of the tempered chocolate by turning the heating pad on and off. If for some reason the chocolate becomes too cold, simply reheat it in the microwave oven on low (10 percent power) for 5- to 10-second intervals. Stir the chocolate for at least 1 minute before rechecking the temperature.

DECORATIVE TECHNIQUES

STRIPED CHOCOLATE CIGARETTES

1. Using a metal spatula, spread the tempered white chocolate thinly over a marble slab. Drag a confectioners' comb through the chocolate (A).

2. After the white chocolate has set slightly, pour a contrasting chocolate over it (B).

3. Using a metal spatula, smooth the chocolate into a thin layer (C).

4. After the chocolate has set but is still pliable, form cigarettes with a bench knife: hold it at a 45-degree angle and shave the chocolate off the slab—it will naturally form into tight cylinder (D and E).

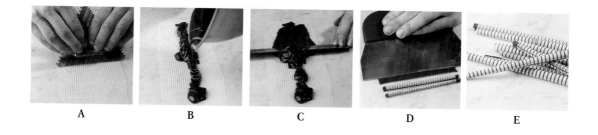

A   B   C   D   E

TRANSFER SHEETS

1. Using a metal spatula, spread a thin layer of tempered chocolate onto parchment paper (A).

2. Press a transfer sheet, print-side-down, onto the chocolate (B).

3. After the chocolate has set completely, peel off the transfer sheet (C).

4. Use cutters or a paring knife to form various shapes for garnish (D and E).

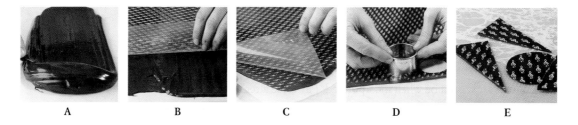

A   B   C   D   E

THE WOOD-GRAIN EFFECT

1. Using a metal spatula, spread the tempered chocolate onto a food-grade acetate band, making it a little wider than the wood-grain tool (A).

2. Drag the wood-grain tool in a rocking motion through the chocolate (B).

3. Once the wood-grained chocolate has set, pour a contrasting chocolate over it and spread into a thin layer (C).

4. Before the second chocolate layer sets, wrap the acetate band around the desired dessert form (D).

5. When the chocolate has set completely, peel off the acetate (E).

A   B   C   D   E

STRIPED CHOCOLATE DESIGNS

1. Using an offset metal spatula, spread the tempered chocolate in a thin layer onto a food-grade acetate. Using a ruler as a guide, draw a confectioner's comb through the chocolate (A).

2. Once the chocolate has set slightly, pour a contrasting chocolate over it (B).

3. Spread the contrasting chocolate into a thin layer (C). Using a cutter or paring knife, cut into desired shapes (D). Allow the chocolate pieces to set completely, and peel off acetate (E).

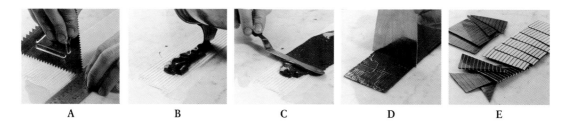

A   B   C   D   E

INGREDIENTS FOR BAKING BASICS

AMARETTO is an almond-flavored liqueur.

BAKING POWDER is a mixture of baking soda, an acid (such as salt crystals) and cornstarch, as a stabilizer. In double-acting baking powder, air pockets form when the powder comes in contact with wet ingredients and then those air pockets expand when they are subjected to heat, causing the product to rise. Pay attention to baking powder's sale date, or test for freshness by adding a teaspoonful to about four ounces of hot water. If it bubbles, the powder is still good.

BUTTER Unsalted butter is used exclusively in the recipes in this book. Some recipes specify the temperature the butter should be when incorporated. Pay close attention and plan ahead. Butter temperature is crucial to finished results. Wrap unused butter in plastic in the refrigerator, or store it in the freezer.

COFFEE In our recipes you will frequently see instant espresso called for; this is truly the best way to deliver intense coffee flavor without too much moisture. If the recipe calls for granules, it does not mean the liquid.

CORNSTARCH is a thickening agent.

CORN SYRUP is a starch extracted from corn kernels; the kernels are treated with an enzyme to create this sweet syrup. Its role in baking is to prevent sugars from crystallizing, which helps the product to retain moisture and extend freshness.

CREAM Use heavy whipping cream, which contains 36 to 40 percent butterfat. It will be pasteurized, but avoid creams that are labeled "ultrapasteurized." This process, designed to extend shelf life, also flattens flavor.

CREAM OF TARTAR is a white powder found, in trace amounts, in baking powder. By itself, it is used to help prevent beaten egg whites from drying out.

CRÈME FRAÎCHE is a French variation of sour cream; it is very rich and slightly fermented. It can be substituted for sour cream, but it is quite expensive.

EGGS Grade AA large eggs are the best choice for baking, for their thick white and strong yolk. Water and protein material make up the white; the white is used to add volume and air to sponge cakes and mousses. The yolk contains cholesterol, fat, protein, vitamins, and minerals; it is used as a thickener and binder in creams and custards. In general, eggs must be brought to room temperature before using. Before beating eggs, be sure the bowl is absolutely clean.

FLOUR Always use the flour called for in a recipe, paying close attention to addendums like "self-rising," "bleached," or "unbleached," and so on. If a recipe does not call for self-rising flour, do not use it. All-purpose flour is the result of a blend of hard and soft wheats, to produce a flour of medium strength and protein content of 10 ½ to 13 percent. Wheat flours contains some gluten, which provides elasticity and strength, as well as certain characteristics in certain pastries—flakiness, for example. Cake flour, milled from soft winter wheat, does not contain gluten; it is more refined than all-purpose and produces a soft, delicate crumb.

GELATIN is used to help set certain mousses and Bavarians. It must be softened before use, which is a simple matter of placing or sprinkling in cold water and waiting for 5 minutes or more until it swells and absorbs the moisture (blooms).

GLUCOSE is used to replace part of the sugar in ice cream and sorbet recipes; it performs the same function as sugar but is not as sweet.

KAHLUA is a coffee-flavored liqueur.

KIRSCH OR KIRSCHWASSER, is cherry brandy.

MASCARPONE is a smooth, rich cream cheese.

NUTS It is crucial that nuts be fresh. Shelled nuts are available natural (raw, with skins intact) or blanched (skins removed). Nuts can be stored in the freezer, well wrapped, for several months (for blanching and roasting information see Basic Techniques).

PHYLLO, or FILO, is pastry dough presented in paper-thin sheets. It is packaged fresh or frozen. Unopened, phyllo will keep in the refrigerator for a month. Once opened, it should be used in two or three days. Phyllo can be frozen for up to one year; thaw completely in the refrigerator before using.

PRALINE PASTE is a combination of almonds and caramelized sugar that is ground to a paste.

RUM Myers's dark rum is preferred for its full flavor.

SALT is used as a flavor enhancer in products containing eggs, butter, and certain fruits, and can cut the sweetness in other desserts when desired.

SOUR CREAM Do not substitute lowfat sour cream.

SUGAR Use the sugar called for in the recipe; when the recipe calls for granulated sugar, use either regular granulated or the superfine variety. Superfine sugar is granulated sugar that has been processed to reduce particle size. Confectioners', or powdered, sugar is granulated sugar that has been milled to powder, with cornstarch added. Brown sugar is granulated sugar with molasses added. Light and dark brown sugar can be used interchangeably, but for precise flavor, use the one called for in our recipes.

VANILLA is a pod fruit from a vine that is in the orchid family, and it produces an irreplaceable sweetness and aroma. Two quality vanillas are Tahitian and Madagascar (or Bourbon). The recipes in this book frequently call for vanilla extract, but when the vanilla flavor must be fresh and impactful, the beans must be purchased, scraped, and the seeds removed, then either the seeds or the seeds and the pod are added to the cooking liquid. Vanilla beans can be stored long-term in the freezer, or short-term in the refrigerator, wrapped tightly in plastic.

BASIC EQUIPMENT FOR THE HOME BAKER AND CANDYMAKER

It is not necessary to run out and buy every piece of equipment shown here in order to make delicious desserts. Not all of the recipes in this book require every device. But if you're serious about applying and improving your skills, you will in time need many of these items. It's a fact of life in kitchens, both professional and at home: pastry-making requires more specialized equipment than savory cooking. This is due, in part, to the delicate chemical reactions that take place, the precise temperatures and mixing times and methods that can spell the difference between success and brilliance.

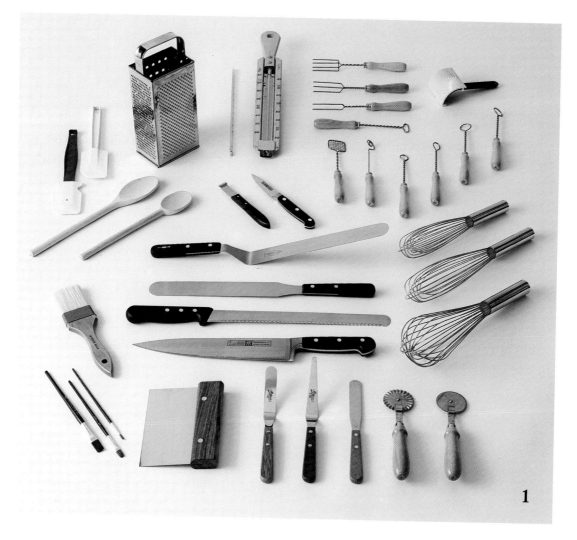

1

PHOTOGRAPH 1

RUBBER SPATULAS For folding and mixing batters as well as scraping down the sides of or bowl. They are produced flat-sided or in a concave, spoon-like shape and are available in rubber or in heat-resistant (up to 500°F) silicone.

WOODEN SPOONS Indispensable kitchen tools for many uses; available slotted, unslotted, flat, or concave. Wood is porous and will absorb odors so it is wise to keep a separate set for savory cooking.

CONFECTIONERS' FORK Also known as a dipping fork. Used for dipping chocolates and other confections into couverture.

CANDY THERMOMETER A thermometer that is used to precisely measure the temperature of cooking sugar.

CHOCOLATE THERMOMETER Should have wide spacing between 1°F increments and need not measure very high temperatures (above 130°F).

LONG SERRATED KNIFE Ideal for slicing a cake on the horizontal and also excellent for chopping chocolate. If the serrations are deep enough, it may be suitable for use in place of a cake comb.

CHEF'S KNIFE The most essential knife in the kitchen. Its long, tapered blade ranges in length from 8 to 14 inches.

PARING KNIFE The 2- to 3-inch, easily manipulated blade makes it useful for tasks such as peeling fruit, splitting vanilla beans, and creating garnishes.

METAL SPATULA May be used for icing or glazing cakes and spreading chocolate into thin sheets for creating decorations and garnish. Available flat or offset and from 4 to 12 inches in length.

METAL SCRAPER A rectangular heavy metal scraper is excellent for cleaning off work surfaces; also great for transferring chopped chocolate to a bowl.

WHISKS Whisks are made in different sizes, suited to different functions: large, for whipping ingredients that require a lot of air to be incorporated and for folding other ingredients into these delicate mixtures; medium to small, for making egg- or starch-based sauces and combining ingredients, such as chocolate and cream for ganache, when you do not want a lot of air incorporated.

PASTRY BRUSHES Broad and flat or thick and round, these brushes are ideal for soaking layers of cake with flavored syrup before assembly or for brushing a thin coating of oil or butter on a pastry prior to baking.

ARTISTS BRUSHES For decorative purposes.

PASTRY WHEEL Also known as a pizza cutter. May be used to cut pastry dough, rolled fondant, and other items.

ZESTER A traditional zester may be used to remove the flavorful outer skin of citrus fruit. A metal ginger grater or the fine side of a box grater covered with plastic wrap (facilitating easy removal of the zest from the grater) will also work well.

BOX GRATER Used to grate chocolate for decoration or garnish, and for the removal of citrus zest.

WOOD GRAIN TOOL A rubber piece with conchoidal ridges that has been adhered to a convex surface attached to a handle. It is used to impart a wood grain-like pattern to chocolate by running it over a spread sheet or strip of melted, tempered chocolate, allowing the chocolate to partially set up and then spreading an alternate color of melted, tempered chocolate over the first layer. Most readily available in hardware or paint stores.

PHOTOGRAPH 2

MIXING BOWLS Glass or stainless steel bowls are equally suited for mixing. Plastic is a porous material and will retain odors and oils, making such bowls unsuitable for fragile egg whites.

DOUBLE BOILER Two pans that fit together. The lower pan holds water, which is heated to a simmer; the top pan contains what is to be heated. A metal (stainless steel) bowl works well. Used for foods that need gentle heat.

CAKE BOARDS Sturdy corrugated cardboard rounds and rectangles in various sizes, used to support a cake at the base. Also available with a wax coating, and in decorative gold and silver with scalloped rims.

COOLING RACKS Work well for cooling baked goods in and out of the pan because they allow for full air circulation around the cake or pastry. They are also ideal to use when glazing because they allow for the excess glaze to drip off the cake, creating a clean bottom edge.

SILICONE BAKING MAT A thin, flexible mat that has been treated with silicone to make its surface nonstick. These mats are reusable and are available in full and half-sheet pan sizes.

TURNTABLE A pedestal approximately 5 inches tall, with a rotating top to facilitate decorating and frosting a cake.

HEAVY-DUTY ELECTRIC MIXER A 4½- to 5-quart bowl is necessary to properly develop volume by the incorporation of air. A stronger machine of 325 to 350 watts is ideal for mixing stiff doughs. A paddle, whip, and dough hook attachment are also important. We recommend the KitchenAid.

2

FOOD PROCESSOR The metal chopping blade is most often used in the pastry kitchen. Indispensable for chopping nuts, mixing doughs and batters, and for the emulsification of ganaches (especially when making truffles).

TARTLET PANS Used for making individual tarts. The sides are usually fluted, but may also be plain. Range in size from 1¼- to 4¾-inch diameter and ⅝- to 1¼-inches in height.

FLEXIPANS Flexible baking pans that are available in varying sizes and shapes. These pans withstand temperatures from -40°F to 536°F and may go from freezer to oven or microwave.

CAKE PANS Aluminum is preferable because it has good heat conductivity, but will not retain heat as do glass pans. Light-colored pans are better because they will not absorb extra heat from the oven.

JELLY ROLL PAN Made of heavy-gauge aluminum with rolled edges to prevent warping and rusting, and to facilitate even heat conduction. Standard size is 11½-by-17½-inches.

ROLLING PINS Available in a wide range of sizes and materials: plastic, metal, glass, marble and hardwood. It is useful to have two types of rolling pins for dessert-making: the hardwood broom-handle type, which is a wooden dowel 18 to 20 inches in length having a diameter of 1¼ to 2 inches, and the hardwood model that is manufactured with a steel rod and a ball bearing system. It is good to have a long and heavy one to ease the task of rolling out doughs.

TART PANS Most commonly available shapes are rectangular (14¾-by-4½ inches), square (9-by-9 inches) and round with an 8-, 9½- or 11-inch diameter; all are approximately 1-inch deep. Extra-deep, round tart pans are also available. Removable bottoms are a necessity.

PHOTOGRAPH 3

PARCHMENT PAPER Available in full-sheet, pan-sized sheets or in rolls. It is used for lining baking pans to provide a nonstick surface.

PARCHMENT TRIANGLES Rolled into cones, they may be used in place of a pastry bag for decorating work.

PLASTIC DOUGH SCRAPER Used for the same applications as a rubber spatula; it covers more surface area but has no handle.

DECORATING COMBS A scraper with scalloped or serrated edges that is used to give a texture or a pattern to the sides and/or top of a cake after frosting. Also used for different applications with chocolate such as creating decorative lines or stripes.

PASTRY BAGS Conical bags that are made of fabric, fabric lined with plastic, nylon, or disposable plastic. Available in various sizes. When fitted with a pastry tip, they are used for decorating and filling pastries, cakes and confections.

PASTRY TIPS Metal, conical fittings that are placed in a pastry bag or attached to the bag with the use of a coupler. The most commonly used tips are the plain and star tips. All tips are available in various sizes and are used, in conjunction with a pastry bag, to fill and decorate cakes, pastries, and confections.

COUPLER   A device that is fitted at the end of a pastry bag so that pastry tips may be changed without having to empty the contents of the bag. Available in various sizes to accommodate the various sizes of pastry bags and tips.

ASSORTED CUTTERS   For cutting cookie dough, cake (to make individual cakes of petits fours), gelée, and chocolate (to make garnishes).

ACETATE STRIP ROLL   Melted, tempered chocolate is spread on this surface so that it may be bent into ribbon-like forms. The ultra-smooth surface will give the chocolate a shiny finish. The strips may also be used to line cake ring molds so that pastries will release easily.

TRANSFER SHEET   An acetate sheet with a cocoa butter visual image. Melted, tempered chocolate is spread on a sheet, allowed to set, then released, and the image adheres to the chocolate.

MARBLE SLAB   This cool, smooth surface is ideal for chocolate work, such as making cigarettes and tempering, and rolling out pastry.

MEASURING EQUIPMENT   It is important to have separate equipment for solid and liquid measure to ensure accurate ingredient amounts.

STRAINERS AND SIEVES   Work well as sifters, are essential for making sauces, and are useful for making slightly overheated chocolate usable.

SQUEEZE BOTTLE Plastic bottles with removable, fine-pointed tops. They are used for distributing sauces and fillings.

RING MOLDS Various heights and diameters make these molds extremely versatile for creating cakes and individual desserts out of mousse, Bavarian cream, ice creams, and the like. Manufactured in metal and plastic.

SCOOPS Scoops with the sweep-blade mechanism are useful for portioning mousses, ice creams, and doughs. Available in round or oval (quenelle) shapes and in various sizes.

SAUCEPANS Heavy-bottomed pans facilitate conduction of heat. They must be made of nonreactive material, such as stainless steel, but not aluminum. When cooking in a saucepan it is important to choose the size of pan that is appropriate for the volume of food to be prepared.

SCALE Balance scales, also known as bakers' scales, are excellent for measuring quantities larger than 1 ounce. They are, however, large and cumbersome, especially for home use. Spring and electronic scales are both of convenient size and are sensitive to fractions of an ounce. The electronic scales use the same type of mechanism as the spring scale, but the digital readout and the ease with which they may be zeroed out so that more than one ingredient can be weighed in the same container make this type of scale the most convenient.

ICE CREAM MACHINE The small machines for home use consist of an insulated container, a paddle, and its motor. The paddle acts to agitate the mixture as it is freezing. An absolute necessity for making frozen desserts, machines are available for less than $50.

BRIOCHE MOLDS Available in various sizes to make individual portions or larger sizes. The fluted sides make them an interesting choice for molding other desserts.

MADELEINE PAN Scalloped-shaped impressions mold the traditional cookies, but these pans may also be used to shape any number of confections. They are available in two sizes. The larger has 12 impressions per pan and the pans for making small madeleines contain 20 impressions per pan.

RAMEKIN Also known as soufflé pan or soufflé dish. Available in various sizes, from large to individual. Used for custard and soufflé desserts that are baked and served in the same container.

PROPANE TORCH (not pictured) A helpful tool for browning or caramelizing the tops of desserts. For some desserts that will be destroyed by the heat of a broiler it is necessary; for others it will simply make the procedure quicker and easier.

BASIC TECHNIQUES

In the creation of fine desserts and candies, certain techniques are used frequently. Following are helpful hints and guidelines to these basic procedures. They will become second nature to you as your skills increase—and your reputation grows.

FROSTING A CAKE Always begin at the top and end at the sides. When the cake is entirely, proportionately frosted, smooth the rim of frosting that will have formed around the top edge of the cake with a spatula. Spread this excess frosting in toward the center of the top of the cake.

LINING CAKE PANS This is a recipe step that prevents a skin of flour from forming on the bottom of the baked cake, and it makes it easier to remove the cake from the pan and invert.

MEASURING DRY INGREDIENTS We measure flour, cocoa, and other dry ingredients by spooning them lightly into the measuring cup and leveling with a spatula or the straight edge of a knife. Do not tap the measuring cup.

TO BLANCH ALMONDS place them in a pot of simmering water for about one minute. Using a strainer, remove them from the simmering water and place them in cold water. By pinching each nut, the skin will slide off. They must be completely dry and cooled before grinding.

TOASTING is important to bring out the full flavor of most nuts, especially almonds and hazelnuts; do not buy pre-roasted nuts; the flavor will drastically affect the dessert.

To toast nuts: Position a rack in the center of the oven and preheat to the temperature called for below. Place the nuts in a single layer on a baking sheet, and shake the pan two or three times during the toasting period. After toasting, place the nuts on a room-temperature baking sheet to cool completely.

To toast and blanch hazelnuts: 8 to 12 minutes in a 350°F. (Extra step: After toasting, wrap the nuts in a clean towel and cool completely. Transfer the nuts to a large sieve and rub them back and forth to remove the loose skins. Remove the nuts from the sieve.)

To toast whole almonds: 10 to 15 minutes in a 350°F oven. Blanched almonds will be golden when done; natural almonds will be a light brown all the way through (cut in half to check).

To toast sliced or slivered almonds: 5 to 10 minutes at 325°F.

To toast walnuts and pecans: 5 to 10 minutes at 350°F.

SPLITTING CAKES TO FORM LAYERS: Make sure that the cake is completely cool, or it will crumble when you attempt to cut it. Set the cake layer on a cake-decorating stand, lazy Susan, or cardboard cake circle. Use a serrated knife that is longer than the diameter of the cake. If a dome has formed on the cake, trim it so that it is flat. Make a small notch lengthwise down the side of the cake layer (you can use this mark later to help you properly align the layers).

Lay one hand lightly on the top of the cake to steady it, place the knife at the midpoint of the side of the cake, and hold the knife in place while turning the cake with the other hand, creating a horizontal, scored line completely around. Using this scored line as a guide, carefully saw straight through the cake layer. Repeat with the second cake layer, if applicable.

W H I T E   C H O C O L A T E

Desserts

White chocolate was first introduced in Switzerland

in the 1920s. During the 1940s and 50s, a few white chocolate bars

appeared on the U.S. market, but it was not until the 1970s that white

chocolate achieved any popularity in the U.S. The flavor of white

chocolate is perhaps best expressed as a "cooked milk" taste, with faint

notes of chocolate and, occasionally, even fainter nutty notes. White choco-

late works best in recipes that use dairy products. It can act as a

sweetener, as a textural enhancer (making creamy items even creamier),

and to add sweetness to balance desserts featuring citrus or spices.

For the lover of white chocolate, it is of course wonderful as the star

of a dessert, but for others, it is best relegated to supporting cast.

Individual Pavlova Cakes Filled with White Chocolate Lemon Curd Mousse

The Pavlova, traditionally a large dessert from which slices are taken, was created by an Australian chef to honor the visiting Russian ballerina, Anna Pavlova. Our individual cakes employ white chocolate lemon curd mousse rather than whipped cream, and adds raspberry sauce. But all of the traditional elements are in place: crisp meringue enclosing a creamy center, with fresh fruit adding its refreshing flavor.

• ◆ •

YIELD: 8 SERVINGS

Preparation: 1½ hours, plus baking, cooling and chilling times

Pavlova Cakes
• ◆ •
5 large egg whites
1 teaspoon fresh lemon juice
⅛ teaspoon salt
1 teaspoon vanilla extract
1¼ cups superfine granulated sugar
1 tablespoon cornstarch, sifted

Raspberry Sauce
• ◆ •
2½ cups fresh raspberries
½ cup granulated sugar
¼ cup water
1 tablespoon raspberry flavored liqueur (optional)

White Chocolate Lemon Curd Mousse
• ◆ •
5 large egg yolks
⅛ teaspoon salt
½ cup granulated sugar
⅔ cup strained fresh lemon juice
Zest of one lemon, peeled in large strips
5 tablespoons unsalted butter, cut into cubes
8 ounces white chocolate, finely chopped
2¼ cups heavy cream

Assembly
• ◆ •
24 whole fresh strawberries, with their leaves intact
56 fresh raspberries
White chocolate curls or shavings
2 kiwi fruit, peeled and cut into small dice (optional)

Make the pistachio praline powder

1. Lightly butter a nonstick baking sheet and set aside. In a medium, heavy saucepan, using a wooden spoon, stir together the sugar and the lemon juice until thoroughly blended. Cook the sugar mixture over medium heat for 4 to 6 minutes, stirring frequently until it liquefies and then turns to a dark amber-colored caramel. Remove the pan from the heat and stir in the pistachios.

2. Quickly scrape the pistachio praline onto the prepared baking sheet and cool for 20 to 30 minutes, until firm. Transfer the praline to a cutting board and coarsely chop it with a large knife. Put the chopped praline into a food processor fitted with the metal chopping blade. Process for 30 to 40 seconds, until finely ground. Transfer the pistachio praline powder to a small bowl and reserve.

Make the white chocolate mousse

1. Finely chop 3 ounces of the white chocolate and set aside. Coarsely chop the remaining 4 ounces of the white chocolate and melt it according to the chocolate melting directions on page 25.

2. Using a handheld electric mixer, beat the heavy cream just until it begins to form soft peaks. Do not overbeat or the mousse will be grainy. Using a large rubber spatula, gently fold one-third of the whipped cream into the melted white chocolate to lighten it. Fold in the remaining cream and the finely chopped white chocolate. Fold in 1 cup of the pistachio praline powder. Cover the bowl with plastic wrap and chill the mousse for 30 minutes.

Make the tuiles

1. Position a rack in the center of the oven and preheat to 400°F. Place the butter in a medium saucepan and cook over medium heat just until golden brown and fragrant, about 5 minutes. Remove from the heat and let cool until tepid.

2. Place the egg whites and sugar in a medium bowl. Using a handheld electric mixer, beat the mixture at medium speed for 2 to 3 minutes, until well blended. At low speed, gradually beat in the vanilla extract, flour, and butter until blended. Transfer about ½ cup of the mixture to a small bowl, blend in the cocoa powder and water, and set aside.

3. Line a baking sheet with parchment paper. Take an 8-inch cardboard square and draw a 6-inch circle in the center of it. With a pair of scissors, cut out the center circle and discard. Place the cardboard with the hole in it in one corner of the prepared baking sheet.

4. Fill the hollow center of the cardboard with 1 to 2 tablespoons of the plain tuile batter, spreading the batter with a spatula so that it fills the circle completely and evenly.

5. Using a small spoon, drizzle the reserved chocolate-flavored batter over the circles, swirling it lightly to create an attractive marbled effect. Carefully lift the cardboard from around the batter and repeat this procedure, placing the cardboard in each corner of the baking sheet.

6. Bake the tuiles 6 to 8 minutes or until the cookies are evenly golden. Remove the sheet pan from the oven. Using a metal spatula, loosen the edges of one of the tuiles and lift it off the baking sheet. Quickly press the cookie into a mini-brioche mold. Immediately repeat the shaping process with the remaining tuiles. If the last tuile is not flexible enough to shape, return the baking sheet to the oven for 15 seconds. Cool the molded tuiles completely, and then gently lift them from the brioche molds. Repeat the above process with the remaining batter. Store the tuiles in an airtight container at room temperature as soon as they are completely cool.

Make the tangerine sauce

1. In a small bowl, using a wire whisk, dissolve the cornstarch in the water and set aside. In a small saucepan, over medium heat, combine the tangerine or orange juice and sugar. Stirring constantly, bring the mixture to a gentle boil and cook for about 1 to 2 minutes. Whisk in the cornstarch mixture and continue cooking over low heat until the mixture thickens. Remove from the heat and cool.

Assemble the dessert

1. Fill a pastry bag fitted with a large open star tip (such as Ateco #8) with the white chocolate mousse. Pipe a generous amount into each tuile cup.

2. Using a pancake spatula, transfer the tuiles to the center of six dessert plates. Carefully spoon some of the tangerine sauce around the base of each tuile. Lightly sprinkle some pistachio praline powder over the tangerine sauce. Garnish each with tangerine slices or 4 or 5 fresh raspberries. Serve immediately.

White Chocolate Chip Fudge Cookies

As chocolaty and fudgy as baking science will allow, these white chocolate–studded cookies include molasses and brown sugar for a pleasantly earthy flavor. They are an ideal offering for a party or picnic.

•◆•

Y I E L D :   3 6   C O O K I E S

Preparation: 25 minutes plus baking and cooling times

2 ounces semisweet chocolate, coarsely chopped
3 ounces unsweetened chocolate, coarsely chopped
2 cups all-purpose flour
1 teaspoon baking soda
½ teaspoon salt
11 tablespoons unsalted butter, at room temperature
1 cup firmly packed light brown sugar
¾ cup plus 2 tablespoons granulated sugar
1 tablespoon unsulphured (mild) molasses
1 tablespoon vanilla extract
2 large eggs, at room temperature
½ cup unsweetened nonalkalized cocoa powder
Three 3-ounce Lindt white chocolate bars, cut into ¼-inch chunks

1. Position a rack in the center of the oven and preheat to 350°F. Line 2 baking sheets with parchment paper.

2. Melt the semisweet and unsweetened chocolates together according to the instructions on page 25. Set aside.

3. In a medium bowl, sift together the flour, baking soda, and salt; set aside.

4. In a 4½-quart bowl of a heavy-duty electric mixer using the paddle attachment, beat the butter until soft, about 1 minute. Gradually beat in the brown sugar and granulated sugar and continue to beat for 1 minute, scraping down the side of the bowl as necessary. Beat in the molasses and vanilla extract.

5. One at a time, beat in the eggs. Sift the cocoa powder and add it to the mixer bowl. Beat until combined. Add the melted chocolates and mix. Decrease the speed to low and blend in half of the flour mixture, scraping the bowl as necessary.

6. Remove the bowl from the mixer and, using a wooden spoon, fold in the remaining flour with the white chocolate chunks. Do not overmix.

7. Drop the dough onto the baking sheets in walnut-sized mounds; flatten each mound slightly. Bake the cookies until the tops are puffed and cracked, about 12 minutes. Do not overbake or the cookies will be dry. Cool the cookies on the baking sheets for 3 to 5 minutes, then transfer them to wire racks to cool completely.

White Chocolate Margarita Mousse

The tangy and tickly flavors of tequila and lime give this creamy mousse an unexpected kick.
Presented in the manner of a Margarita—with sugar on the rim sweetly substituting for salt—this
is an adults-only dessert, perfect for summer evenings of the soul.

•◆•

YIELD: 6 SERVINGS

Preparation: 1 hour plus cooling times
Special Equipment: 6 martini glasses, for serving mousse

White Chocolate Margarita Mousse
•◆•
10 ounces white chocolate, chopped
½ cup granulated sugar
¼ cup water
4 large egg whites
2 tablespoons orange liqueur
1 tablespoon tequila
1 teaspoon grated lime zest
Pinch of salt
1¼ cups heavy cream

Garnish
•◆•
1 lime
¾ cup granulated sugar
⅓ cup water

Assembly
•◆•
1 cup granulated sugar
Water

Make the mousse

1. Melt the chocolate according to the directions on page 25. Let it cool, stirring once or twice.

2. Combine the sugar and water in a small heavy-bottomed saucepan and cook over medium-low heat, stirring until the sugar dissolves, about 3 to 4 minutes. Raise the heat to medium-high and bring the mixture to a boil. Cook, without stirring, until the syrup registers 240°F on a candy thermometer, about 8 minutes. When the syrup reaches 230°F, start beating the egg whites.

3. In a 4½-quart bowl of a heavy-duty electric mixer, using the wire whip attachment, beat the egg whites at low speed until frothy. Increase the speed to medium-high, beating until stiff peaks form.

4. At this point, the sugar syrup should register 240°F on a candy thermometer. While beating at medium-low speed, gradually pour the syrup in a slow, steady stream near the side of the bowl onto the beaten whites. Increase the speed to medium-high and beat for 5 to 8 minutes, or until the mixture is completely cool and forms stiff, glossy peaks when the wire whip is lifted.

5. Pour the melted white chocolate onto the egg whites and beat on low speed until the chocolate is just incorporated. Beat in the orange liqueur, tequila, lime zest, and salt, and set aside.

6. In a clean, chilled 4½-quart bowl of a heavy-duty electric mixer, using the wire whip attachment, beat the heavy cream until stiff peaks form.

7. Using a large rubber spatula, gently but quickly fold the whipped cream into the egg white-chocolate mixture. Cover the bowl with plastic wrap and chill the mousse for at least 3 hours.

Make the garnish

1. Using a small, sharp knife, cut the lime into very thin slices. Set aside.

2. Combine the sugar and water in a small heavy-bottomed saucepan and cook over medium-low heat, stirring until the sugar dissolves, about 3 to 4 minutes. Raise the heat to medium-high and bring the mixture to a boil. Cook, without stirring, until the mixture thickens to a light syrup, about 2 minutes. Add the lime slices and simmer until they are candied and the peels appear translucent, about 2 to 3 minutes.

3. Using a slotted spoon, remove the lime slices from the sugar syrup and place them on a wire rack to cool and dry.

Assemble the desserts

1. Spread the sugar out evenly in a small dish (it should be at least ⅛-inch deep). Place ⅛-inch of water in another small dish. Dip the rim of each martini glass first into the water, then into the sugar.

2. Carefully spoon some mousse into each prepared glass.

3. Garnish the mousse with the lime slices. Serve immediately or refrigerate until ready to serve.

White Chocolate Soufflé with Lemon Custard and Espresso Whipped Cream

The promise of a soon-to-be-served soufflé generates excitement, and the unexpected nature of this one is bound to intrigue. The pleasing bite of espresso is the flavor undercurrent to this creamy, sweet-and-sour combination of white chocolate and lemon.

•◆•

YIELD: 6 TO 8 SERVINGS

Preparation: 55 minutes, plus baking, cooking, and cooling times

Lemon Custard Sauce
•◆•

2 cups whole milk
1½ tablespoons finely grated lemon zest
5 large egg yolks
¼ cup granulated sugar

Espresso Whipped Cream
•◆•

¼ teaspoon instant espresso powder
2 teaspoons hot water
¾ cup cold heavy cream
2 tablespoons confectioners' sugar

White Chocolate Soufflé
•◆•

3 tablespoons unsalted butter
3½ tablespoons all-purpose flour
Pinch of salt
¾ cup whole milk
4 ounces white chocolate, finely chopped
5 large eggs, separated, at room temperature
1 teaspoon vanilla extract
⅓ cup granulated sugar

Make the lemon custard sauce

1. In a small saucepan set over medium heat, scald the milk. Remove the pan from the heat, stir in the lemon zest, and set aside for 15 minutes.

2. In a medium bowl, beat the egg yolks and sugar with a handheld electric mixer until thick and fluffy, 3 to 4 minutes. Gently stir in the warm milk. Return the mixture to the saucepan and cook over

moderately low heat, stirring constantly, until the mixture reaches 160°F on a thermometer and coats the back of a spoon, about 5 minutes. Strain the custard through a fine sieve into a bowl. Let cool completely, then cover and refrigerate for at least 2 hours or up to 3 days.

Make the espresso whipped cream

1. In a medium bowl, stir together the espresso powder and water until blended. Pour in the heavy cream, add the sugar, and beat with an electric mixer until soft peaks form; do not overbeat. Use immediately or cover and refrigerate for up to 3 hours, rebeating if necessary.

Make the white chocolate soufflé

1. Preheat the oven to 375°F. Tear off a piece of 12-inch-wide aluminum foil, long enough to fit around a 1½-quart soufflé dish with 2 inches to spare. Fold the foil in half lengthwise and wrap it around the outside of the dish; be sure the foil extends 3 inches above the rim. Roll and pinch the two ends of the strip of foil together to connect them securely. Grease the dish and collar, and coat with a dusting of granulated sugar. Set aside on a baking sheet.

2. In a medium saucepan set over medium heat, melt the butter. Whisk in the flour and salt; stir constantly for 2 minutes to cook the starch. Gradually whisk in the milk, then bring to a boil, stirring often. Remove the pan from the heat, add the white chocolate, and whisk occasionally until smooth. Beat in the egg yolks and vanilla extract.

3. In a dry, grease-free 4½-quart bowl of a heavy-duty electric mixer, using the whip attachment, whip the egg whites until frothy. Gradually sprinkle in the sugar while continuing to whip, until all the sugar is added; continue beating until stiff.

4. Gently whisk ¼ of the whites into the yolk mixture until blended. Gently fold in the remaining whites just until no streaks remain. Scrape the batter into the prepared dish. Bake for about 35 minutes, until puffed and golden. Serve at once with lemon custard sauce and espresso whipped cream.

White Chocolate Opera Cake

By placing white chocolate at center stage of this opera cake, we have had to change the classic opera flavors of coffee and chocolate. But we have retained the exquisite opera texture and created a flavor system that sings: full-bodied white chocolate and sweet honey, with almond as a back note, are presented in paper-thin layers of cake, buttercream, and mousse.

•◆•

YIELD: 8 SERVINGS

Preparation: 1 hour, 50 minutes, plus baking, cooling, and chilling times

Almond Biscuit
•◆•
¾ cup slivered almonds
½ cup plus 1 tablespoon granulated sugar, divided
2 large eggs, at room temperature
3 large egg whites, at room temperature
¼ cup cake flour
2 tablespoons unsalted butter, melted

Sugar Syrup
•◆•
⅓ cup water
¼ cup granulated sugar
¼ cup honey
1 tablespoon B&B liqueur

Honey Buttercream
•◆•
1 cup (2 sticks) unsalted butter, softened
3 large egg yolks, at room temperature
¼ cup honey

White Chocolate Mousse
•◆•
7 ounces Swiss white chocolate, coarsely chopped
1 cup plus 3 tablespoons heavy cream, divided
1 tablespoon B&B liqueur

White Chocolate Glaze
•◆•
7 ounces Swiss white chocolate, coarsely chopped
¼ cup heavy cream

Chocolate Decor
•◆•
1 ounce bittersweet chocolate

Make the almond biscuit

1. Position a rack in the center of the oven and preheat to 400°F. Butter a 17½-by-11½-inch jelly roll pan and line the bottom with parchment paper. Lightly butter and flour the sheet, shaking off the excess flour. Set aside.

2. Using a food processor fitted with a metal chopping blade, process the almonds to a very fine cornmeal-like texture. Place the ground almonds in a medium bowl and stir in ½ cup of the sugar.

3. Using a handheld electric mixer, beat 1 whole egg into the almond mixture. Beat the mixture on high speed for 1 minute. Add the second egg and beat on high speed for another minute. Scrape down the sides of the bowl and the beaters. The mixture should be pale yellow in color.

4. Place the egg whites in a 4½-quart bowl of a heavy-duty electric mixer fitted with the wire whisk attachment. Beat the whites on high speed until they are frothy. Slowly add the reserved tablespoon of sugar and beat until the whites are slightly glossy and stiff peaks form.

5. Sift the flour over the egg-almond mixture and, using a large rubber spatula, fold in the flour until incorporated. Gently fold in the whites in two batches. Fold in the melted butter, making sure it is completely incorporated into the batter.

6. Pour the mixture onto the prepared pan in an even layer approximately ¼-inch thick. Tap the pan lightly on the counter and smooth to remove any air pockets.

7. Bake the cake for 10 minutes, or until lightly browned. Remove from the oven and cool on a wire rack for 10 minutes. Invert the cake onto a wire rack, peel off the parchment paper and cool completely. Cut the cake into 3 equal portions, each 5½-inches wide. If the cake will not be assembled until the following day, wrap securely in plastic wrap, placing a piece of waxed paper in between each layer.

Make the sugar syrup

1. In a small heavy saucepan, combine the water, sugar, and honey. Bring to a boil and boil for 2 to 3 minutes, until the sugar is dissolved and the syrup is clear. Remove from heat and add the B&B liqueur; set aside.

Make the honey buttercream

1. Place the butter into a medium bowl and cream, using a handheld electric mixer, until completely softened and smooth; set aside.

2. In a 4½-quart bowl of a heavy-duty electric mixer fitted with the wire whisk attachment, beat the yolks on medium speed until pale yellow in color.

3. Spray a heatproof glass measure or ramekin with nonstick cooking spray. Place the honey in a small saucepan. Stirring constantly, bring the honey to a rolling boil over medium-high heat. Immediately pour the honey into the empty glass measure or ramekin to stop the cooking. Pour half of the honey onto the yolks, turn the mixer to high, and beat for 1 minute. Turn off the mixer, add the remaining honey and beat until the bowl feels cool, about 5 minutes. Scrape down the sides of the bowl well with a rubber spatula. Add the softened butter and beat until completely smooth. Scrape into a small bowl, cover, and reserve.

Make the white chocolate mousse

1. Melt the chopped white chocolate and the 3 tablespoons of heavy cream according to the directions on page 25. Whisk gently and let cool to room temperature.

2. Place the remaining heavy cream into a 4½-quart bowl of a heavy-duty electric mixer fitted with the wire whisk attachment. Add the B&B liqueur. Beat on high speed until soft peaks form.

3. Using a wire whisk, gently stir in about 1 cup of the whipped cream to the cooled white chocolate mixture. Using a rubber spatula, fold in the remaining cream. Do not over-mix or the mousse will become grainy. Cover and refrigerate until ready to use.

Assemble the cake

1. Place one of the biscuit rectangles onto a cake board of the same size. Using a pastry brush, generously soak the cake with the sugar syrup. Reserve 2 tablespoons of the honey buttercream for decoration. Place the remaining honey buttercream onto the cake and using a long, straight spatula, smooth into an even layer.

2. Place the next layer of biscuit on top and press gently into the honey buttercream layer. Again, soak with the sugar syrup. Scrape half of the white chocolate mousse onto the layer of biscuit and smooth into an even layer.

3. Place the final layer of biscuit on top and soak with the sugar syrup. Smooth the remaining white chocolate mousse on top. Place the cake into the refrigerator for at least 30 minutes.

Make the white chocolate glaze

1. Melt the white chocolate with the heavy cream according to the directions on page 25. Whisk gently until smooth. Let cool for 10 minutes and then pour over the chilled cake. Using a long metal cake spatula, smooth out into an even layer. Place the cake into the refrigerator for 30 minutes to set.

Make the chocolate decor

1. Line a baking sheet with parchment paper. Temper the chocolate according to the instructions on page 27. Make a small paper cone with a tiny opening at the tip and fill with the tempered bittersweet chocolate. Pipe twenty or so musical notes and or clefs onto the parchment paper. Let harden completely.

Finish the cake

1. Remove the cake from the refrigerator. Using a long sharp knife that has been heated, either in hot water (and wiped dry) or over a gas flame, slice approximately ¼ inch off of each side of the cake to make a perfect rectangle. Slice the cake lengthwise down the center and then crosswise to make 8 equal portions.

2. Place the remaining 2 tablespoons of honey buttercream into another small paper cone with a slightly larger opening at the tip. Pipe a small dot of honey buttercream onto the center of each piece. Using a gloved hand, peel back the chocolate decor from the parchment paper and place it on the dot of buttercream. Serve immediately or refrigerate and bring to room temperature before serving.

White Chocolate Raspberry Cheesecake

Cheesecake is one of America's unacknowledged most-favorite desserts, and this one is an elegant variation of the standard form. A chocolate graham cracker crust supports a white chocolate cheesecake filling swirled with tart, colorful raspberry sauce.

•◆•

YIELD: 10 SERVINGS

Preparation: 1 hour, plus baking and cooling times

Chocolate Graham Cracker Crust
•◆•

11 whole chocolate graham crackers (⅓ of a 1-pound box), broken into
1-inch pieces
4 tablespoons unsalted butter, melted
2 tablespoons granulated sugar

White Chocolate Cheesecake Filling
•◆•

8 ounces white chocolate, chopped
¼ cup heavy cream
Five 8-ounce packages cream cheese, at room temperature
1 cup granulated sugar
3 large eggs

Raspberry Coulis
•◆•

2 pints raspberries
½ cup granulated sugar
1 tablespoon eau de framboise or kirsch
1 teaspoon fresh lemon juice

Garnish
•◆•

White chocolate curls
½ pint raspberries

Make the chocolate graham cracker crust

1. Preheat the oven to 350°F. Place the graham crackers in a food processor fitted with the metal chopping blade. Process until they form fine crumbs. Transfer to a 10-inch springform pan. Add the melted butter and the sugar. Toss together well, then press into the bottom of the pan. Bake for 10 minutes, then set on a wire rack and cool completely.

Make the white chocolate cheesecake filling

1. In a small saucepan, melt the white chocolate with the cream over low heat, stirring occasionally until smooth. Set aside to cool.

2. In the 4½-quart bowl of a heavy-duty electric mixer using the paddle attachment, beat the cream cheese and sugar until well blended. Beat in the eggs one at a time; continue mixing for 3 minutes. Pour in the cooled white chocolate mixture. Mix at low speed until incorporated. Pour the filling into the pan and smooth the top.

3. Bake the cheesecake for 1 hour and then turn off the oven without opening the door. Allow the cake to cool in the oven for 2 hours. Remove the cake from the oven and place it on a rack to cool completely. Cover and refrigerate for at least 8 hours or up to 3 days.

Make the raspberry coulis

1. Place the raspberries in a medium bowl. Sprinkle the sugar, eau de framboise or kirsch, and lemon juice on top; let rest for 15 minutes. Mash the berry mixture with a fork, then push through a fine mesh sieve, discarding the seeds.

2. Before serving, uncover the cake. Garnish the top of the cake with white chocolate curls. Arrange the berries all over the curls. (May be refrigerated for up to 3 hours uncovered before serving.) Cut the cake into slices and serve with the raspberry coulis swirled on each serving plate.

Cashew White Chocolate Meringue Cake

The pleasing earthiness of cashew—reinforced by toasted cashews—infuses slender meringue discs which sandwich silky white chocolate buttercream. Guaranteed that even the most experienced dessert lover will not have tried anything like this simple but ingenious offering.

•◆•

YIELD: 10 SERVINGS

Preparation: 1 hour, 45 minutes, plus baking and cooling times

Cashew Meringues
•◆•
1⅓ cups raw cashews
3 tablespoons cornstarch
1½ cups granulated sugar, divided
8 large egg whites, at room temperature

White Chocolate Buttercream
•◆•
1½ cups (3 sticks) unsalted butter, softened
8 ounces premium white chocolate, such as Lindt
4 large egg whites
1 cup granulated sugar
½ cup water

Garnish
•◆•
1 cup raw cashews
2 tablespoons unsweetened cocoa powder

Make the cashew meringues

1. Line 2 baking sheets with parchment paper. Using a pencil, trace the outline of an 8-inch cake pan directly onto the parchment paper. Repeat 3 more times to make a total of four 8-inch circles. (Only 3 meringue circles will be needed; the fourth is in case of breakage). Invert the parchment paper on the baking sheets and set aside. Preheat the oven to 200°F.

2. Place the cashews in a food processor fitted with a metal chopping blade. Add the cornstarch and half of the sugar. Pulse until the cashews are finely ground.

3. Place the egg whites into a 4½-quart bowl of a heavy-duty electric mixer fitted with the whisk attachment. Beat the egg whites on high speed until soft peaks form. Add the remaining sugar and beat until the whites are firm and glossy.

4. Using a large rubber spatula, gently fold in the dry ingredients. Place the meringue into a large pastry bag fitted with a ½-inch plain tip (such as Ateco #6). Holding the pastry bag in a vertical position over one of the traced circles, pipe the meringue in a spiral motion toward the circle's outer edge, until it is completely filled. Fill in the remaining 3 circles and then pipe eight 3-inch discs in the empty spaces on the baking sheets (these will be crushed for garnish). Bake the meringues for 1 to 1½ hours, or until dry.

Make the white chocolate buttercream

1. Place the butter in a medium bowl and, using a handheld electric mixer, beat until completely smooth. Set aside.

2. Melt the white chocolate according to directions on page 25. Set aside to cool.

3. Place the egg whites into a 4½-quart bowl of a heavy-duty electric mixer fitted with the whisk attachment.

4. Place the sugar and the water in a medium, heavy saucepan. Cook over high heat, brushing down the sides of the pan with cold water to prevent the sugar from crystallizing. Cook the syrup until it registers 250°F on a candy thermometer.

5. Meanwhile, begin beating the egg whites at medium-high speed. When the sugar has reached the desired temperature, reduce the speed of the mixer to medium and slowly drizzle in the hot sugar syrup between the side of the bowl and the whisk. Beat on high for 2 minutes and then lower to medium speed and beat until completely cool.

6. At medium speed, beat in the butter a little bit at a time until completely incorporated. (If the egg-sugar mixture is even slightly warm when the butter is added, the buttercream may separate. In that case, place the buttercream over a bowl of ice water and whisk until cool.)

7. Beat in the melted and cooled white chocolate until completely incorporated. Store the buttercream in an airtight container for up to one day at room temperature.

Assemble and garnish the cake

1. Preheat the oven to 375°F. Place the cashews on a baking sheet and bake for 8 to 10 minutes or until golden brown. Remove from the oven and cool.

2. Place a dab of buttercream in the center of an 8-inch round cardboard cake disc. Place an 8-inch meringue on top. Frost with approximately one-quarter of the buttercream. Place another meringue disc on top, pressing down gently but firmly. Continue with another layer of buttercream and the last meringue. With the remaining buttercream, frost the side and top of the cake.

3. Place the cashews in a food processor fitted with a metal chopping blade. Pulse until the cashews are finely chopped.

4. Place the 8 small meringue discs in a medium bowl and crush with your hands. Add the chopped and toasted cashews and blend well. Press the crumbs into the side and top of the cake. Refrigerate for 1 hour or until 30 minutes before serving. Sift the cocoa powder over the top of the cake and serve. Slice the cake using a serrated knife.

White Chocolate Strawberry Mousse Cake

White chocolate again plays the foil, this time for the beloved flavor of strawberry, here delivered in the form of smooth and lustrous mousse. A flavorful almond cake provides the frame for the white chocolate and strawberry mousses. A summer dessert without peer.

•◆•

YIELD: 12 SERVINGS

Preparation: 3 hours, plus baking, cooling, and chilling times
Special Equipment: One-gold flecked transfer sheet

Toasted Almond Sponge Cake
•◆•
½ cup blanched almonds, toasted (see page 41)
½ cup cake flour
¼ cup plus 1 tablespoon granulated sugar, divided
⅛ teaspoon salt
6 large eggs, separated, at room temperature
¼ cup confectioners' sugar
2 teaspoons vanilla extract

Strawberry Mousse
•◆•
1½ teaspoons unflavored powdered gelatin
½ cup strawberry fruit purée, at room temperature
1 cup heavy cream
¼ cup granulated sugar

White Chocolate Mousse
•◆•
¼ cup water
1 envelope unflavored powdered gelatin
¼ cup cornstarch
2 cups milk, divided
2 large eggs plus 1 large egg yolk
¼ cup granulated sugar
6 ounces Swiss white chocolate, such as Lindt, finely chopped
2 tablespoons unsalted butter, cut into ½-inch pieces
2 teaspoons vanilla extract
2 cups heavy cream

White Chocolate Triangles
•◆•
6 ounces Swiss white chocolate, such as Lindt, coarsely chopped

Garnish
•◆•
1½ cups sliced almonds
1 pint strawberries, hulled

Make the toasted almond spongecake

1. Position a rack in the center of the oven and preheat to 350°F. Lightly butter the side of a 9-inch round cake pan. Line the bottom of the pan with a circle of parchment or waxed paper. Dust the side of the pan with flour and tap out the excess.

2. In a food processor fitted with the metal chopping blade, combine the toasted almonds, cake flour, 1 tablespoon of the granulated sugar, and salt. Process for 30 to 40 seconds, or until the almonds are finely ground.

3. In the 4½-quart bowl of a heavy-duty electric mixer using the wire whisk attachment, beat the egg yolks at medium speed until blended. While continuing to beat, add the confectioners' sugar, 1 tablespoon at a time. Increase the speed to high and continue beating the egg yolk mixture for 4 to 7 minutes, until it is pale yellow. Beat in the vanilla extract.

4. In a clean 4½-quart bowl of a heavy-duty electric mixer, using the wire whisk attachment, beat the egg whites until frothy. Gradually increase the speed to medium-high and beat the whites until soft peaks start to form. One teaspoon at a time, add the remaining ¼ cup granulated sugar and continue beating the whites until stiff, shiny peaks form.

5. Using a balloon whisk or rubber spatula, fold one-third of the egg white mixture along with one-third of the almond-flour mixture into the egg yolk mixture. In two more additions, fold in the remaining egg white and almond-flour mixture, being careful not to deflate the batter.

6. Scrape the batter into the prepared pan and smooth the top. Bake for 30 to 35 minutes or until the center of the cake springs back when gently pressed. Cool the cake in the pan set on a wire rack for 10 minutes. Run the tip of a small knife around the edge of the cake to loosen it from the side of the pan. Invert the cake onto a wire rack and remove the pan. Carefully peel off the paper and invert the cake again onto another wire rack. Cool the cake completely. Using a long serrated knife, cut the cake horizontally into three equal layers. Set aside.

Make the strawberry mousse

1. In a small heatproof measuring cup, place the gelatin and ¼ cup fruit purée, and allow to sit for 5 minutes. Set the cup in a pan of simmering water for a few minutes, stirring occasionally until the gelatin is dissolved. Remove the cup and stir the gelatin mixture into the remaining purée. The mixture should be cool to the touch.

2. In a chilled bowl beat the heavy cream with a handheld electric mixer just until it starts to mound softly when dropped from a spoon. Gradually add the sugar. Add the purée and beat just until stiff peaks form when the beater is raised.

Make the white chocolate mousse

1. Place the water in a small heatproof cup. Sprinkle the gelatin over the water and let the mixture soften while you prepare the mousse.

2. In a medium bowl, whisk the cornstarch and ½ cup milk until smooth. Whisk in the eggs and egg yolk until blended. In a heavy, noncorrosive saucepan, combine the remaining 1½ cups milk and sugar. Cook over medium heat, stirring occasionally, until small bubbles form around the side of the pan. Gradually whisk 1 cup of the hot milk mixture into the cornstarch/egg mixture until blended. Pour this mixture back into the saucepan.

3. Continue cooking over medium heat, whisking constantly until the mixture starts to form bubbles. Continue stirring and boil the mixture for 2 minutes. Take the pan off the heat. Add the chocolate and the gelatin mixture. Whisk until smooth. Stir in the butter until blended.

4. Strain the mixture through a sieve into a large bowl. Stir in the vanilla extract. Place the bowl over a bowl of ice water and stir for 5 to 10 minutes, until cool. Remove the white chocolate mixture from the bowl of the iced water.

5. In a chilled large bowl, using a handheld electric mixer set at medium speed, beat the cream until soft peaks begin to form. Do not overwhip the cream. Using a rubber spatula, fold one-third of the whipped cream into the white chocolate mixture to lighten it. Fold in the remaining whipped cream.

Assemble the cake

1. Remove the side from a 9-inch springform pan. Trim a 10-inch cardboard cake circle so that it fits snugly within the curved lip of the bottom of the springform pan. Reattach the side of the springform pan. Remove the paper from the bottom of the cake layers. Place one of the cake layers into the prepared pan.

2. Scrape 3 cups of the white chocolate mousse over the cake layer in the pan. Using a small offset metal cake spatula, spread the mousse in an even layer over the cake. Make sure that the mousse is evenly distributed within the narrow space between the side of the pan and the edge of the cake layer.

Place the second cake layer over the white chocolate mousse. Scrape the strawberry mousse over the cake layer in the pan. Using a small offset metal cake spatula, spread the mousse in an even layer over the cake. Place the third cake layer over the strawberry mousse. Scrape 1½ cups of the remaining white chocolate mousse or enough mousse to fill the space between the top layer of the cake and the top edge of the pan. Spread the mousse in an even layer over the cake using the rim of the pan as a guide. With a long metal cake spatula scrape off any excess mousse. Transfer the remaining white chocolate mousse to a small bowl and cover with plastic wrap. Refrigerate the assembled cake and reserved mousse for at least 4 hours, or overnight.

Make the white chocolate triangles

1. Line a flat baking sheet with a piece of parchment paper. Draw a 9-inch circle on the parchment paper. Place the transfer sheet on top of the parchment paper. Tape the 4 corners of the transfer sheet to the baking sheet to hold it in place.

2. Temper the white chocolate according to the instructions on page 27. Pour the tempered chocolate into the center of the traced circle on the transfer sheet. Using a small offset cake spatula, spread the chocolate evenly until it fills in the circle. Refrigerate the baking sheet for 5 to 10 minutes, until the chocolate feels firm, but not brittle.

3. With a long sharp knife, cut the circle into 12 wedges. Using an offset metal cake spatula, gently peel the wedges off the transfer sheet and transfer them to a waxed paper-lined baking sheet. If the wedges become soft while you are cutting them, return the baking sheet to the refrigerator briefly until the chocolate is firm again.

Unmold the cake

1. Using a portable blow-dryer or damp (not wet) very hot towel, carefully heat the outside of the springform pan until the edge of the mousse melts slightly. Release the clamp on the side of the springform pan and gently lift it up and remove it from around the side of the cake.

Decorate the cake

1. Reserve about ¾ cup of the chilled white chocolate mousse for piping on top of the cake. Using an offset metal spatula, spread a thin layer of the remaining mousse around the side of the cake to coat the exposed cake layers.

2. Lift up the cake on the cardboard circle, supporting the bottom of the cake in one hand. Use a metal spatula to lift up the almonds and press them against the side of the cake, working around the cake until the side is completely covered with the sliced almonds. Put the cake on a serving plate.

3. Fill a pastry bag fitted with a large closed star tip (such as Ateco #4) with the reserved ¾ cup of white chocolate mousse. Pipe one rosette in the top center of the cake and 12 rosettes evenly spaced around the top outer edge of the cake. Top each of the 12 rosettes with a fresh strawberry, point side up.

4. Place 12 triangles around the top of the cake. Place each triangle so that the widest portion rests at a slight angle on the strawberry on a piped rosette at the edge of the cake. Place a large strawberry in the middle of the cake on the single piped rosette. Refrigerate the cake until ready to serve.

Mini White Chocolate Orange Cheese Tarts

Although these are mini-tarts, they pack a flavor wallop: spicy gingersnap crust supports a filling of assertive farmer's cheese, sweet white chocolate, and refreshing orange, with cranberry sauce providing moisture and a tart undernote. These are grown-up flavors, but give the kids a bite—it's never too soon to refine the palate.

•◆•

YIELD: EIGHT 4-INCH TARTS

Preparation: 1½ hours, plus baking and cooling times

Special Equipment: Eight 4-inch diameter-by-1-inch deep fluted tartlet pans with removeable bottoms; two 6-inch-square pieces of food-safe accetate; 6-inch wide decorator's comb or serrated knife with ⅛-inch wide teeth

Gingersnap Crusts
•◆•

One 12-ounce box prepared gingersnap cookies, finely ground
1¼ cups whole toasted almonds, finely ground
⅓ cup granulated sugar
10 tablespoons (1¼ sticks) unsalted butter, melted

White Chocolate Cheese Filling
•◆•

1 pound, 3 ounces farmer's cheese,* at room temperature
¾ cup granulated sugar
3 tablespoons all-purpose flour
2 large eggs, at room temperature
2 large egg yolks, at room temperature
7½ ounces white chocolate, melted
1 teaspoon orange extract
2 tablespoons Cointreau, or other orange liqueur
½ cup heavy cream

Cranberry Sauce
•◆•

6 ounces fresh cranberries
2 cups water
1 cup granulated sugar
½ teaspoon orange extract

Wavy Chocolate Lines
•✦•
3 ounces white chocolate, tempered (see tempering instructions on page 27)
3 ounces bittersweet chocolate

*Note: If farmer's cheese is not available at your local market, cream cheese may be substituted.

Make the gingersnap crusts

1. In a large mixing bowl, combine the ground gingersnaps, ground almonds, and sugar. Drizzle the melted butter over the mixture and stir to combine.

2. Place 2 to 3 tablespoons of the gingersnap mixture into a 4-inch-by-1-inch fluted tartlet pan with removable bottom. Press the mixture onto the bottom and sides of the pan, adding more crumbs if necessary. Repeat with the remaining 7 tartlet pans.

3. Set the tartlet pans on a baking sheet and refrigerate until ready to fill. Place a rack in the center of the oven and preheat to 350°F.

Make the white chocolate cheese filling

1. In the 4½-quart bowl of a heavy-duty mixer fitted with the paddle attachment, beat the farmer's cheese on low speed, until light and fluffy. Add the sugar and flour, and continue at low speed until the mixture is smooth and fluffy. One at a time, add the eggs and egg yolks, mixing on low to medium speed until each is incorporated. Scrape down the sides of the bowl as necessary. Add the melted white chocolate and mix to combine. Add the orange extract, Cointreau, and heavy cream, and mix until the batter is smooth. (Do not beat at too high of a speed or air bubbles will form in the batter.)

2. Fill the chilled tartlet pans with batter, stopping ⅛ inch below the top of the crust. Place the baking sheet with the tart pans in the oven and bake for 30 to 35 minutes, until the filling is set and slightly puffed. Cool over a baking rack until just warm before removing the cheese tarts from the pans and serving.

Make the cranberry sauce

1. In a medium, heavy saucepan combine the cranberries, water, and sugar over medium-high heat. Bring to a boil, stirring with a wooden spoon until the sugar is dissolved. Boil for 10 minutes or until the liquid is reduced by one-third. Purée and strain the mixture and return to the saucepan. Bring to a boil once again and skim any foam off the surface. Remove from the heat and stir in the orange extract. Refrigerate the sauce if not using immediately. Rewarm the sauce before serving.

Make the wavy chocolate lines

1. Spray a clean work surface with nonstick cooking spray and place two 6-inch-square pieces of food-safe acetate side by side over the sprayed surface (so they won't slip). Spread the white chocolate along the edge of one piece of acetate with an offset spatula. Using a six-inch-wide decorating comb with ⅛-inch-wide teeth or a serrated knife, comb the chocolate along the acetate, weaving the comb back and forth to make wavy lines. Repeat the bittersweet type of chocolate. Let the chocolate set before using the lines to garnish the tarts.

Garnish the tarts

1. Place each tart on a dessert plant. Place three wavy chocolate lines vertically into each tart and serve immediately.

Tahitian Vanilla Swirls

Inside a dark chocolate swirl form is a white chocolate cream center kissed lightly with cognac and distinctively flavored with tiny seeds from a Tahitian vanilla bean. It is important to split the vanilla beans and infuse them in heavy cream the night before preparing the ganache filling.

YIELD: 64 CHOCOLATES

Preparation: 3 hours, plus infusing, chilling, freezing, and setting times. Allow time for the Tahitian vanilla cream to infuse overnight.

Special Equipment (see mail order sources on page 302): digital thermometer; heating pad with temperature control dial (such as the type used for backaches); two clear, rigid polycarbonate chocolate molds, each containing 32 oval swirl-shaped mold cavities; ¼-inch natural-bristle flat pastry brush; flexible straight-edged steel baker's scraper; 8-inch offset metal cake spatula; cotton gloves.

Tahitian Vanilla Cream

2 Tahitian vanilla beans, split in half lengthwise
1 cup heavy cream

Tahitian Vanilla Ganache

12 ounces Swiss white chocolate, such as Lindt*
2 teaspoons invert sugar, such as Nulomoline**
2 tablespoons unsalted butter, softened
2 teaspoons cognac

Hollow Dark Chocolate Swirls

2 pounds bittersweet chocolate couverture, such as Valrhona Caraque or Caraibe (see mail order sources on page 302)

*Note: Use 3-ounce Lindt Swiss white chocolate bars for preparing the ganache. This particular chocolate contains just the right amount of cocoa butter to enable the ganache filling to set up properly.

**Note: Invert sugar acts as a softener and helps to prolong the freshness of the ganache filling. See a mail order source for Nulomoline on page 305.

Prepare the Tahitian vanilla cream

1. Using the sharp tip of a small knife, scrape the paste of tiny black seeds from inside the split vanilla bean. Combine the vanilla bean paste and heavy cream in a small, heavy saucepan. Add the scraped pods to the cream. Bring the mixture to a gentle boil over medium heat. Remove from the heat and pour the mixture into a glass measuring cup. Cool for 15 minutes, stirring occasionally. Cover with plastic wrap and refrigerate 12 hours or overnight.

THE NEXT DAY

Make the Tahitian vanilla ganache

1. Coarsely chop the white chocolate and put it in a food processor fitted with the metal chopping blade. Process the chocolate for 15 to 20 seconds and leave the chocolate in the work bowl.

2. Scrape the chilled Tahitian vanilla-infused cream into a small, heavy saucepan and add the invert sugar. Heat the cream mixture until it comes to a gentle boil. Using tongs, remove the vanilla bean pods and discard. Pour the hot cream over the chopped white chocolate. Using a rubber spatula, press down on the chocolate so that it is completely submerged in the hot cream. Let the mixture stand for 1 minute.

3. Add the butter and replace the lid of the food processor. Pulse 4 to 6 times, until the mixture is creamy and smooth. Scrape down the sides of the work bowl, and add the cognac. Pulse 2 to 3 times until blended.

4. Scrape the ganache onto a baking sheet, letting it spread into a thin layer. Cover the surface with plastic wrap and freeze for at least 2 hours, until firm.

Prepare the hollow dark chocolate swirls

1. Temper the bittersweet chocolate. (Refer to the tempering instructions on page 27.)

2. Thoroughly clean the inside of each oval cavity in the 2 chocolate molds with a lint-free cloth or a cotton ball.

3. With a ¾-inch flat, dry pastry brush, using a quick dabbing brush stroke, paint the inside of each mold cavity with a thin, even layer of tempered chocolate. Try to work quickly and avoid creating air bubbles.

4. Using a flexible straight-edged steel baker's scraper, level the edges of chocolate-lined cavities by scraping the surface of the chocolate mold. Hold the scraper at a slight angle and run the scraper over the length of mold. Let the chocolate set at room temperature for 3 to 10 minutes, until the chocolate starts to harden but is still slightly tacky. Leave the brush on the heating pad so that the chocolate will not harden on the bristles.

5. Brush the inside of each swirl cavity with a second thin layer of chocolate and level the edges with the baker's scraper. Allow the hollow chocolate swirls to harden at room temperature while preparing the ganache filling. Keep the tempered chocolate warm, stirring occasionally and monitoring the temperature with a digital thermometer. Do not let the chocolate get too hot (above 92°F), or it will go out of temper.

Whip the Tahitian vanilla ganache

1. Remove the plastic wrap from the chilled ganache. Gently warm the bottom of the baking sheet by passing it back and forth a few times over a gas flame or electric range top set on medium. Heat the pan only until the ganache starts to melt slightly so that it can be easily removed from the pan. Using a rubber spatula, scrape half (about 1 cup) of the ganache into the bowl of a heavy-duty electric mixer.

2. Set the bowl over another bowl of hot, not simmering water (the water must touch the bottom of the bowl) for 30 seconds to 2 minutes, stirring constantly with a rubber spatula until the ganache reads 65°F on an instant-read thermometer and has softened to the consistency of handmade mayonnaise. Be careful not to overheat the ganache. If the ganache becomes warmer than 65°F, place the bowl over a bowl of ice water for 2 to 4 seconds. Stir the ganache with a rubber spatula, just until it starts to thicken. Remove the bowl from the ice water.

3. Using the wire whip attachment, whip the softened ganache at medium speed for 30 seconds to 2 minutes, or until it lightens in color and forms soft peaks. It should have the texture of a fluffy vanilla buttercream frosting. If the whipped ganache becomes too firm and appears grainy, replace the bowl over the hot water for 2 to 4 seconds, and stir gently until it softens enough to be re-whipped. Conversely, if the ganache is too soft and will not form soft peaks, place it over the bowl of ice water and stir for 2 to 4 seconds, until it just starts to thicken. Continue whipping until the ganache reaches the proper consistency.

Fill the hollow chocolate swirls

1. Scrape the whipped Tahitian vanilla ganache on top of one end of one of the chocolate-lined molds. Using an 8-inch offset metal cake spatula, carefully spread the ganache over the surface of the mold and press a portion of it into each of the mold cavities. Try to avoid creating air pockets. Holding the spatula at a 90° angle, scrape the excess filling off the surface of the mold.

2. Using the remaining chilled ganache, repeat the process, filling the second chocolate mold. (Stir the excess ganache from the first batch of filling into the second batch of softened ganache before whipping.) Refrigerate the filled molds for 20 to 30 minutes, until the ganache is firm. Then let the molds sit at room temperature for 15 minutes before sealing with tempered chocolate.

Seal the bottoms of the filled chocolate swirls

1. Check the temperature and fluidity of the tempered bittersweet chocolate. It needs to be between 89°F and 91°F—a little warmer than usual—so that it is easy to seal the bottoms of the filled mold cavities with a thin covering of chocolate.

2. Rest one end of a chocolate mold on the edge of the bowl of tempered chocolate. Pour about ⅓ cup of tempered chocolate over the top half of the mold. Using an 8-inch offset metal cake spatula and holding it at a slight angle, spread the chocolate in a thin, even layer over the filled chocolate swirls. Still holding the spatula at a slight angle, scrape the excess chocolate back into the bowl, leaving behind a thin layer of chocolate capping each mold cavity. Turn the mold around and seal the remaining chocolate swirls with tempered chocolate. Repeat the process with the second chocolate mold. Refrigerate the chocolate molds for 1½ hours.

3. Pour the remaining tempered chocolate onto a waxed paper-lined baking sheet and refrigerate for 10 to 15 minutes, until firm. Let the chocolate stand at room temperature for 30 minutes. Break into pieces and store in a zip-lock bag.

Unmold the chocolates

1. Pad a work surface with a folded kitchen towel or a double thickness of paper towels. Remove 1 of the chocolate molds from the refrigerator. Holding a mold upright, check underneath the mold to see if the surface of the chocolate that is against the surface of each swirl cavity is uniformly frosty. If there are any clear spots, return the chocolate molds to the refrigerator and check again in about 30 minutes.

2. Carefully invert the molds, one at time, over the padded surface, and if necessary gently tap each mold on the work surface to release the swirls. (If they do not release from the molds after a gentle tap, it could be one of three reasons: the chocolate has not set sufficiently; there is excess chocolate around the mold cavities, or the chocolate was not properly tempered. If the problem is excess chocolate, it will be obvious. You will see a layer of chocolate on the surface of the mold surrounding the swirl cavities. Tap the pan firmly on the work surface until the swirls release from the mold. If the swirls are still not releasing from the mold, this is an indication that the chocolate was not in temper when you brushed the mold cavities with chocolate to form the hollow chocolate swirls. If this should happen, do not attempt to scrape the chocolate from the molds. Simply heat the chocolate in each mold cavity with a portable hair dryer until it melts and wipe the entire mold clean. You will have to start over with newly tempered chocolate couverture. Let the unmolded swirls come to room temperature for 30 minutes.)

3. Sometimes the unmolded swirls need to be trimmed, especially if there was excess chocolate on the mold during the unmolding process. Wearing cotton gloves and using a small, sharp knife, carefully trim around the base of each chocolate. Store the Tahitian Vanilla Swirls in an airtight container at cool room temperature for up to 5 days, or in the refrigerator for up to 2 weeks. Allow the chocolates to come to room temperature in the storage container before serving.

Summer Truffles

Flavors we normally associate with Asian cuisine—lemongrass and coconut milk—are showcased in a white chocolate ganache center, coated in white chocolate with crunchy wisps of toasted coconut. A cool and distinctive addition to your candy repertoire.

•◆•

YIELD: APPROXIMATELY 50 TRUFFLES

Preparation: 2 hours, plus infusing, cooling, chilling, freezing, and setting times. Allow time for the lemongrass, coconut milk, and heavy cream to infuse overnight before preparing the ganache.

Special Equipment (see mail order sources on page 302): Disposable pastry bag; ½-inch plain decorating tip (such as Ateco #6); digital thermometer; heating pad with temperature control dial (such as the type used for backaches); 2 silicone baking mats; cotton gloves.

Lemongrass Coconut Cream
•◆•
2 stalks fresh lemongrass
¾ cup heavy cream
⅓ cup plus 2 tablespoons well-stirred canned unsweetened coconut milk

Lemongrass Coconut Ganache
•◆•
12 ounces coarsely chopped Swiss white chocolate, such as Lindt*
2 teaspoons invert sugar, such as Nulomoline**
1 tablespoon unsalted butter, softened
Confectioners' sugar

White Chocolate Coconut Coating
•◆•
1¼ cups sweetened shredded coconut
1 pound Swiss white chocolate couverture, from the large 13-ounce Lindt bars (see mail order sources, page 302)

*Note: Use 3-ounce Lindt Swiss white chocolate bars for preparing the ganache. This particular chocolate contains just the right amount of cocoa butter to enable the ganache filling to set up properly.

**Note: Invert sugar acts as a softener and helps to prolong the freshness of the ganache filling. See a mail order source for Nulomoline on page 305.

THE NIGHT BEFORE

Prepare the lemongrass coconut cream

1. Remove the outer leaves from the lemongrass stalks and trim the ends. Rinse and dry the stalks well before cutting into thin slices. In a small saucepan, combine the heavy cream, coconut milk, and lemongrass. Bring to a gentle boil, stirring often. Remove from the heat and pour the mixture into a glass measuring cup. Cool for 20 minutes, stirring occasionally. Cover with plastic wrap and refrigerate 12 hours or overnight.

THE NEXT DAY

Prepare the lemongrass coconut ganache

1. In a food processor fitted with the metal chopping blade, process the white chocolate until finely chopped.

2. Scrape the chilled lemongrass coconut cream into a small saucepan and add the invert sugar. Bring the mixture to a full boil, stirring often. Immediately pour the hot cream through a fine-meshed sieve over the chopped chocolate. Using a spoon, press down on the lemongrass to extract every bit of the infused cream. With a rubber spatula, make sure that the white chocolate is completely submerged in the hot cream. Let the mixture stand 1 minute.

3. Add the softened butter and replace the lid of the food processor. Pulse 6 to 8 times, until the mixture is creamy. Scrape down the sides of the work bowl, and pulse 4 more times, until blended.

4. Scrape the ganache onto a baking sheet letting it spread into a thin layer. Cover the surface of the ganache with plastic wrap and freeze for at least 2 hours, until firm.

Prepare the truffle centers

1. Remove the ganache from the freezer and let it soften at room temperature for 30 to 45 minutes, or until it is soft enough to pipe, about 68°F.

2. Cut the pointed end off of a disposable pastry bag and insert a ½-inch plain decorating tip (such as Ateco #6). Twist the portion of the pastry bag that is just above the wider opening of the plain tip. Tuck the twisted portion into the wider opening. (This will prevent the ganache from leaking out of the end of the tip before you are ready to pipe.) Turn down the top 2 to 4 inches of the pastry bag and place it into a 2-cup liquid measuring cup. (The cup will support the bag as you fill it with the ganache.)

3. Scrape the softened ganache into the prepared pastry bag. Pipe ⅞-inch mounds with pointed peaks onto a clean baking sheet. Cover the mounds loosely with a piece of plastic wrap and refrigerate for 15 to 25 minutes, until they are firm enough to roll.

4. Sift a light dusting of confectioners' sugar over the chilled centers. Lightly coat the palms of your hands and fingertips with confectioners' sugar. With your fingertips, pinch a truffle center into a round, then roll it gently between your palms into a ⅞-inch ball. Place the rolled center onto a waxed paper-lined baking sheet. Roll the remaining truffle centers. Loosely cover the prepared centers with a piece of waxed paper and let them stand at room temperature for 45 to 60 minutes to form a thin, dry crust.

Toast the coconut

1. Position a rack in the center of the oven and preheat to 350°F. Spread the coconut in an even layer on a baking sheet. Toast for 8 to 12 minutes, stirring frequently, until it is lightly browned. Cool completely.

Seal-coat the truffle centers

1. Temper the white chocolate. (See tempering instructions on page 27.) Line a baking sheet with a silicone baking mat with the textured side facing up. If you are right-handed, arrange your work area so that the baking sheet with the uncoated truffle centers is on the left side of the bowl of tempered chocolate and the lined baking sheet is on the right side of the tempered chocolate. If you are left-handed, reverse the positions of uncoated truffle centers and the baking sheet.

2. Remove a dab (about 1 tablespoon) of tempered white chocolate with the fingers of one hand and put it on the palm of the other hand. Touch the two palms together a couple of times so that there is a thin layer of white chocolate on both palms. Pick up a truffle center and gently roll it between both palms until it is coated with an almost tissue-thin, even layer of white chocolate. Using your forefinger and second finger of one hand, place the coated center on the silicone baking mat-lined baking sheet, withdrawing your the second finger last with a twisting motion. Pick up another truffle center and coat it with white chocolate in the same manner; place the coated truffle on the baking sheet. Dab the palm of one hand with more white chocolate, touch the palms together a couple of times and one at a time, coat two more truffle centers. Continue to seal-coat the remaining truffle centers in the same manner. Allow the coating to set for 15 minutes. Disregard any small cracks that may appear on the surface of some of the truffles; these cracks will be completely covered by a second coating of white chocolate that is textured with toasted coconut.

3. Meanwhile, line a second baking sheet with a silicone baking mat with the textured side facing up. Monitor the temperature and check the temper of the white chocolate.

4. Stir 1 cup of the toasted coconut into the white chocolate. With your left hand pick up a truffle center that had previously been coated with the first thin layer of white chocolate and gently drop it on the surface of the tempered coconut-white chocolate mixture. With the forefinger and second finger of your right hand, dip the center into the chocolate. (If you are left-handed, reverse the procedure.) Roll the center gently between your fingers on the surface of the chocolate to get an even coating that is textured with bits of the toasted coconut. Lift up the coated center; move your fingers in a scissor-type motion to release any drips and gently scrape your fingertips along one edge of the bowl. Place the coated center onto the second lined baking sheet, withdrawing your last finger with a twisting motion. Make sure that the small, flat bottom created by setting down the truffle with the first coating of chocolate is also the base when you set it down after the second coating of chocolate; otherwise your truffles will be oddly shaped.

5. If necessary, when all the truffles are coated, let them set at room temperature for about 1 hour, or until they can be lifted from the baking mat easily and the undersides of the truffles are glossy.

6. Pour the remaining tempered white chocolate onto a waxed paper-lined baking sheet and refrigerate for 10 to 15 minutes, until hardened. (If desired, you may stir 1 cup of whole or sliced roasted almonds to make Coconut-Almond Bark.) Let the chocolate stand at room temperature for 1 hour and then break into pieces. Store in an airtight container for up to 1 month.

7. Store the Summer Truffles in an airtight container at cool room temperature for up to 5 days, or in the refrigerator for up to 2 weeks. Allow the chocolates to come to room temperature in the storage container before serving.

Noel Bars

Sweet, creamy milk chocolate contrasts with the colorful, fruity tart flavors of dried California apricots, dried cranberries, and candied orange peel. Roasted almonds and green pistachio nuts add color and nutty crunch to this festive chocolate bar. Friand molds are sometimes used to make dainty almond cakes, called Financiers. They are also the perfect size for making individual chocolate bars.

·•·

YIELD: 16 CHOCOLATE BARS

Preparation: 1½ hours, plus chilling and setting times

Special Equipment: (see mail order sources on page 302): Digital thermometer; heating pad with temperature control dial (such as type used for backaches); sixteen 3⅞-by-2-inch rectangular metal Friand molds; cotton gloves.

1½ pounds Swiss white chocolate couverture, from the large 13-ounce
Lindt bars (see mail order sources on page 302)
⅔ cup whole almonds, roasted (see page 41)
⅔ cup unsalted shelled pistachio nuts
⅔ cup dried cranberries
⅔ cup diced dried California apricots
⅓ cup European candied diced orange peel (see mail order sources
on page 302)

Make the chocolate bars

1. Temper the white chocolate. (Refer to the tempering instructions on page 27.)

2. With a lint-free cloth or cotton ball, rub the inside of sixteen 3⅞-by-2-inch rectangular metal Friand molds until shiny.

3. Gently stir the almonds, pistachios, cranberries, apricots, and orange peel into the tempered white chocolate.

4. Carefully spoon the chocolate mixture into the Friand molds. Do not overfill. As you fill each mold, gently tap the mold on the work surface to remove air pockets and to level the chocolate mixture. Wipe up any chocolate spills that may have splashed on the molds. Place the filled molds on a baking sheet and refrigerate for 4 hours, or until the chocolate contracts slightly from the sides of the molds.

Unmold the chocolate bars

1. Pad a work surface with a folded kitchen towel or a double thickness of paper towels. Invert one of the Friand molds over the padded surface, and gently tap the mold on the work surface. The chocolate bar should release easily from the mold. If the bar does not release from the mold after a gentle tap, it could be one of two reasons: the chocolate has not set sufficiently, or the chocolate was not properly tempered. Return the mold to the refrigerator. Try again after another 30 minutes.

2. Tap the mold firmly on the work surface until the chocolate bar releases from the mold. (If the chocolate bar still does not release from the mold, this is an indication that the chocolate was out of temper when you spooned the chocolate mixture into the mold. If this should happen, do not attempt to scrape the chocolate from the mold. Simply heat the chocolate in the mold with a portable hair dryer until it melts and wipe the mold clean. You will have to start over with newly tempered chocolate couverture.) Unmold the remaining chocolate bars in the same manner.

3. Let the bars come to room temperature for 30 minutes. If desired, wrap each bar individually in gold confectioners' foil and then in a band of colorful paper. Store the Noel Bars in an airtight container at cool room temperature for up to 6 weeks.

White and Dark Chocolate Scallop Shells with Mocha Ganache

A fluted scallop shell mold traditionally used for baking small French cakes is employed to make these realistic-looking chocolate shells. The mottled pattern on the shells is created with a small piece of a dry, cellulose sponge dipped in tempered bittersweet chocolate. Inside it is a creamy mocha ganache with the infused flavor of fresh roasted coffee beans, contrasting nicely with the sweetness of the white chocolate.

YIELD: 16 LARGE CHOCOLATES

Preparation: 4 hours, plus setting, infusing, and chilling times.

Special Equipment (see mail order sources on page 32): Digital thermometer; heating pad with temperature control dial (such as the type used for backaches); two metal scallop shell molds, each containing eight 2½-inch fluted scallop shell-shaped cavities; one new medium-sized cellulose sponge, rinsed and dried; 1½-inch natural-bristle flat pastry brush; flexible straight-edged steel baker's scraper; 8-inch offset metal cake spatula; cotton gloves.

White and Dark Chocolate Scallop Shells

12 ounces bittersweet chocolate couverture, such as Valrhona Caraque
(see list of mail order sources on page 302)
2 pounds white chocolate couverture, such as Valrhona Ivoire (see mail
order sources on page 302)

Mocha Ganache

¾ cup plus 2 tablespoons heavy cream
3 tablespoons fresh roasted Sumatra coffee beans, coarsely ground
⅛ teaspoon ground cinnamon
1 vanilla bean, split in half lengthwise
8 ounces Swiss dark chocolate, such as Lindt*
2 teaspoons invert sugar, such as Nulomoline**
1 tablespoon unsalted butter, softened
1 tablespoons coffee liqueur, such as Kahlua or Tia Maria
1 tablespoon cognac

*Note: Use 3-ounce Lindt Swiss dark chocolate bars for preparing the ganache. This particular chocolate contains just the right proportion of cocoa solids and cocoa butter to enable the ganache filling to set up properly.

**Note: Invert sugar acts as a softener and helps to prolong the freshness of the ganache filling. See a mail order source for Nulomoline on page 305.

Prepare the white and dark chocolate scallop shells

1. Separately temper the bittersweet and white chocolates. (Refer to the tempering instructions on page 27.) Keep both the tempered bittersweet and white chocolates in separate bowls on the heating pad and carefully monitor the temperature and fluidity of the chocolates to prevent them from going out of temper.

2. Wipe the insides of the 8 shell-shaped mold cavities in each of the two scallop shell molds with a lint-free cloth or a cotton ball, until each mold cavity is shiny.

3. Cut the sponge into ½-by-1-inch sections. Dip the ½-inch end of one of the sponge strips into the bittersweet chocolate. Remove the sponge at a slight angle following the curve of the bowl to release any excess chocolate.

4. Pressing firmly, dab the inside surface of one of the shell mold cavities with the dark chocolate-coated sponge. Dab the mold cavity a couple of times before coating the end of the sponge with more tempered chocolate. To create a mottled shell pattern, sponge paint the entire inside surface of each scallop shell mold cavity, dabbing the sponge in alternating directions.

5. Using a flexible straight-edged steel baker's scraper, level the edges of chocolate-lined cavities by scraping the surface of the scallop shell mold. Hold the scraper at a slight angle and run the scraper over the length of the pan—one row of four cavities at a time. Wipe the edge of the scraper off on a paper towel before leveling the edges of the second row of four scallop shell cavities. Repeat with the second scallop shell mold. Let the bittersweet chocolate-coated shells set at room temperature for 5 to 10 minutes, until hardened.

6. Meanwhile, pour the remaining bittersweet chocolate onto a waxed paper-lined baking sheet and refrigerate for 10 to 15 minutes, until hardened. Let the chocolate stand at room temperature for 30 minutes. Break into pieces and store in a zip-lock bag.

7. With a 1½-inch flat, dry pastry brush, using a quick dabbing brush stroke, paint the inside of each scallop shell cavity with a thin, even layer of tempered white chocolate, carefully covering the mottled bittersweet chocolate pattern without melting it. Using the baker's scraper, level the edges of choco-late-lined cavities using the same technique as above. Let the chocolate set at room temperature for 3 to 10 minutes, until the chocolate shells start to harden but are still tacky. Leave the brush on the heating pad so that the chocolate will not harden on the bristles.

8. Brush the inside of each scallop shell with a second thin layer of white chocolate and level the edges with the baker's scraper. Allow the chocolate shells to harden at room temperature while preparing the filling. Keep the tempered white chocolate warm, stirring occasionally and monitoring the temperature. Do not let the chocolate get too hot (above 92°F), or it will go out of temper.

Prepare the mocha ganache

1. In a small saucepan, combine the heavy cream, coffee beans, and cinnamon. Using the sharp tip of a small knife, scrape the paste of tiny black seeds from inside the split vanilla bean. Reserve the vanilla bean paste in a small bowl and add the scraped pods to the cream mixture. Bring the mixture to a gentle boil over medium heat. Remove from the heat, cover the pan, and let the mixture infuse for 10 minutes.

2. Meanwhile, coarsely chop the dark chocolate and put it in a food processor fitted with the metal chopping blade. Process the chocolate for 15 to 20 seconds, until finely chopped. Remove the lid of the food processor and leave the chocolate in the work bowl.

3. Add the invert sugar to the cream mixture and reheat until it comes to a gentle boil. Take the pan off the heat and pour the hot cream through a fine-meshed strainer over the chopped chocolate. Using a rubber spatula, press down on the chocolate so that it is completely submerged in the hot cream. Add the reserved vanilla seed paste to the chocolate cream mixture. Let the mixture stand for 1 minute.

4. Add the butter to the chocolate-cream mixture. Replace the lid of the food processor and pulse 4 to 6 times, until the mixture is creamy. Scrape down the sides of the work bowl, and add the coffee liqueur and cognac. Pulse 4 more times, until blended. Scrape the ganache into a medium bowl.

5. Check the temperature of the ganache; it should read between 80°F to 84°F. If it is warmer than 84°F, allow the ganache to cool before filling the chocolate scallop shells.

Fill the scallop shells

1. Spoon the mocha ganache into the chocolate shells, filling each shell $\frac{1}{16}$-inch below its rim. Do not overfill.

2. Gently tap the scallop shell molds on the work surface to release any large air bubbles and to level the ganache. Refrigerate the scallop shell molds for 15 to 25 minutes, until the ganache filling is firm. Then let the molds sit at room temperature for 15 minutes.

Seal the bottoms of the filled scallop shells

1. Check the temperature and fluidity of the tempered white chocolate. It needs to be 89°F to 91°F—a little warmer than usual—so that it is easy to seal the bottoms of the filled scallop shells with a thin covering of white chocolate.

2. Rest one end of a scallop shell mold on the edge of the bowl of tempered white chocolate. Pour about ⅓ cup of tempered chocolate over the top half of the mold. Using an 8-inch offset metal cake spatula and holding it at a slight angle, spread the chocolate in a thin, even layer over four of the scallop shells. Still holding the spatula at a slight angle, scrape the excess chocolate back into the bowl, leaving behind a thin layer of chocolate sealing each filled scallop shell. Turn the mold around and seal the remaining scallop shells in the same manner. Repeat the process with the second scallop mold. Refrigerate the molds for about 1 hour.

3. Pour the remaining white chocolate onto a waxed paper-lined baking sheet and refrigerate for 10 to 15 minutes until hardened. Let the chocolate stand at room temperature for 30 minutes. Break into pieces and store in a zip-lock bag.

Unmold the scallop shells

1. Pad a work surface with a folded kitchen towel or a double thickness of paper towels. Carefully invert the molds, one at a time over the padded surface, and if necessary gently tap each mold on the work surface to release the shells. (If they do not release from the molds after a gentle tap, it could be one of three reasons: the chocolate has not set sufficiently; there is excess chocolate around the mold cavities, or the chocolate was not properly tempered. If the problem is excess chocolate, it will be obvious. You will see a layer of chocolate on the surface of the mold surrounding the shell cavities. Tap the pan firmly on the work surface until the shells release from the mold. If the shells are still not releasing from the mold, this is an indication that the chocolate was not in temper when you sponge-painted the mold cavities with bittersweet chocolate. If this should happen, do not attempt to scrape the chocolate from the molds. Simply heat the chocolate in each mold cavity with a portable hair dryer until it melts and wipe the entire mold clean. You will have to start over with newly tempered chocolate couverture.) Let the unmolded shells come to room temperature for 30 minutes.

2. Sometimes the unmolded shells need to be trimmed, especially if there was excess chocolate on the mold during the unmolding process. Wearing cotton gloves and using a small, sharp knife, carefully trim around the base of each shell. Place the scallop shells in an airtight container between layers of waxed paper. Store at cool room temperature for up to 5 days, or in the refrigerator for up to 2 weeks. Allow the chocolates to come to room temperature before serving.

MILK CHOCOLATE
Desserts

*M*ilk chocolate—a love story. In 1819, Francois-Louis Cailler opened the first chocolate factory in Switzerland. In the 1830s, he was the first among many chocolatiers throughout Europe who were trying to find a way to combine milk with chocolate in solid form. In 1863, a candle-maker's apprentice named Daniel Peter married Cailler's daughter and began to learn a new skill. In 1879, it was Daniel Peter who found a way to combine Henri Nestlé's milk powder with chocolate to produce the world's first milk chocolate. Today, milk chocolate is the world's favorite chocolate. Although it is delicious in candy form, milk chocolate presents a problem in desserts. Because of its milk solids, it cannot tolerate high heat, and therefore cannot be cooked or baked. Also, the chocolate flavor is so muted that it can be lost when combined with other ingredients. It is best as you find it the following recipes—in cookies and as the star of rich chocolate tarts and cakes.

Chocolate Hazelnut Brownies with Milk Chocolate Hazelnut Frosting

America's own brownie meets the classic Italian favorite of chocolate and hazelnuts, in these moist and eminently nosh-able treats. A touch of hazelnut liqueur reinforces the perfect flavor blend. The kids will love this, but adults will be more likely to appreciate the nuances.

•◆•

YIELD: NINE 2 1/2 - INCH BROWNIES

Preparation: 30 minutes, plus baking and setting times

Chocolate Hazelnut Brownies
•◆•
3 ounces bittersweet chocolate, coarsely chopped
½ cup (1 stick) unsalted butter
2 large eggs
¾ cup plus 2 tablespoons granulated sugar
2 tablespoons Italian hazelnut liqueur, such as Frangelico
½ cup all-purpose flour
1 cup (5 ounces) skinless hazelnuts, toasted and coarsely chopped

Milk Chocolate Hazelnut Frosting
•◆•
5 ounces Lindt milk chocolate, finely chopped
1 tablespoon unsweetend alkalized cocoa powder
⅓ cup heavy cream
1 tablespoon Italian hazelnut liqueur, such as Frangelico

Make the brownies

1. Preheat the oven to 350°F. Butter the bottom and sides of an 8-inch square baking pan. Line the bottom of the pan with parchment or waxed paper and coat the paper with butter.

2. Place the chocolate and the butter in the top of a double boiler over hot, not simmering water. Stir the mixture until it is completely melted and smooth. Remove the top part of the double boiler from the bottom and allow the mixture to cool.

3. In a medium bowl, whisk together the eggs and sugar. Whisk in the cooled chocolate and the hazelnut liqueur. With a rubber spatula, stir in the flour until just blended. Stir in the hazelnuts. Scrape the batter into the prepared pan. Smooth over the top with a rubber spatula. Bake the brownies for 25

to 30 minutes, or until a toothpick inserted in the center comes out with a few moist crumbs clinging to it. Cool the brownies on a wire rack for 15 minutes. Run a paring knife around the edges of the pan and carefully invert the brownies onto a flat surface. Peel off the paper, and then reinvert the brownies onto a cooling rack. Cool completely.

Make the frosting

1. Place the chocolate in a medium bowl. Sift the cocoa powder over the chocolate. In a small saucepan or in the microwave, bring the cream to a boil. Pour the hot cream over the chocolate and gently whisk until smooth. Stir in the hazelnut liqueur and allow the mixture to cool to a spreadable consistency, about 2 hours.

2. Using a metal spatula, spread the frosting over the top of the brownies. Using a long serrated knife, trim approximately ¼ to ½ inch off each side. Cut the brownies into 9 squares. Store in an airtight container.

Espresso-Flavored Milk Chocolate and Walnut Bars

The perfect take-along for an outdoor concert on a summer's evening: On an espresso-flavored shortbread cookie sits a meringue-like topping that packs plenty of crunch, courtesy of chopped walnuts, and plenty of flavor, thanks to milk chocolate and a wicked hint of rum.

•◆•

YIELD: THIRTY-FIVE 1½-INCH SQUARES

Preparation: 1 hour, plus baking and cooling times

Special Equipment: 9-by-13-inch baking pan; candy thermometer

Espresso-Flavored Shortbread Layer
•◆•
1¼ cups all-purpose flour

¼ cup cornstarch

¼ cup dark brown sugar

2 tablespoons granulated sugar

1½ teaspoons instant espresso powder

¼ teaspoon salt

10 tablespoons (1¼ sticks) unsalted cold butter, cut into ½-inch cubes

Milk Chocolate and Walnut Topping
•◆•
Two 3-ounce Lindt Swiss milk chocolate bars, divided

2½ cups chopped walnuts (about 10 ounces), divided

⅓ cup heavy cream

6 tablespoons (¾ stick) unsalted butter, cut into tablespoons

½ cup light corn syrup

½ cup granulated sugar

2 tablespoons Myers' dark rum

1 teaspoons instant espresso powder

1 teaspoon vanilla extract

2 large eggs

Make the espresso-flavored shortbread layer

1. Position a rack in the center of the oven and preheat to 350°F. Butter the bottom and sides of a 9-by-13-inch baking pan and line the pan with parchment paper so that the paper extends about 1 inch above the long sides of the pan.

2. Place the flour, cornstarch, brown sugar, granulated sugar, espresso powder, and salt in the bowl of a food processor fitted with the steel blade. Process for a few seconds to mix. Scatter the cubes of cold butter over the flour mixture and pulse the machine until the mixture resembles coarse meal.

3. Press the flour-butter mixture into the prepared pan in an even layer and bake the shortbread for about 20 minutes or until set and lightly colored. It will not be completely baked.

4. Place the shortbread layer in the pan on a wire rack and allow to cool to room temperature.

Make the milk chocolate and walnut topping

1. Lower the temperature of the oven to 300°F. Cut 4 ounces of the milk chocolate into ⅓-inch chunks. Place the chunks in a small bowl and refrigerate while the shortbread layer is cooling.

2. Break the remaining 2 ounces of milk chocolate into small pieces. Place the pieces of chocolate and 1½ cups of the chopped walnuts in the bowl of a food processor fitted with the metal chopping blade. Pulse the machine until the mixture is coarsely ground. Place the ground chocolate-nut mixture in a bowl and set aside.

3. In a medium-sized heavy saucepan, combine the cream, butter, corn syrup, and sugar. Cook over medium heat, stirring constantly with a wooden spoon, until the butter melts and the sugar dissolves. Increase the heat and bring the syrup to a boil. Insert a candy thermometer and cook, without stirring, for about 3 to 4 minutes or until the candy thermometer registers 230°F. Remove the pan from the heat and stir in the ground chocolate-nut mixture and the remaining chopped walnuts. Transfer the nut-sugar mixture to a medium-sized heatproof bowl and let cool for 5 minutes.

4. In a small bowl, using a wire whisk, whisk the rum, espresso powder, and vanilla extract until the espresso powder dissolves. Add the eggs and whisk until well blended. Using a wooden spoon, stir the egg mixture into the nut-sugar mixture, then fold in the chilled chocolate chunks.

5. Pour the topping onto the shortbread layer and spread evenly with a small, metal offset spatula. Bake about 35 minutes or until the topping is set. Remove the pan from the oven and place on a rack. Allow to set, at room temperature, for at least 6 hours or, preferably, overnight (cover the pan with foil).

6. Run a thin knife between the cooled bar and the unlined sides of the pan to loosen. Invert onto a baking sheet and remove the parchment paper. Invert onto a work surface. Using a sharp, serrated knife and a ruler, trim the edges; then cut into 1½-inch squares. Alternatively, the bars may be cut using small heart-shaped or round cookie cutters. To store, place the bars in a single layer in a baking pan. Keep at room temperature, tightly covered with foil, for up to 2 days.

Gianduja Marjolaine

A 20th-century classic from France, the marjolaine offers an exquisite flavor and textural experience—chewy meringue, smooth chocolate, creamy mousse. Ours is only a slight variation of the classic, with mocha buttercream offering yet another note to the symphony created by chocolate and hazelnut.

•◆•

YIELD: 12 SERVINGS

Preparation: 2½ hours, plus baking and cooling times

Hazelnut Meringues
•◆•
½ cup hazelnuts, toasted
¼ cup almonds, toasted
2 tablespoons cornstarch
8 large egg whites, at room temperature
1¼ cups granulated sugar
¼ teaspoon salt
1 teaspoon vanilla extract

Chocolate for Coating Meringues
•◆•
12 ounces semisweet chocolate, chopped

Gianduja Mousse
•◆•
8 ounces gianduja chocolate
4 ounces unsweetened chocolate
7 large egg whites, at room temperature
⅔ cup granulated sugar
½ cup water
1½ cups heavy cream

Mocha Buttercream
•◆•
2½ ounces unsweetened chocolate, chopped
1 tablespoon plus 1 teaspoon instant coffee granules
¼ cup hazelnut praline paste
2 cups (4 sticks) unsalted butter, divided
8 large egg yolks, at room temperature
⅔ cup granulated sugar
½ cup water
1 teaspoon vanilla extract

Chocolate Ganache
•◆•
10 ounces semisweet chocolate, chopped
1 cup heavy cream

Garnish
•◆•
16 whole hazelnuts for garnish

Make the hazelnut meringues

1. Place 2 racks, at least 4 inches apart, near the center of the oven and preheat to 250°F. Line a large baking sheet with parchment paper. Trace three 12-by-4-inch rectangles onto the parchment paper. Spray the baking sheet with nonstick cooking spray to adhere the parchment paper. Reverse the parchment so that the ink side faces down, away from the food but still visible.

2. Place the hazelnuts, almonds, and cornstarch in the bowl of a food processor fitted with the chopping blade and process the nuts until finely ground. Set aside.

3. Place the egg whites, granulated sugar, and salt in the 4½-quart bowl of a heavy-duty electric mixer. Place the mixing bowl over a larger bowl of hot water and stir the mixture until it is warm and the sugar has begun to dissolve. Remove the bowl with the eggs and dry off the bottom. Attach the bowl to the mixer stand and beat at medium-high speed using the whisk attachment until the egg whites form soft peaks. Beat in the vanilla extract.

4. Fold the ground nuts into the meringue. Fill a pastry bag fitted with a ½-inch plain tip (such as Ateco #6) with the meringue. Pipe the meringue along the outline of each rectangle and spiral inward.

5. Bake the meringues for 2 hours, or until the center of each is hard to the touch. Cool the meringues completely before storing in an airtight container.

Coat the meringues with chocolate

1. Temper the semisweet chocolate according to the instructions on page 27. Place the meringues 1 inch apart on a piece of parchment paper on a flat work surface or baking sheet.

2. Using a pastry brush, brush the top side of each meringue with the chocolate. Allow the chocolate to set, then turn the meringues over and coat the other side with chocolate. When the chocolate has set, wrap the meringues in plastic and store at room temperature until ready to assemble the marjolaine.

Make the gianduja mousse

1. Melt the gianduja and unsweetened chocolates together according to the directions on page 25.

2. Place the egg whites in the 4½-quart bowl of a heavy-duty electric mixer fitted with the whisk attachment and splatter shield. In a small heavy saucepan, combine the sugar and water over medium-high heat. Stir until the sugar has dissolved and bring to a boil. Cover the syrup and cook for 2 minutes. Meanwhile, beat the egg whites at medium-high speed until they form soft peaks. Uncover the syrup after 2 minutes and continue to cook until the temperature registers 240°F on a candy thermometer.

3. Increase the mixer speed to medium and carefully pour the syrup down the side of the pouring shield into the egg whites. Do not allow the syrup to come into contact with the whisk attachment or it will splatter. Continue to beat the egg whites until they cool to room temperature, about 5 to 8 minutes.

4. In a medium bowl, beat the heavy cream with a hand-held electric mixer until soft peaks form.

5. Transfer the melted chocolates to a large mixing bowl. Fold in one-quarter of the whipped egg whites to lighten the chocolate. Gently fold in another one-quarter of the egg whites and then the whipped cream. Fold in the remaining egg whites. Cover the bowl with plastic wrap and refrigerate for at least 3 hours.

Make the mocha buttercream

1. Melt the chocolate according to the instructions on page 25. Add the instant coffee granules and stir until dissolved. Strain into another bowl and set aside until cooled.

2. Place the hazelnut praline paste into a small mixing bowl. Fold in ¼ cup (½ stick) of the butter until smooth. Stir in the cooled chocolate mixture and set aside.

3. Place the egg yolks in the bowl of a 4½-quart heavy-duty electric mixer. Fill a wider, shallow bowl with hot water and set the bowl with the egg yolks directly over it, letting the water touch the bottom of the bowl to warm the yolks. Stir gently for one minute until the yolks are warm.

4. Remove the bowl with the yolks from the water and dry the bottom. Attach the bowl to the mixer stand along with the splatter-shield and whisk attachment and beat at medium-high speed for 5 to 7 minutes. The yolks should be tripled in volume and a ribbon falling off the beater should remain on the surface of the yolk mixture for a few seconds. While the eggs are mixing, prepare the syrup.

5. In a medium heavy saucepan, combine the granulated sugar and water over medium-low heat. Stir with a wooden spoon to dissolve the sugars. Increase the heat to medium-high and bring the mixture to a boil. Continue to boil, unstirred, until the mixture reaches 240°F on a candy thermometer.

6. With the mixer running at medium speed, carefully pour the hot syrup down the side of the pouring spout, being sure to avoid splattering the syrup onto the whisk. Continue to beat the eggs until they have cooled to room temperature, about 5 to 10 minutes.

7. Once the egg mixture is cool, lower the speed and gradually add the butter, one to two tablespoons at a time. The buttercream will look lumpy or curdled when half of the butter has been added, but it will smooth out at the end. Beat in the vanilla extract and praline-chocolate mixture.

Assemble the gianduja marjolaine

1. Cut out a 12-by-4-inch cardboard rectangle and cover it with waxed paper. Place a chocolate-covered meringue rectangle onto the cardboard rectangle. Place approximately 1 cup of the mocha buttercream into a pastry bag fitted with a medium plain tip (such as Ateco #5). Pipe the buttercream around the outer edge of the meringue rectangle, then repeat, making a border to hold the mousse that is one inch high. Chill for a minute or two to stiffen the buttercream before filling with mousse. Fill the center of the rectangle with ½ of the mousse, and place a meringue rectangle on top. Repeat the process with the second layer and place the third meringue on top.

2. Reserve about 1 cup of the buttercream; use the rest to frost the top and sides of the marjolaine, creating a perfect rectangle. Chill the marjolaine for 30 minutes before glazing with the ganache.

Make the ganache

1. Place the chopped chocolate in a medium heatproof bowl. Pour the heavy cream into a small saucepan over medium heat and bring to a boil. Pour the heavy cream over the chocolate and let stand for 30 seconds. Stir gently until the chocolate is melted and the mixture is smooth. Strain into a measuring cup with a pouring spout.

2. Remove the marjolaine from the refrigerator and place it on a cooling rack set over a baking sheet. Pour the ganache over the marjolaine, directing the glaze down the sides to evenly coat the dessert. Allow the ganache to set before garnishing.

3. Place the remaining buttercream in a piping bag fitted with a leaf tip. Pipe 3 leaves at each corner. Pipe 12 pairs of leaves down the center of the marjolaine. Place a toasted hazelnut in the center of each pair of leaves. Chill the marjolaine until ready to serve.

Milk Chocolate and Golden Almond Cakes

A sophisticated dessert experience is created out of the simplest and most traditional elements: devil's food cake encloses milk chocolate almond ganache and amaretto mousse. The cake is frozen, then served at room temperature with dollops of amaretto cream and a shower of walnuts. The mellow flavor of almond meets voluptuous chocolate in a textural experience that is sure to intrigue.

·•·

YIELD: 8 INDIVIDUAL SERVINGS

Preparation: 1 hour, plus baking and chilling times
Special Equipment: Eight 3-inch diameter by 1¼-inch high ring molds

Devil's Food Cake
·•·
1½ cups cake flour
¼ cup unsweetened nonalkalized cocoa powder
1 teaspoon baking powder
¼ teaspoon salt
½ cup (1 stick) unsalted butter, softened
1 cup granulated sugar
2 large eggs
½ cup heavy cream
1 teaspoon vanilla extract

Milk Chocolate Golden Almond Ganache
·•·
13 ounces Lindt milk chocolate, coarsely chopped
½ cup slivered almonds, toasted
2 tablespoons unsweetened nonalkalized cocoa powder
2 cups heavy cream, divided
2 tablespoons amaretto liqueur

Amaretto Syrup
·•·
¼ cup water
¼ cup granulated sugar
¼ cup amaretto liqueur

Milk Chocolate Cream Glaze
·•·
12 ounces Lindt milk chocolate, coarsely chopped
1 cup heavy cream
¼ cup amaretto liqueur

Amaretto Cream
•◆•
1 cup heavy cream
2 tablespoons amaretto liqueur

Garnish
•◆•
2 cups slivered almonds, toasted and chopped
Milk chocolate curls, made from 6 ounces of Lindt milk chocolate

Make the devil's food cake

1. Position a rack in the center of the oven and preheat to 350°F. Butter a 17½-by-11½-inch jelly roll pan. Line the bottom of the pan with parchment or waxed paper and butter the paper.

2. Sift the cake flour, cocoa powder, baking powder, and salt into a medium bowl.

3. In a 4½-quart bowl of a heavy-duty electric mixer using the paddle attachment, cream the butter and sugar on medium speed until well blended, about 1 minute. Scrape down the sides of the bowl with a rubber spatula. Add the eggs, one at a time, beating well after each addition. Turn off the mixer and add the heavy cream and the vanilla extract. Beat the mixture at medium speed for 1 minute until well mixed. Add the sifted dry ingredients and beat the mixture on high speed for 1 minute. Scrape down the sides and bottom of the bowl well.

4. Scrape the batter into the prepared pan and smooth it into an even layer. Bake the cake for 12 to 15 minutes, until a toothpick inserted into the center of the cake comes out clean. Cool the cake in the pan completely on a wire rack.

Make the milk chocolate golden almond ganache

1. Place the chopped milk chocolate, slivered almonds, and cocoa powder into the bowl of a food processor fitted with a metal chopping blade. Pulse until the chocolate and almonds are finely ground. Transfer to a medium bowl.

2. Place 1 cup of the heavy cream in a medium saucepan and bring just to a boil. Reserve remaining heavy cream for assembly. Pour the hot cream over the chopped chocolate and almond mixture and let stand for 1 minute. Stir with a wire whisk until the chocolate is completely melted. Stir in the amaretto liqueur. Let cool at room temperature for 2 to 3 hours, until it reaches a spreadable consistency.

Make the amaretto syrup

1. Place the water and sugar in a small saucepan and bring to a boil. Boil for 3 minutes or until the sugar has completely dissolved. Stir in the amaretto liqueur. Cool.

Assemble the cakes

1. Using one of the 3-inch ring-molds, cut out 16 circles from the devil's food cake (you may need to piece together the sixteenth circle). Place the 8 ring molds on a parchment-lined baking sheet. Place 1 piece of cake into the bottom of each ring mold. Using a pastry brush, soak each cake round well with the amaretto syrup. Place a heaping tablespoon of ganache on top of each cake round (there should be approximately 1 cup of ganache left). Dip a spoon in cold water and shake off the excess. Use the spoon to spread the ganache evenly over each cake layer. Place another cake round on top of the ganache in each ring mold and press down firmly. Soak each round with the amaretto syrup.

2. Place the remaining 1 cup of heavy cream and the amaretto in a 4½-quart bowl of a heavy-duty electric mixer fitted with the whisk attachment. Beat on high speed until soft peaks form. Using a wire whisk, gently blend the whipped cream into the remaining 1 cup of ganache. Spoon the mousse on top of each of the 8 ring molds and level the surface with a spatula. Place in the freezer for 1 hour.

Make the milk chocolate cream glaze

1. Place the chopped milk chocolate in a medium bowl. Place the heavy cream in a small saucepan and bring to a boil. Pour the hot cream over the chopped chocolate and let stand for 1 minute. Whisk until the chocolate is completely melted. Stir in the amaretto liqueur.

Glaze the cakes

1. Line a large baking sheet with foil and set a large cake rack over it. Remove the cakes from the freezer. One by one, run a thin knife around the inside of the mold and push the cake up from the bottom to release the mold. Place them on the rack with at least 1 inch between each cake. If any of the tops were damaged in the process, smooth the frozen mousse with a warm, dry knife.

2. Using a 2- to 3-ounce ladle, pour the glaze over each individual cake, concentrating the glaze especially on the sides. Pour slowly and deliberately so the top and sides are fully coated. It may be necessary to repour the glaze that has drizzled onto the foil liner. In that case, pick up the cake rack from the baking sheet and place it on another foil-lined baking sheet. Lift the two ends of the chocolate-covered foil and drizzle the recycled glaze over the remaining cakes to completely cover them.

Make the amaretto cream

1. Place the heavy cream in a 4½-quart bowl of a heavy-duty electric mixer fitted with the whisk attachment. Add the amaretto and beat on high speed until stiff peaks form.

Garnish the cakes

1. Line a clean baking sheet with parchment paper. Use a wide metal spatula to lift each cake off the rack. With your other hand, place handfuls of the remaining 2 cups of toasted chopped almonds around the entire side of each cake. Place the cakes on the prepared baking sheet.

2. Cover the tops of the cakes with milk chocolate curls. Serve the cakes at room temperature with the amaretto cream. They may be refrigerated for up to 5 days.

Milk Chocolate and Hazelnut Bark

Bark is not only a great candy, it is also an easy way to use up tempered chocolate that is left over from other candy-making or baking. Here, the flavor created by the European favorite combination of milk chocolate and hazelnut is deepened with bittersweet chocolate.

•◆•

YIELD: 1¼ POUNDS

Preparation: 20 minutes, plus setting time

12 ounces milk chocolate, chopped
1½ cups lightly toasted hazelnuts (see page 41), coarsely chopped
4 ounces bittersweet chocolate, chopped

1. Line a baking sheet with parchment paper.

2. Temper the milk chocolate according to the directions on page 27. Stir the chopped hazelnuts into the tempered chocolate.

3. Pour the chocolate-nut mixture onto the baking sheet. Using an offset spatula, smooth the mixture into a thin, even layer. Set aside.

4. Temper the bittersweet chocolate according to the directions on page 27. Immediately pour the tempered bittersweet chocolate in a thin stream over the milk chocolate to create a decorative pattern. Let the chocolate bark stand at room temperature until set, about 6 hours.

5. When the bark is set, break it into pieces. Store the bark in an airtight container at room temperature for up to 5 days.

Milk Chocolate Transfer Cookies

Every child in the neighborhood and every buyer at the bake sale will be clamoring for more of these beauty-with-brains chocolate chip and peanut cookies. Using transfer sheets to create patterns in the chocolate ensures that these cookies will be treasured right up to the moment they disappear.

•◆•

YIELD: 22 COOKIES

Preparation: 1 hour, plus baking, cooling, and tempering times

Special Equipment: Transfer sheets; 1½-ounce ice cream scoop

Milk Chocolate and Peanut Cookies
•◆•

2 cups all-purpose flour

¼ teaspoon baking soda

¾ cup salted, roasted, skinned peanuts, such as Planters cocktail peanuts

1 large egg

1 large egg yolk

1 teaspoon vanilla extract

1 cup (2 sticks) unsalted butter, softened

⅔ cup granulated sugar

⅓ cup barley malt syrup

Three 3-ounce Lindt Swiss milk chocolate bars, cut into ⅓-inch chunks

Milk Chocolate Coating
•◆•

1½ pounds milk chocolate couverture

Make the milk chocolate and peanut cookies

1. Place the flour, baking soda, and peanuts in the bowl of a food processor, fitted with the metal chopping blade. Pulse the machine until the nuts are finely ground.

2. Combine the egg, yolk, and vanilla extract in a small bowl and beat lightly with a fork until just blended.

3. In the 4½-quart bowl of a heavy-duty electric mixer, fitted with the paddle attachment, beat the butter and sugar at medium speed until blended, about one minute. Add the blended eggs and barley malt syrup and continue beating until the mixture is uniformly blended, about 1 or 2 minutes.

3. Place the ground hazelnuts, remaining flour, and salt into a large bowl and combine using a whisk. Make a well in the center and add the confectioners' sugar, brown sugar, and egg yolks. Using your fingers or a wooden spoon, combine the sugars and the yolks, mixing in the well until the sugars begin to dissolve. Add the softened butter and begin to incorporate the flour. Combine it well by picking up handfuls and rubbing the mixture between the palms of your hands. When it is well combined, form it into a ball and knead the dough two or three times on a lightly floured surface. Flatten the dough into a disc and wrap it securely in a piece of waxed paper. Refrigerate for 1 hour.

4. Lightly flour the top and bottom of the dough and roll out between 2 sheets of parchment paper into a circle approximately 14 inches in diameter. Turn the dough out into the prepared tart shell and press gently to line the sides. Trim the excess dough from the top edge using a sharp knife. Freeze the tart shell for 10 minutes. Preheat the oven to 400°F.

5. Place a baking sheet on the center rack of the preheated oven. Line the inside of the tart shell with a piece of aluminum foil. Place 3 cups of dried beans or rice on top of the foil and place the tart shell on the baking sheet in the preheated oven. Bake for 15 minutes. Remove the tart shell from the oven. Cool on a rack, leaving the beans inside. When completely cool, remove the foil and beans. Reduce the oven temperature to 325°F.

Make the milk chocolate filling

1. Place the milk into a medium saucepan. Heat until scalding and pour the hot milk over the chopped milk and bittersweet chocolates. Let sit for 30 seconds and then whisk gently. Whisk in the vanilla extract.

2. In a large bowl, whisk the eggs, yolks, and sugar until blended. Gradually whisk in the chocolate mixture. Using a fine mesh sieve, strain the filling into the cooled pie shell. Bake in the preheated oven for 20 minutes or until set. Remove the tart from the oven and cool on a rack. When cool, place in refrigerator until ready to serve.

3. Just before serving, sprinkle the sugar evenly over the top of the tart. Smooth it into an even layer right up to the sides of the tart. Using a propane torch, hold the flame approximately 5 inches from the top of the tart and caramelize the sugar turning it a golden brown. To prevent the crust from burning, hold a knife or metal spatula against the crust to prevent the flame from coming in contact with it. Cut the tart into 8 portions and serve with vanilla bean ice cream.

The "Sunflower"

Brilliant to behold and wickedly delicious, this unusual dessert's dramatic appearance promises complex, satisfying flavor—and delivers. A chocolate dome encloses milk chocolate mousse and orange cake; the orange-chocolate flavor is reinforced with Grand Marnier syrup and orange segments. Toasted sunflower seeds and milk chocolate caramel sauce provide texture, flavor, and a visual accent.

•◆•

YIELD: 10 SERVINGS

Preparation: 3 hours, plus baking, cooling, tempering, and chilling times
Special Equipment: Ten 2¾-inch diameter, 4-ounce capacity, flexipan demisphere molds

Sugared Sunflower Seeds
•◆•

½ large egg white
⅛ teaspoons salt
1 cup hulled sunflower seeds
¼ cup granulated sugar

Milk Chocolate Caramel Sauce
•◆•

3 ounces milk chocolate, chopped
½ cup crème fraîche
½ cup heavy cream, divided
⅓ cup water
¾ cup granulated sugar

Milk Chocolate Domes
•◆•

1½ pounds milk chocolate couverture

Orange Butter Cake
•◆•

1 cup all-purpose flour
1 teaspoon baking powder
¼ teaspoon salt
1 large egg
1 large egg yolk
1 teaspoon vanilla extract
1 tablespoon finely minced orange zest
8 tablespoons (1 stick) unsalted butter, softened
⅔ cup granulated sugar
⅓ cup whole milk

Grand Marnier Syrup
⬧
⅓ cup water
3 tablespoons granulated sugar
3 tablespoons Grand Marnier or other orange-flavored liqueur

Milk Chocolate Mousse
⬧
⅓ cup crème fraîche
½ cup heavy cream
6 ounces milk chocolate, finely chopped
4 tablespoons (½ stick) unsalted butter, cut into cubes, at room temperature
⅓ cup dry white wine
4 large egg yolks
¼ cup granulated sugar

Assembly
⬧
10 navel oranges, about 10 to 12 ounces each

Make the sugared sunflower seeds

1. Position a rack in the center of the oven and preheat to 325°F.

2. In a medium bowl, lightly whisk the egg white with the salt until frothy. Add the sunflower seeds to the mixture and stir until the seeds are evenly moistened. Stir in the sugar and toss to coat.

3. Place the seeds in a single layer in a jelly roll pan and bake, stirring and turning frequently with a metal spatula, for about 15 minutes or until the seeds are golden. Place the pan on a wire rack and allow to cool completely. Store the sugared sunflower seeds in an airtight container in the freezer.

Make the milk chocolate caramel sauce

1. Melt the chocolate according to the directions on page 25.

2. Place the crème fraîche and ¼ cup of the heavy cream in a small saucepan and whisk to combine. Cook over medium heat until it comes to a gentle boil. Remove the pan from the heat.

3. In a medium-sized heavy saucepan, combine the water and sugar. Cook over medium heat, stirring constantly with a wooden spoon, until the sugar dissolves. Increase the heat to medium-high and continue to cook, without stirring, for 4 to 6 minutes, until the syrup begins to brown. Lower the heat to medium-low and continue to cook, swirling the pan, until the syrup turns a light amber color.

Remove the pan from the heat and slowly add the warm cream (be careful as the mixture may bubble up). Return the pan to medium heat and stir until any bits of hardened caramel are completely melted and the caramelized syrup is smooth. Stir in the remaing heavy cream. Add the melted chocolate and whisk until the sauce is smooth and well-blended.

4.   Strain the sauce into a heatproof bowl; then pour the sauce into a squeeze bottle and allow to cool to room temperature. (The sauce can be made up to 3 days ahead and stored in the refrigerator, but should be used at room temperature.)

Make the milk chocolate domes

1.   Have ready ten 3-inch diameter ring molds (at least 1¼ inches high) or 10 cups of the same dimensions. These are necessary to support the flexipan demisphere molds.

2.   Temper the milk chocolate according to the directions on page 27. One at a time, fill each demisphere mold halfway with the tempered chocolate and swirl to coat the mold evenly. Allow the excess chocolate to drip back into the bowl of tempered chocolate. Place the coated mold into a ring or cup and place the supported mold onto a jelly roll pan. Let set at room temperature for 1 hour. Chill the coated molds for at least 1 hour or overnight. (When the chocolate has chilled, cover the pan of chocolate-coated domes with plastic wrap.)

Make the orange butter cake

1.   Position a rack in the center of the oven and preheat to 350°F. Lightly butter the bottom and sides of an 8-inch square cake pan. Line the bottom with parchment paper.

2.   In a medium bowl, using a wire whisk, stir the flour, baking powder, and salt until well-blended. Set aside.

3.   Combine the egg, yolk, vanilla extract, and orange zest in a small bowl and beat lightly with a fork just until blended.

4.   In the 4½-quart bowl of a heavy-duty electric mixer fitted with the paddle attachment, beat the butter and sugar at medium speed for about 4 to 5 minutes until the mixture is light and fluffy. Scrape down the sides of the bowl with a rubber spatula as necessary. Add the egg mixture in two additions, beating well after each addition.

5.   On low speed, beat half the flour mixture into the butter mixture. Gradually beat in the milk, beating only until absorbed. Fold in the remaining flour mixture with a rubber spatula.

6. Scrape the batter into the prepared pan. Bake for about 25 minutes, or until a tester inserted into the center of the cake comes out clean. Place the baking pan on a wire rack and allow to cool for 5 minutes. Invert the cake onto a wire rack and carefully remove the parchment paper. Cool the cake completely.

7. When the cake is completely cool, place it in a clean 8-inch square cake pan and wrap with plastic wrap. (The wrapped cake may remain at room temperature for one day or frozen for a longer period.)

Make the Grand Marnier syrup

1. In a small heavy saucepan, combine the water and sugar. Cook over medium heat, stirring constantly with a wooden spoon, until the sugar dissolves. Bring to a boil; remove the pan from the heat and set aside to cool. Whisk in the Grand Marnier. Place the syrup in a covered container and store in the refrigerator until needed. (The syrup will keep for several days.)

Make the milk chocolate mousse

1. Place the crème fraîche and heavy cream in a chilled bowl and whisk together until blended. Using a handheld mixer set at medium speed, whip the cream mixture until soft peaks form. Be careful not to over-whip this mixture because the crème fraîche may break. Chill until needed.

2. Melt the milk chocolate according to the directions on page 25. Whisk in the room-temperature butter.

3. Place the white wine and egg yolks in the 4½-quart bowl of a heavy-duty mixer. Use a wire whisk to blend the yolks and wine. Slowly whisk in the sugar. Set the bowl over a saucepan of simmering water making sure that the bottom of the bowl does not touch the water. Whisk the mixture for 3 to 4 minutes until thickened and increased in volume. During this time, remove the bowl from the pan 3 or 4 times to whisk for a few seconds off the heat; this ensures even heating and that the bottom will not overcook. Attach the bowl to the mixer and, using the whip attachment, whip for 3 to 5 minutes until the mixture has cooled, thickened, and will hold a soft peak when the whip is lifted.

4. Thoroughly fold about ½ cup of the yolk mixture into the chocolate mixture. Fold the lightened chocolate mixture into the remaining yolk mixture. Fold in the whipped cream.

Assemble the domes

1. Cut the cake into 5 rounds using a 2¾-inch biscuit cutter. Remove the cake rounds from the pan and using a serrated knife, cut each round in half horizontally. (Any unused cake may be placed in the bowl of a food processor, fitted with the metal blade, and pulsed until the cake is reduced to fine crumbs. Store the crumbs in an airtight container in the freezer and use for other purposes.) Place the rounds, cut side up, on a baking sheet and use a pastry brush to moisten each round with some of the Grand Marnier syrup.

2. Fill the chocolate-coated domes with the milk chocolate mousse to within ½-inch of the top. Top with a round of cake, placing the moistened side against the mousse and pressing down lightly on the cake.

3. Cover the filled molds with plastic wrap and chill until set, at least 3 hours. (This may be done up to 2 days ahead.)

Plate the dessert

1. Using a very sharp knife, remove the rind and pith from one of the navel oranges. Cut between the membranes of the orange to produce 20 thin segments. (Do this over a bowl to collect the juice and reserve the juice for another purpose.) Repeat for each orange. Place the segments on a tray lined with paper towels to absorb excess moisture.

2. Unmold one of the mousse-filled domes onto the center of a large flat plate, such as a dinner plate. Paint 3 "leaves" of chocolate sauce around the dome. Arrange about 20 orange segments around the dome to resemble the petals of a sunflower. Center a 3½-inch diameter biscuit cutter over the dome, resting it lightly on the orange segments. Evenly distribute about 4 teaspoons of sugared sunflower seeds in the space between the edges of the cutter and the dome to form a ring of seeds around the dome. Carefully remove the cutter. Repeat to make 10 desserts.

Milk Chocolate Rocky Road Ice Cream with Chocolate Almond Biscotti

The American lust for over-the-top additions to its candies and ice creams reaches its pinnacle with Rocky Road ice cream. We throw in extra chewiness and chocolate kick with a dark chocolate cup. Super-crunchy and flavorful biscotti is like the adult chaperone to this back-to-childhood ice cream experience.

•◆•

Y I E L D :   6   S E R V I N G S

Preparation: 2 hours, plus baking and chilling times
Special Equipment: Ice cream machine; six 4-inch mini-brioche molds

M i l k   C h o c o l a t e   R o c k y   R o a d   I c e   C r e a m
•◆•
5 ounces milk chocolate, chopped
1 ounce unsweetened chocolate, chopped
6 large egg yolks, at room temperature
½ cup granulated sugar
1 pint milk
1 cup heavy cream
½ vanilla bean, split and scraped
1 tablespoon plus 1 teaspoon unsweetened nonalkalized cocoa powder
Pinch of salt
⅔ cup mini-marshmallows
2 ounces (⅔ of a 3-ounce bar) Toblerone milk chocolate
candy bar, chopped
¼ cup roasted slivered almonds (see page 41), chopped

C h o c o l a t e   A l m o n d   B i s c o t t i
•◆•
1½ cups granulated sugar, divided
1½ cups all-purpose flour, divided
⅔ cup unsweetened nonalkalized cocoa powder
2 teaspoons baking powder
½ teaspoon baking soda
½ teaspoon salt
1½ cups whole roasted almonds, divided
1 cup miniature semisweet chocolate chips
4 large eggs, at room temperature, divided
2 tablespoons vegetable oil
1 tablespoon plus 1 teaspoon almond extract

D a r k   C h o c o l a t e   C u p s
•◆•
12 ounces bittersweet chocolate

Make the milk chocolate rocky road ice cream

1. Melt the chopped chocolates together according to the instructions on page 25. Set aside.

2. Whisk the egg yolks together in a small heatproof bowl and set aside. In a medium, heavy saucepan combine the sugar, milk, heavy cream, and vanilla bean over low to medium heat. Once the sugar has dissolved, increase the heat slightly and bring the mixture to a boil, stirring frequently. Once the mixture reaches a boil, lower the heat and gradually pour a cup of the hot liquid into the egg yolks, whisking constantly. In a slow, steady stream whisk the tempered egg mixture into the hot milk and cream, stirring constantly. Stir the mixture over medium heat with a wooden spoon until the mixture thickens slightly. The mixture will be ready when a line drawn across the back of the spoon remains uncovered with sauce.

3. Remove pan from the heat and add the melted chocolates to the pan, stirring until smooth. Sift the cocoa powder and salt over the mixture and stir until incorporated. Strain the mixture into a medium, heatproof bowl and chill until cold, about 6 hours.

4. Place the chilled ice cream base into the chilled bowl of an ice cream maker and process according to the manufacturer's directions. When the ice cream is almost halfway through the chilling process, add the mini-marshmallows, chopped Toblerone bar, and almonds to the machine. If hard ice cream is desired, place the finished ice cream in the freezer for an hour or 2 longer.

Make the chocolate almond biscotti

1. Place a rack in the center of the oven and preheat to 325°F; line a baking sheet with parchment paper; set aside. In a large mixing bowl, combine 1¼ cups of the sugar, 1 cup of the flour, the cocoa powder, baking powder, baking soda, and salt. Place ¼ cup of the roasted almonds along with the remaining ½ cup flour in the bowl of a food processor and pulse until finely ground. Add the ground almonds to the dry ingredients.

2. Coarsely chop the remaining ¾ cup roasted almonds. Stir the chopped almonds and the mini-chocolate chips into the dry ingredients. In a liquid measuring cup with a pouring spout, stir together three of the eggs, the vegetable oil, and almond extract. Pour the liquid ingredients into the dry ingredients in thirds, stirring after each addition. Knead the dough briefly to combine. If the dough is overly crumbly and will not stick together, add ½ of the remaining egg, beaten.

3. Divide the dough in half. With each half, form a log 2 inches wide, 1 inch high and about 12 inches long. Place the logs on the prepared baking sheet, spaced at least 4 to 5 inches apart. Brush the logs with the remaining beaten egg and sprinkle with the remaining ¼ cup sugar. Bake for 35 to 40 minutes, until the dough is set in the middle and beginning to brown at the edges. Remove the baking sheet from the oven and turn the heat down to 300°F. Let the cookies rest for 20 to 30 minutes before slicing crosswise on the diagonal into ½- to ¾-inch-wide strips. Bake the slices for 20 to 30 minutes longer, until firm and dry.

Make the chocolate cups

1. Temper the chocolate according to the directions on page 27. Place a cooling rack over a jelly roll pan and have six 4-inch mini-brioche molds ready. Working with 1 mold at a time, fill the mold halfway with chocolate and tip the mold to swirl the chocolate evenly throughout. Pour out the excess chocolate and place the mold face down on the rack to set. After 10 minutes the chocolate should be set if it was correctly tempered. Place the molds in the refrigerator for 5 minutes before removing the chocolate cups from the molds.

2. To remove the cups, place 2 fingers onto the chocolate on the side of each mold and gently ease the chocolate cup out of the mold.

3. Serve the ice cream in the chocolate cups with 1 or 2 biscotti on the side.

Milk Chocolate Mousse Roulade

The combination of milk chocolate and hazelnut is presented in a most sophisticated and subtle way, in this rich, moist roulade. Hazelnut and chocolate cake batters are baked and rolled with velvety milk chocolate mousse for a memorable flavor experience that can stand on its own.

•◆•

YIELD: 16 SERVINGS

Preparation: 1 hour, plus baking and cooling times
Special Equipment: Candy thermometer; 12-by-17-inch silicone baking mat;
12-inch decorating comb

Milk Chocolate Mousse
•◆•
6½ ounces milk chocolate, coarsely chopped
1½ ounces unsweetened chocolate, coarsly chopped
4 large egg whites, at room temperature
⅔ cup granulated sugar
⅓ cup water
1 cup heavy cream

Chocolate Sponge Cake Batter
•◆•
6 tablespoons unsalted butter, at room temperature
¾ cup confectioners' sugar, sifted
3 large egg whites, at room temperature
1 teaspoon vanilla extract
2 tablespoons unsweetened alkalized cocoa powder
⅓ cup plus 1 tablespoon bread flour

Hazelnut Sponge Cake Batter
•◆•
½ cup toasted hazelnuts
2 tablespoons plus 2 teaspoons bread flour
¼ teaspoon salt
2 large eggs, at room temperature
⅓ cup confectioners' sugar
2 large egg whites, at room temperature
2 tablespoons unsalted butter, melted

Make the milk chocolate mousse

1. Melt the milk and unsweetened chocolates together according to the directions on page 25. Place in a large mixing bowl and set aside.

2. Place the egg whites in the 4½-quart bowl of a heavy-duty mixer fitted with the whisk attachment and a splatter-shield. Place the sugar and water in a small, heavy saucepan and bring to a boil, stirring to dissolve the sugar. After the syrup reaches a boil, cover with a lid and continue to boil for 2 minutes. Meanwhile, begin whipping the egg whites; turn the mixer off after the egg whites have reached the soft-peak stage. Uncover the syrup after 2 minutes and check the temperature with a candy thermometer; stop cooking at 240°F. Immediately turn on the mixer to medium speed and very carefully pour the hot syrup down the pouring spout in the splash guard. Leave the mixer running until the egg whites have cooled to room temperature, about 7 minutes.

3. In a medium bowl using a handheld electric mixer, whip the heavy cream to soft peaks. Fold one-third of the egg whites into the melted chocolate to lighten it. Fold in the remaining egg whites. Fold the whipped cream into the mixture. Chill the mousse for at least 2 hours before filling the cake.

Make the chocolate sponge cake batter

1. In a large mixing bowl, cream the butter and confectioners' sugar together with a handheld electric mixer. One at a time, add the egg whites, beating after each addition. Beat in the vanilla extract. Sift the cocoa powder and flour over the batter. Mix to combine. If the batter is thin, refrigerate briefly to thicken it. Otherwise, proceed with the recipe.

2. Place a 12-by-17-inch silicone baking mat on a 12-by-17-inch jelly roll pan. Spread one-half of the chocolate batter along one 12-inch side, leaving an empty edge ¼-inch wide. Hold the 12-inch decorating comb behind the batter along the empty ¼-inch edge. Pressing the comb firmly against the mat, drag the comb slowly and steadily down the mat, pushing the batter towards the opposite edge. Remove any excess batter and chill the silicone mat on the baking sheet in the refrigerator while preparing the hazelnut sponge batter. There is twice the amount of necessary batter for combining in case the first attempt isn't perfect.

Make the hazelnut sponge cake batter

1. Place a rack in the lower third of the oven and preheat to 475°F. Combine the toasted hazelnuts, flour, and salt in a food processor and pulse to finely grind the hazelnuts. Sift this mixture onto a piece of waxed paper, discarding any lumps that won't fall through, and set aside.

2. Place the whole eggs and confectioners' sugar in the 4½-quart bowl of a heavy-duty mixer, and put the bowl in a smaller bowl filled with hot water. Whisk the eggs until the sugar is dissolved. Dry the bottom of the 4½-quart bowl and place on the mixer stand fitted with the whisk attachment. Whip at medium-high speed until the mixture has tripled in volume and a ribbon of batter will rest on the surface for 10 seconds.

3. With a handheld electric mixer, beat the egg whites in a medium bowl until soft, but not stiff, peaks form. Fold the dry ingredients into the whole egg-sugar mixture, then fold in the melted butter. Fold the egg whites into the hazelnut mixture.

4. Spread the hazelnut batter evenly over the chilled chocolate batter with a metal offset spatula. Bake for 5 to 8 minutes, until the center springs back and the edges are barely browned. Invert the cake onto a parchment-covered cooling rack to cool. After 1 or 2 minutes, peel the silicone mat off of the cake and spray the cake lightly with nonstick cooking spray. Trim any overly browned edges. Place a sheet of parchment on top of the cake, and a baking sheet over that. Invert the cake so the stripes face down. Gently roll the cake up lengthwise (between the 2 pieces of parchment paper), jelly-roll fashion, beginning with one 17-inch side. Cool completely before filling.

Assemble the roulade

1. Gently unroll the cake and spread the chilled mousse in a ¼-inch layer over the entire surface. Roll the cake up jelly-roll fashion once again and chill for at least 2 hours before serving. To serve the cake, slice the roulade diagonally at 1-inch intervals.

Milk Chocolate Toasted Almond Shortbread Sandwiches

Deceptively rich, these sandwich cookies showcase the pairing of milk chocolate and almonds, which have been sweetened and toasted to bring out their full flavor. The buttery shortbread is the perfect canvas for this almond chocolate treat.

•◆•

YIELD: 24 COOKIES

Preparation: 1½ hours, plus baking and cooling times

Shortbread Cookies
•◆•
1 cup blanched whole almonds, toasted
1 cup confectioners' sugar, divided
2 cups all-purpose flour
Pinch of salt
1 cup (2 sticks) unsalted butter, softened
2 teaspoons brandy

Milk Chocolate Filling
•◆•
4 ounces milk chocolate, finely chopped
½ cup sour cream

Toasted Almond Filling
•◆•
½ cup blanched whole almonds, toasted (see page 41)
½ cup confectioners' sugar
½ cup (1 stick) cold unsalted butter, cut into ½-inch cubes
1 teaspoon brandy

Garnish
•◆•
4 ounces milk chocolate, chopped
½ cup natural (unblanched) almonds

Make the shortbread cookies

1. Combine the almonds and ¼ cup of the confectioners' sugar in a food processor and pulse until the almonds are finely ground. Do not overprocess.

2. In a medium bowl, whisk together the flour and salt.

3. In the 4½-quart bowl of a heavy-duty electric mixer, using the paddle attachment, beat the butter for 30 seconds at medium speed, or until creamy. Add the remaining ¾ cup confectioners' sugar and continue beating for 2 minutes, or until the mixture is light in texture and color. Scrape down the sides of the bowl with a rubber spatula. Beat in the brandy.

4. At low speed, beat in the flour mixture a third at a time, scraping down the sides of the bowl after each addition. Beat in the ground almonds, scraping down the sides of the bowl once or twice.

5. Divide the dough into quarters. Shape each piece into a disc about 4 inches in diameter, wrap in waxed paper, and refrigerate for 1 hour, or until firm enough to roll.

6. Position one rack in the top third and another in the bottom third of the oven and preheat to 350°F.

7. Place 1 piece of the chilled dough in between 2 sheets of waxed paper (leave the other pieces of dough in the refrigerator). Using a rolling pin, roll out the dough so that it is approximately ⅛-inch thick. Remove the top piece of waxed paper and lay it loosely back on top of the dough. Turn the dough over and peel off the second piece of waxed paper. Using a 2-inch plain or scalloped cookie cutter, cut out as many cookies as possible from the dough. Carefully transfer the cookies to an ungreased baking sheet, spacing them about 1½ inches apart. Gather the scraps of dough together into a ball and flatten into a disc. Wrap the dough in plastic wrap and refrigerate until firm. Reroll the scraps one time only to make more cookies (discard excess dough). Repeat with remaining pieces of dough.

8. Bake the cookies for about 13 minutes, or until set; switch the positions of the cookie sheets halfway through the baking time for even baking. Cool the cookies on the baking sheets on wire racks for 2 minutes. Using a metal spatula, gently transfer the cookies to the wire racks and cool completely.

Make the milk chocolate filling

1. Place the chocolate in a medium bowl and melt according to the directions on page 25. Whisk in the sour cream. Set aside to cool slightly.

Make the toasted almond filling

1. Combine the almonds and confectioners' sugar in a food processor and pulse until the almonds are finely ground. Add the butter cubes and brandy and process until the mixture is smooth, stopping the machine to scrape down the sides once or twice.

Assemble the cookies

1. Spread a teaspoon of the milk chocolate filling onto the bottom of a cookie; spread a teaspoon of the toasted almond filling onto the bottom of another cookie. Sandwich the cookies together so that the fillings touch. Repeat with remaining cookies.

Garnish the cookies

1. Temper the chocolate according to the directions on page 27. Using a fork, drizzle the cookies with some of the tempered chocolate. Dip the almonds halfway in the remaining tempered chocolate, then place on top of each cookie. Let the cookies stand at room temperature for 1 hour to set the chocolate. Store the cookies in an airtight container with pieces of waxed paper between the layers for up to 3 days.

Milk Chocolate Glazed Black Forest Petits Fours

Petits fours are making a major comeback in fine restaurants and hotels, and there is no reason they cannot be presented at home; they are the perfect accompaniment to coffee or tea. Here, all the elements of the Black Forest cake—the classic combination of chocolate and cherry—are in place. This item stands on its own, or can be served with other petits fours, cookies, or chocolates.

•✦•

YIELD: 16 PETITS FOURS

Preparation: 1 hour, plus baking and cooling times

Special Equipment: Four 1¼-inch cutters in assorted shapes

Dark Chocolate Sponge Cake
•✦•
2 tablespoons cake flour
1 tablespoon unsweetened alkalized cocoa powder, plus additional for dusting
¼ teaspoon salt
4 large egg yolks, at room temperature
¼ cup granulated sugar
5 large egg whites, at room temperature
⅓ cup semisweet chocolate chips, melted

Cherry Filling
•✦•
½ cup cherry preserves
2 tablespoons kirsch

Milk Chocolate Glaze
•✦•
8 ounces milk chocolate, chopped
5 ounces heavy cream

White Chocolate Garnish
•✦•
2 ounces white chocolate, melted

Other Garnishes
•✦•
Candied violets, candied rose petals, and candied mint leaves

Make the dark chocolate sponge cake

1. Preheat the oven to 350°F and place a rack in the lower third of the oven. Butter the bottom of a 10-inch-by-15-inch jelly roll pan and line with parchment paper. Butter the paper.

2. Sift the cake flour, cocoa powder, and salt together; set aside. Place the egg yolks and sugar in the 4½-quart bowl of a heavy-duty electric mixer. Place the bowl over a smaller bowl of hot water and

whisk until the mixture is warm and the sugar has dissolved. Dry the bottom of the bowl and place it on the mixer stand, fitted with the whip attachment; whip at medium-high speed until the mixture has tripled in volume and a ribbon of batter can stand on the remaining batter for 10 seconds.

3. With a handheld electric mixer, beat the egg whites until soft, but not stiff, peaks form. With a rubber spatula, place a dollop of the egg yolk mixture into the melted chocolate and fold together. Very gently, fold the melted chocolate mixture into the remaining egg yolk mixture. Sift the dry ingredients over the egg yolk mixture and begin to fold together. Before the dry ingredients are fully combined, fold half of the egg whites into the chocolate-yolk mixture. Fold in the remaining egg whites and, working carefully not to deflate it, spread the batter into the prepared pan with a metal offset spatula. Bake the sponge cake for 10 to 15 minutes, until the center springs back when touched.

4. Dust the top of the cake lightly with cocoa powder. Place a piece of parchment paper and a baking sheet over the jelly roll pan and invert the cake. Remove the jelly roll pan and let the cake cool for a minute or 2 before peeling the greased parchment paper off the cake. Cover the cake with a clean, dry cloth until ready to use.

Assemble the petit-fours

1. In a small saucepan, melt the cherry preserves with the kirsch. Bring to a boil, then remove the pan from the heat. Set aside.

2. Using four 1¼-inch cutters, such as a diamond, square, flower, and circle cutter, cut out 48 pieces of cake (12 for each cutter). Using a pastry brush, brush a little cherry preserves over one piece of cake and top with a second piece of cake. Cover the second piece of cake with preserves and top with a third piece of cake. Set the 3-tiered petit-four on a cooling rack and repeat process until there are 16 petits fours.

Glaze and garnish the petits fours

1. Place the chopped milk chocolate in a heatproof bowl. In a small saucepan, bring the heavy cream to a boil. Pour the heavy cream over the chocolate and let stand 1 minute. Stir until smooth.

2. Set the cooling rack with the petits fours over a jelly roll pan. Spoon the glaze over each petit four, letting the glaze slide down the sides to coat each cake completely.

3. Make a parchment cone and fill with the melted white chocolate. Snip the end of the cone to open it and garnish each shape with a different design and the candied petals and leaves. Let the cakes stand to set the glaze. Because the glaze is actually a ganache, it will not become hard. Chill the petits fours briefly before covering them with plastic wrap.

Peanut Butter Milk Chocolate Pie

Peanut butter is America's favorite item to pair with chocolate, and here that marriage is presented in all its glory and simplicity. In a chocolate crust pie, and with a layer of caramel to deepen the flavor, the flavor duo shimmers in a silky dessert experience. Perfect any time.

•◆•

YIELD: 8 TO 10 SERVINGS

Preparation: 1 hour, 15 minutes, plus baking, cooling, and setting times

Chocolate Pastry Crust
•◆•
1¼ cups all-purpose flour
¼ cup unsweetened nonalkalized cocoa powder
5 large egg yolks
¼ cup granulated sugar
¼ cup firmly packed light brown sugar
1 teaspoon vanilla extract
½ cup (1 stick) unsalted butter, softened

Caramel Layer
•◆•
1 cup heavy cream
1½ cups granulated sugar
⅓ cup light corn syrup

Milk Chocolate Ganache Layer
•◆•
6 ounces Lindt milk chocolate
½ cup heavy cream
¼ cup sour cream
½ cup skinless, roasted peanuts, coarsely chopped, divided

Peanut Butter Mousse
•◆•
1¼ cups whole milk
¾ cup smooth peanut butter
1 large egg
1 large egg yolk
¼ cup light brown sugar
2 tablespoons all-purpose flour
1 teaspoon vanilla extract
½ cup heavy cream

Stabilized Whipped Cream
•◆•

1¼ teaspoons unflavored powdered gelatin
3 tablespoons water
2 cups heavy cream
¼ cup granulated sugar
1 teaspoon vanilla extract

Milk Chocolate Drizzle
•◆•

2 ounces milk chocolate
3 tablespoons heavy cream

Make the chocolate pastry crust

1. Preheat the oven to 350°F. Butter a 9-inch pie plate. In a large bowl, sift together the flour and the cocoa. Make a well in the center and place the egg yolks, both sugars, and vanilla extract into the well. With a rubber spatula or your fingers, pull the flour-cocoa mixture into the yolks until most of the dry ingredients have been incorporated. Break the butter into small pieces and add to the mixture. Take handfuls of the mixture and rub between your palms to incorporate the butter into the dry ingredients until well blended. You should be able to form the dough into a ball. Knead the pastry 2 or 3 times on a clean work surface. Flatten the dough into a disc and wrap in waxed paper. Refrigerate for 20 minutes.

2. Roll the dough out into an 11-inch circle between 2 pieces of waxed paper that have been dusted lightly with flour. Remove the top sheet of paper and turn the dough into the prepared pie plate. Trim and flute the edges. Line the pie crust with aluminum foil and fill with dried beans or blind-baking weights. Bake in the preheated oven for 20 minutes. Remove the pie crust from the oven and let cool with the beans inside. Remove the beans from the pie shell.

Make the caramel layer

1. Place the heavy cream, sugar, and light corn syrup into a large, heavy saucepan. Bring to a boil, stirring occasionally with a wooden spoon. Stop stirring when the sugar has dissolved. Bring the temperature to 244°F and immediately pour the mixture into a medium stainless steel bowl. Cool to 120°F, stirring occasionally, and pour the caramel into the prepared chocolate crust. Spread it into an even layer using a small offset spatula.

Make the milk chocolate ganache layer

1. Chop the milk chocolate and place into a small bowl. Place the heavy cream and sour cream into a small saucepan and bring just to a boil. Pour over the chopped chocolate and stir until all of the chocolate has melted; stir in ¼ cup of the chopped peanuts. Reserve the remaining ¼ cup for the garnish. Cool to room temperature, stirring occasionally, and pour on top of the caramel layer. Spread it into an even layer using a small offset spatula. Place the pie into the refrigerator to chill.

Make the peanut butter mousse

1. Place the milk and the peanut butter in a medium heavy saucepan. Bring the mixture just to a boil, whisking it to a smooth consistency. Meanwhile, in a medium bowl, whisk together the egg, egg yolk, brown sugar, flour, and vanilla extract. When the milk mixture has reached a boil, pour half of it into the egg mixture and whisk until smooth. Pour it all back into the remaining milk mixture and whisk constantly over medium high heat until the mixture boils. Boil for two minutes, whisking constantly. (The mixture will be very thick and the bubbles will be large and slow moving.)

2. Remove from the heat and whisk in the heavy cream until smooth. Place in a small bowl and cover with plastic wrap. Refrigerate until cold, stirring occasionally.

Make the stabilized whipped cream

1. Place the powdered gelatin in a small microwave-safe bowl. Add the water and let stand for 5 minutes. Microwave on high (100%) power for 30 seconds, stirring after each 10-second interval, until the gelatin is dissolved. Let the gelatin cool to room temperature.

2. Place the 4½-quart bowl of a heavy-duty electric mixture and the wire whisk attachment into the freezer for at least 5 minutes. Remove the bowl and the whisk attachment from the freezer and place the heavy cream and the sugar in it. Beat on high speed until you can see a trail made by the whisk attachment. At that point, slowly pour the cooled gelatin mixture into the whipped cream, beating on high speed, until soft peaks form. Add the vanilla and beat for 20 more seconds. Refrigerate until ready to use.

Finish the peanut butter mousse

1. When the peanut butter mixture is cool, gently whisk in a whisk-full of the stabilized whipped cream. Whisk until smooth. Using a rubber spatula, fold in more whipped cream, using a total of half of the whipped cream. Spoon the peanut butter mousse on top of the chocolate ganache layer, smoothing it just to the sides of the crust.

2. Spoon the remaining stabilized whipped cream on top of the mousse layer, leaving a ½ inch of peanut butter mousse showing around the edge of the pie. Refrigerate for at least 4 hours.

Make the milk chocolate drizzle

1. Chop the milk chocolate and place into a small bowl. Place the heavy cream into a microwave-safe container and microwave on high (100%) power for 30 seconds or until it comes to a boil. Pour over the chopped chocolate and stir until smooth. Cool to room temperature.

Finish the pie

1. Sprinkle the top of the pie with the reserved ¼ cup of chopped peanuts. Drizzle the cooled milk chocolate drizzle over the top of the pie. Serve the pie immediately, or refrigerate for up to 3 days before serving.

Milk Chocolate Hazelnut Praline Mice

A heavenly hazelnut praline ganache is piped into teardrop shapes, with round milk chocolate bases. Coated in a thin sheath of tempered milk chocolate, the candy centers are transformed into whimsical creatures with sliced almonds for ears and piped dark chocolate forming the eyes, noses, and coiled tails.

•◆•

YIELD: ABOUT 60 MICE

Preparation: 4 hours, plus infusing, freezing, chilling, and setting times

Special Equipment (see mail order sources on page 302): Flat metal cake spatula; closed star decorating tip (such as Ateco #2); ⅛-inch plain decorating tip (such as Ateco #8); disposable pastry bags; digital thermometer; 2 silicone baking mats; 3-pronged chocolate dipping fork; heating pad with temperature control dial (such as the type used for backaches); cotton gloves.

Hazelnut Praline Mousse Ganache
•◆•
Vegetable oil, for oiling baking sheet
½ cup sifted granulated sugar
¾ teaspoon lemon juice
½ cup roasted and skinned hazelnuts (see page 41)
1 vanilla bean, split in half lengthwise
1 cup plus 2 tablespoons heavy cream
12 ounces Swiss dark chocolate, such as Lindt*
2 teaspoons invert sugar, such as Nulomoline**
2 tablespoons cognac
⅛ teaspoon Fiori di Sicilia***

Round Chocolate Bases
•◆•
6 ounces milk chocolate couverture, such as Valrhona Lactée
(see mail order sources on page 302)

Milk Chocolate Coating
•◆•
1¾ pounds milk chocolate couverture, such as Valrhona Lactée
(see mail order sources on page 302)

Decoration
•◆•
Sliced almonds, for mouse ears
4 ounces dark chocolate couverture, such as Valrhona Caraque
(see mail order sources on page 302)

Note: Use 3-ounce Lindt Swiss dark chocolate bars for preparing the ganache. This particular chocolate contains just the right proportion of cocoa solids and cocoa butter to enable the whipped hazelnut praline ganache to set up properly. The piped center will be just firm enough to be coated in a thin, crisp shell of tempered milk chocolate. Yet when the chocolate-coated mouse is bitten into, it will yield a soft and creamy filling.

**Note: Invert sugar acts as a softener and helps to prolong the freshness of the ganache filling. See a mail order source for Nulomoline on page 305.*

***Note: Fiori di Sicilia is an oil-based flavoring that exudes the aromas of vanilla, fresh citrus, and flowers. A tiny bit of this flavoring adds a lovely nuance to the hazelnut praline ganache. See mail order sources on page 302.*

Make the hazelnut praline ganache

1. Lightly oil a heavy baking sheet and a flat metal cake spatula.

2. In a small, nonstick saucepan or skillet, combine the sugar and lemon juice. Stir with a wooden spoon until the sugar is evenly moistened. Cook over medium heat, swirling the pan frequently, until the mixture liquefies and turns to an amber-colored caramel. Gently stir in the hazelnuts. Continue to cook until the mixture is fluid again and the hazelnuts are evenly coated with the caramel.

3. Pour the hot hazelnut praline onto the prepared baking sheet. Set the baking sheet on a cooling rack and allow the praline to cool for 3 minutes.

4. Using the oiled cake spatula, carefully loosen the undersides of the caramel to prevent it from sticking to the baking sheet. Let the caramel cool until it hardens completely.

5. Coarsely chop the praline and put it into a food processor fitted with the metal chopping blade. Process for 15 to 20 seconds, until it is finely ground. Continue to process for 2 to 3 minutes, until the mixture forms a crumbly paste. Scrape the praline paste into a small, heavy saucepan. (Do not clean the work bowl or metal blade, as you will be using it again to chop the chocolate.)

6. Using the tip of a small knife, remove the paste of tiny black seeds from inside the split vanilla bean. Add the scraped vanilla pod and seeds to the saucepan. Add the heavy cream and stir with a wooden spoon until blended. Cook over medium heat, stirring constantly until the praline paste is completely dissolved and the mixture is scalding hot. Remove the pan from the heat and allow the mixture to infuse for 30 minutes.

7. Meanwhile, coarsely chop the dark chocolate. Put the chocolate in the food processor with the metal chopping blade. Process for 15 to 20 seconds, until finely chopped. Remove the lid of the food processor and leave the chocolate in the work bowl.

8. Add the invert sugar to the praline-cream mixture and reheat, stirring frequently until the mixture comes to a gentle boil. Using tongs, remove the vanilla bean pods and discard. Pour the hot cream over the chopped chocolate in the food processor work bowl. With a rubber spatula, press down on the chocolate so that it is almost completely submerged in the hot cream. Let the mixture stand for 1 minute. Replace the lid of the food processor and pulse 6 to 8 times, until the mixture is creamy. Scrape down the sides of the work bowl, and add the cognac and Fiori di Sicilia. Pulse 4 to 6 more times, until smooth. Scrape the ganache onto a baking sheet, letting it spread into a thin layer. Cover the surface with plastic wrap and freeze for at least one hour, until firm.

Make the round chocolate bases

1. Temper the milk chocolate using the quick tempering instructions on page 30. The working temperature for making the milk chocolate bases should be 89°F to 91°F, slightly higher than the normal dipping temperature for milk chocolate. (The process of spreading the chocolate into a thin layer will continue to temper the chocolate.)

2. Place a 12-by-16-inch rectangle of baking parchment or waxed paper on a flat Formica or wood work surface, with the long sides lying parallel in front of you. (Do not lay paper on a marble, granite, or a metal countertop, as the chocolate will set up too quickly on any of these work surfaces.)

3. Pour half (3 ounces) of the tempered milk chocolate in a thin line about 8 inches long down the center of the paper. Using an 8-inch offset metal cake spatula, quickly spread the chocolate into a paper-thin rectangle, about ¹⁄₃₂-inch thick, leaving about a ¼-inch border around the edge of the paper. Continue moving the spatula back and forth over the chocolate rectangle for 10 to 20 seconds, or until the chocolate starts to feel tacky and begins to loose its sheen.

4. As the milk chocolate starts to set, press the 1-inch round open end of a closed star decorating tip (such as Ateco #2) into the chocolate rectangle, leaving about ½-inch of space between each circle. Continue using the tip as a cutter, until you have pressed thirty-five 1-inch rounds. Leave the round chocolate bases attached to the paper. Cover the bases with a sheet of baking parchment or waxed paper and weight with a heavy baking sheet. (The weight will prevent the chocolate bases from curling up as the chocolate contracts while it hardens.) Leave the round chocolate bases under the baking sheet until ready to pipe the chocolate mice centers.

5. Using the remaining 3 ounces of tempered milk chocolate, repeat steps 2 though 4 of making the round chocolate bases. Place the second sheet of paper with round chocolate bases on top of the first sheet of chocolate bases and cover with a piece of parchment or waxed paper. Replace the baking sheet on top of the chocolate bases.

Whip the hazelnut praline mousse ganache

1. Cut the pointed end off a disposable pastry bag and insert a ⅜-inch plain decorating tip (such as Ateco #8). Twist the portion of the pastry bag that is just above the wider opening of the tip. Tuck this twisted portion of the bag into the wider opening of the tip. (This will prevent the whipped ganache from leaking out the end of the decorating tip before you are ready to pipe.) Place the bag into a 2-cup glass measuring cup. Turn down the top 2 to 3 inches of the pastry bag, forming a cuff around the outside of the measuring cup. (The cup will support the bag as you fill it with the whipped ganache.)

2. Remove the plastic wrap from the chilled ganache. Gently warm the bottom of the baking sheet by passing it back and forth a few times over a gas flame or electric range top set on medium. Heat the pan only until the ganache starts to melt slightly so that it can be easily removed from the pan. Using a rubber spatula, scrape half (about 1 cup) of the ganache into the bowl of a heavy-duty electric mixer.

3. Set the bowl over another bowl of hot, not simmering water (the water must touch the bottom of the bowl) for 30 seconds to 2 minutes, stirring constantly with a rubber spatula until the ganache reads 65°F on a digital thermometer and has softened to the consistency of handmade mayonnaise. Be careful not to overheat the ganache. If the ganache becomes warmer than 65°F, place the bowl over a bowl of ice water for 2 to 4 seconds. Stir the ganache with a rubber spatula, just until it starts to thicken. Remove the bowl from the ice water.

4. Using the wire whip attachment, whip the softened ganache at medium speed for 30 seconds to 2 minutes, or until it lightens in color and forms soft peaks. It should have the texture of a fluffy chocolate buttercream frosting with a good piping consistency. If the whipped ganache becomes too firm and appears grainy, replace the bowl over the hot water for 2 to 4 seconds and stir gently until it softens enough to be rewhipped. Conversely, if the ganache is too soft and will not form soft peaks, place it over the bowl of ice water and stir for 2 to 4 seconds, until it just starts to thicken. Continue whipping until the ganache reaches the proper consistency.

Pipe the whipped ganache

1. Immediately scrape the ganache into the prepared pastry bag. Work quickly as the ganache will start to set up shortly after it is whipped. Remove the baking sheet and paper covering a sheet of chocolate bases. Hold the tip of the piping bag in at a 20-degree angle, barely touching the middle of a round chocolate base. Pipe the ganache into a 1¼-inch teardrop-shaped mound with an accentuated point—the head section of the mousse. Quickly finish piping the ganache onto the remaining chocolate bases.

2. Using the remaining chilled ganache, repeat steps 3 and 4 of whipping the hazelnut praline mousse ganache, and step 1 of piping the whipped ganache onto the sheet of remaining chocolate bases.

3. To form mouse ears, break a sliced almond in half and insert the broken ends of each half into the head portion of a piped mouse. Insert two almond ears into each of the remaining mice. Cover the mice with plastic wrap and refrigerate for 10 to 20 minutes, until firm.

4. Individually transfer the chilled mice centers (still attached to their chocolate bases) to a paper-lined baking sheet. The leftover chocolate trimmings can be saved for another use. Cover the mice centers loosely with a sheet of waxed paper or baking parchment and let them stand at room temperature for 1 hour before coating.

Coat the chocolate mice

1. Temper the milk chocolate using one of the tempering methods on page 27. Put the tempered chocolate into a 1-quart glass bowl and set it on a heating pad set to low heat to maintain the correct coating temperature. Line 2 baking sheets with silicone baking mats with the textured side facing up. Arrange the work area so that the uncoated centers are to the left of the tempered chocolate, with the mat-covered baking sheet on the right. Reverse these positions if you are left-handed.

2. Gently drop a mouse center (still attached to its round chocolate base) with the head facing up, onto the surface of the melted chocolate. Slide the prongs of a 3-pronged dipping fork underneath the mouse and at an angle, gently submerge the mouse into the chocolate until it is completely coated. Lift the coated mouse out of the chocolate and tilt the fork slightly so that it slips about an eighth of the way off the end of the fork. Level the fork and gently tap the bottom of the fork in a forward circular motion, barely touching the surface of the chocolate. Tap several times until very little chocolate is being pulled from the bottom of the mouse.

3. Lift the fork away from the surface of the chocolate and lightly touch the edge of the bowl with the bottom of the fork. Hold the fork at a slight angle and follow the curve of the bowl with it to remove any excess chocolate that is left on the bottom of the fork.

4. Place the coated mouse on the upper right-hand corner of the baking mat and pull the fork away with a quick but gentle motion. Coat the remaining mice in the same manner, setting them on the baking mats in straight rows.

Decorate the chocolate mice

1. Temper the dark chocolate using the quick tempering instructions on page 30. Make a small paper cone with a tiny opening at the tip. Fill the cone with some of the tempered dark chocolate. Pipe tiny dots for the eyes and nose on the face of each mouse. Pipe a curled tail on the back of each mouse. Let the Chocolate Mice set for at least 1 hour before removing them from the silicone mat.

2. Spread the remaining tempered milk and dark chocolates into even layers onto waxed paper-lined baking sheets and refrigerate for 10 to 15 minutes, until hardened. Let the chocolate stand at room temperature for 30 minutes. Break into pieces and store in zip-lock bags.

3. Store the Chocolate Mice in an airtight container for up to 5 days at room temperature, or in the refrigerator for up to 2 weeks. Allow the chocolates to come to room temperature in the storage container before serving.

Peanut Gianduja

This is an all-American twist on a European favorite: gianduja, which is the result of a blend of hazelnut paste and milk chocolate. Since Americans' favorite is the peanut, we've made a creamy filling of peanut butter and milk chocolate and encased it in a delicate chocolate coating.

• ❖ •

YIELD: 64 SMALL BARS

Preparation: 2½ hours, plus chilling and setting times

Special Equipment (see list of mail order sources on page 302): Two 4⅛-by-14¼-inch stainless steel, open-bottomed rectangular flan forms (for molding peanut gianduja filling); 4½-inch offset metal cake spatula; digital thermometer; heating pad with temperature control dial (such as the type used for backaches); 8-inch offset metal cake spatula.

Peanut Gianduja Filling
• ❖ •
⅓ cup plus 1 tablespoon low-salt, low-sugar peanut butter, such as Jif
1 tablespoon canola oil
10 ounces Swiss milk chocolate, such as Lindt
⅓ cup coarsely chopped, lightly salted dry-roasted peanuts

Milk Chocolate Coating
• ❖ •
2 ounces cocoa butter, finely chopped (see mail order sources, page 302)
1½ pounds Swiss milk chocolate, such as Lindt

Dark Chocolate Piping
• ❖ •
6 ounces dark chocolate couverture

Make the peanut gianduja filling

1. Tear off a 16-inch-long piece of aluminum foil. Fold it in half lengthwise and slit it in half along the fold with a sharp knife. Line a heavy, flat baking sheet with the 2 strips of aluminum foil. Set a 4⅛-by-14¼-inch rectangular flan form on top of each of the foil strips. Create a foil bottom for each flan form by tightly folding the excess foil up to cover the 4 outer sides of each flan form.

2. In a small bowl, combine the peanut butter and oil. Whisk until smooth.

3. Temper the milk chocolate. (Refer to the tempering instructions on page 27.)

4. Gently stir the peanut butter mixture into the bowl of tempered milk chocolate and whisk until smooth. Stir in the peanuts.

5. Divide the peanut gianduja filling mixture evenly between the 2 flan forms. Using a small, offset metal cake spatula, spread the filling into a thin, even layer. Carefully cover the surface of the filling with plastic wrap. Using a plastic scraper, smooth the plastic wrap so that it is flush with the surface of the filling. Refrigerate for 10 to 20 minutes, until firm.

Coat the gianduja rectangles

1. Put the cocoa butter in a 1 cup microwave-safe glass measuring cup. Microwave at medium (50 percent) power for 2 to 5 minutes, until completely melted. Temper the milk chocolate, adding the melted cocoa butter to the unmelted milk chocolate chunks. (Refer to the tempering instructions on page 27.)

2. Remove the baking sheet with the gianduja rectangles from the refrigerator.

3. Transfer the gianduja rectangles to a large cutting board and remove the plastic wrap. Heat the blade of a small, sharp knife over a gas flame or under hot running water (wipe the blade dry) and quickly cut around the edges of one of the flan forms to loosen the gianduja rectangle. Remove the flan form. With the tip of the knife, cut around the base of the gianduja rectangle and remove the excess foil. Trim the slight ridge on the top edge of the rectangle so that the surface is level. Repeat the unmolding and trimming process with the second flan form.

4. Cut four pieces of cardboard that measure the size of the unmolded gianduja rectangles and cover with aluminum foil. Slip a long metal cake spatula underneath one of the gianduja rectangles (the foil is still attached to the bottom of the rectangle) and transfer it to one of the foil-covered pieces of cardboard. Repeat with the second gianduja rectangle.

5. Check the temperature and fluidity of the tempered milk chocolate. It needs to be between 89°F and 91°F—a little warmer than usual—so that it is very fluid, making it easy to cover the surface of the gianduja rectangles with a thin layer of milk chocolate. Carefully reheat the tempered milk chocolate if necessary.

6. Lift up one of the gianduja rectangles (still on the cardboard) and, holding the bottom with the palm of one hand, rest one end of the rectangle on the edge of the bowl of tempered milk chocolate. Spoon a scant ¼ cup of tempered milk chocolate over the top of the front half of the gianduja rectangle. Using an 8-inch offset metal cake spatula and holding it at a slight angle, spread the chocolate in a thin, even layer over the front half of the rectangle. Still holding the spatula at a slight angle, scrape the excess milk chocolate back into the bowl. Turn the gianduja rectangle around and cover the remaining top half with a thin layer of tempered milk chocolate. Repeat the process with the second gianduja rectangle.

7. Let the chocolate-coated rectangles set at room temperature for 3 to 5 minutes, until the tempered chocolate is no longer wet.

8. Place the third foil-covered cardboard rectangle over the top of one of the milk chocolate-coated gianduja rectangles and invert. Remove the foil-covered cardboard and carefully peel off the foil that is adhered to the bottom of the gianduja. (If for some reason you have trouble removing the foil because the gianduja has softened, simply chill the rectangle for 5 to 10 minutes and try again.) Repeat with second chocolate-coated gianduja rectangle.

9. Coat the second side of each of the gianduja rectangles with a thin layer of tempered milk chocolate using the same method as described above. Allow the chocolate to set at room temperature for 3 to 5 minutes, until no longer wet. The gianduja is now sandwiched between 2 thin layers of milk chocolate.

Decorate the gianduja

1. Temper the dark chocolate couverture according to the directions on page 27. Prepare 2 small paper cones with tiny openings at their tips. Fill one of the cones with some of the dark chocolate and pipe thin, delicate lines of dark chocolate on a diagonal, over one of the milk chocolate-coated rectangles. Turn the rectangle 90 degrees and pipe more thin diagonal lines of chocolate, forming a lattice pattern. Fill the second paper cone and decorate the second rectangle in the same manner. Let the chocolate lattice pattern set for 2 to 3 minutes at room temperature.

2. Pour the remaining tempered milk and dark chocolates onto waxed paper-lined baking sheets and refrigerate for 10 to 15 minutes, until hardened. Let the chocolate stand at room temperature for 30 minutes. Break into pieces and store in zip-lock bags.

Cut the gianduja

1. Using a long metal cake spatula or knife, transfer one of the rectangles to a cutting board. Using a long, thin-bladed knife (such as a slicing knife), carefully trim about ⅛-inch from all 4 edges of the rectangle. Wipe the knife blade clean between each cut.

2. Cut the trimmed rectangle in half lengthwise. Cut each half into small 1½-by-1-inch bars. Cut the second gianduja rectangle in the same manner. Store the Peanut Gianduja between layers of waxed paper in an airtight container for up to 3 weeks.

Viennese Walnut Squares

*A soft, silky dark chocolate ganache is flavored with caramelized walnuts, a whisper of coffee,
and a hint of Tahitian vanilla and dark rum. This European-style candy is enrobed
in milk chocolate and the delicate square crowned with a walnut.*

•◆•

YIELD: 60 SQUARES

Preparation: 3 hours, plus setting, infusing, freezing, and chilling times

*Special Equipment (see list of mail order sources on page 302): Two 4⅜-by-14¾-inch
stainless steel, open-bottomed flan forms (for molding the ganache filling); digital
thermometer; heating pad with temperature control dial (such as the type used for
backaches); 4½-inch offset metal cake spatula; 8-inch offset metal cake spatula;
thin-bladed slicing knife; two silicone baking mats; 3-pronged chocolate
dipping fork; cotton gloves.*

Viennese Walnut Ganache
•◆•

⅓ cup sifted granulated sugar
½ teaspoon lemon juice
⅓ cup walnut halves, coarsely chopped
1 vanilla bean, split in half lengthwise
1 cup heavy cream
10 ounces Swiss dark chocolate*
2 teaspoons instant coffee crystals
2 teaspoons invert sugar, such as Nulomoline**
2 tablespoons dark rum

Milk Chocolate Coating
•◆•

1¾ pounds milk chocolate couverture,
such as Valrhona Lactée (see mail order sources on page 302)

Decoration
•◆•

60 perfect walnut halves

**Note: Use 3-ounce Lindt Swiss dark chocolate bars for preparing the ganache.
This particular chocolate contains just the right proportion of cocoa solids and
cocoa butter to enable the whipped ganache to set up properly.*

***Note: Invert sugar acts as a softener and helps to prolong the freshness of the
ganache filling. See a mail order source for Nulomoline on page 305.*

Prepare the Viennese walnut ganache

1. Lightly oil a heavy baking sheet and a flat metal cake spatula.

2. In a small, nonstick saucepan or skillet, combine the sugar and lemon juice. Stir with a wooden spoon until the sugar is evenly moistened. Cook over medium heat, swirling the pan frequently, until the mixture liquefies and turns to an amber-colored caramel. Gently stir in the walnuts. Continue to cook until the mixture is fluid again and the walnuts are evenly coated with the caramel.

3. Pour the hot walnut praline onto the prepared baking sheet. Set the baking sheet on a cooling rack and allow the praline to cool for 3 minutes.

4. Using the oiled cake spatula, carefully loosen the undersides of the praline to prevent it from sticking to the baking sheet. Let the praline cool until it hardens completely.

5. Coarsely chop the praline and put it into a food processor fitted with the metal chopping blade. Process for 15 to 20 seconds, until it is finely ground. Continue to process for 2 to 3 minutes, until the mixture forms a crumbly paste. Scrape the praline paste into a small, heavy saucepan. (Do not clean the workbowl or metal blade, as you will be using it again to chop the chocolate.)

6. Using the tip of a small knife, remove the paste of tiny black seeds from inside the split vanilla bean. Add the scraped vanilla pod and seeds to the saucepan. Add the heavy cream and stir with a wooden spoon until blended. Cook over medium heat, stirring frequently until the praline paste is completely dissolved and the mixture is scalding hot. Remove the pan from the heat and allow the mixture to infuse for 30 minutes.

7. Meanwhile, coarsely chop the dark chocolate. Put the chocolate in the food processor with the metal chopping blade. Process for 15 to 20 seconds, until finely chopped. Remove the lid of the food processor and leave the chocolate in the work bowl.

8. Add the instant coffee and invert sugar to the praline-cream mixture and reheat, stirring frequently until the mixture comes to a gentle boil. Using tongs, remove the vanilla pods and pour the hot cream over the chopped chocolate in the food processor workbowl. With a rubber spatula, press down on the chocolate so that it is almost completely submerged in the hot cream. Let the mixture stand for 30 seconds. Replace the lid of the food processor and pulse 6 to 8 times, until the mixture is creamy. Scrape down the sides of the work bowl, add the dark rum, and pulse 4 to 6 more times until smooth. Scrape the ganache onto a baking sheet, letting it spread into a thin layer. Cover the surface with plastic wrap. Freeze for at least 1 hour, until firm.

Whip the Viennese walnut ganache

1. Tear off a 16-inch-long piece of aluminum foil. Fold it in half lengthwise and slit it in half along the fold with a sharp knife. Line a heavy, flat baking sheet with the 2 strips of aluminum foil. Set a 4⅜-by-14¾-inch rectangular flan form on top of each of the foil strips. Create a foil bottom for each flan form by tightly folding the excess foil up to cover the 4 outer sides of each flan form.

2. Remove the plastic wrap from the chilled ganache. Gently warm the bottom of the baking sheet by passing it back and forth a few times over a gas flame or electric range top set on medium. Heat the pan only until the ganache starts to melt slightly so that it can be easily removed from the pan. Using a rubber spatula, scrape the ganache into the bowl of a heavy-duty electric mixer.

3. Set the bowl over another bowl of hot, not simmering, water (the water must touch the bottom of the bowl) for 30 seconds to 2 minutes, stirring constantly with a rubber spatula until the ganache reads 65°F on a digital thermometer and has softened to the consistency of handmade mayonnaise. Be careful not to overheat the ganache. If the ganache becomes warmer than 65°F, place the bowl over a bowl of ice water for 2 to 4 seconds. Stir the ganache with a rubber spatula, just until it starts to thicken. Remove the bowl from the ice water.

4. Using the wire whip attachment, whip the softened ganache at medium speed for 30 seconds to 2 minutes, or until it lightens in color and forms soft peaks. It should have the texture of a fluffy chocolate buttercream frosting with a smooth spreading consistency. If the whipped ganache becomes too firm and appears grainy, replace the bowl over the hot water for 2 to 4 seconds and stir gently until it softens enough to be rewhipped. Conversely, if the ganache is too soft and will not form soft peaks, place it over the bowl of ice water and stir for 2 to 4 seconds, until it just starts to thicken. Continue whipping until the ganache reaches the proper consistency.

5. Immediately divide the whipped ganache between the two prepared flan forms (about 1½ cups for each form). Using a small, offset metal cake spatula, spread the ganache into an even layer. Work quickly as the ganache will start to set up shortly after it is whipped. Carefully cover the surface of the ganache with plastic wrap. Using a plastic scraper, smooth the plastic wrap so that it is flush with the surface of the filling. Refrigerate for 15 to 25 minutes, until firm.

Coat the ganache rectangles

1. Temper the milk chocolate using one of the tempering methods on page 27. Put the tempered chocolate into a 1-quart glass bowl and set it on a heating pad set to low heat to maintain the correct coating temperature.

2. Remove the baking sheet with the ganache rectangles from the refrigerator and peel off the plastic wrap. Heat the blade of a small, sharp knife over a gas flame or under hot running water (wipe the blade dry) and quickly cut around the inside edges of one of the flan forms to loosen the ganache filling. Fold down the foil and remove the flan form. With the tip of the knife, trim the excess foil around the base of the ganache rectangle and discard. Trim the slight ridge on the top edge of the ganache rectangle so that the surface of the rectangle is level. Repeat the unmolding and trimming process with the second flan form.

3. Cut 4 pieces of cardboard that measure the size of the unmolded ganache rectangles and cover with aluminum foil. Slip a long metal cake spatula underneath one of the ganache rectangles (the foil is still attached to the bottom of the rectangle) and transfer it to one of the foil-covered pieces of cardboard. Repeat with the second ganache rectangle.

4. Check the temperature and fluidity of the tempered milk chocolate. It needs to be between 89°F and 91°F—a little warmer than usual—so that it is very fluid, making it easy to cover the surface of the ganache rectangles with a thin layer of milk chocolate. Carefully adjust the temperature of the tempered milk chocolate if necessary.

5. Lift up one of the ganache rectangles (still on the cardboard), and holding the bottom with the palm of one hand, rest one end of the rectangle on the edge of the bowl of tempered milk chocolate. Spoon a scant ¼ cup of tempered milk chocolate over the top of the front half of the ganache rectangle. Using an 8-inch offset metal cake spatula and holding it at a slight angle, spread the chocolate in a thin, even layer over the front half of the rectangle. Still holding the spatula at a slight angle, scrape the excess milk chocolate back into the bowl. Turn the ganache rectangle around and cover the remaining top half with a thin layer of tempered milk chocolate. Repeat the process with the second ganache rectangle.

6. Let the chocolate-coated rectangles set at room temperature for 3 to 5 minutes, until they are no longer wet.

7. Place the third foil-covered cardboard rectangle over the top of one of the chocolate-coated ganache rectangles and invert. Remove the foil-covered cardboard and carefully peel off the foil that is adhered to the ganache filling. (If for some reason you have trouble removing the foil because the ganache has softened, simply chill the rectangles for 5 to 10 minutes, and then try again.) Repeat with second chocolate-coated ganache rectangle.

8. Coat the second side of each of the ganache rectangles with a thin layer of tempered milk chocolate using the same method as described above. Allow the chocolate to set at room temperature for 3 to 5 minutes, until no longer wet. The ganache filling is now sandwiched between 2 thin layers of milk chocolate. Keep the milk chocolate in temper while cutting the ganache rectangles into squares.

Cut the milk chocolate-covered ganache rectangles into squares

1. Using a long metal cake spatula or knife, transfer one of the rectangles to a cutting board. Heat a long, thin-bladed knife (such as a slicing knife) under hot running water and wipe dry. Carefully trim ⅛ inch from all 4 edges of the rectangle. Rinse the knife under hot water and wipe the knife dry between each cut. Continue to cut the trimmed rectangle into 1¼-inch strips. Cut each strip into three 1¼-inch squares. Transfer the cut squares to a baking sheet, with the flat, smooth surface of each square facing up. Trim and cut the remaining ganache rectangle into 1¼-inch squares and transfer them to the baking sheet.

Coat the sides of the ganache squares in milk chocolate

1. Line 2 baking sheets with silicone baking mats with the textured side facing up. Arrange your work area so that the baking sheet of ganache squares is to the left of the tempered chocolate, with a silicone baking mat-covered baking sheet on the right. Reverse these positions if you are left-handed.

2. Pick up a ganache square with your left hand and gently drop it on the surface of the chocolate so that the flat surface without cracks or smudges is facing up. With the tip of a finger, gently press down on the center of the ganache square until just the side of it is evenly submerged in the chocolate. (The top of the square has already been coated.) Slide the prongs of a 3-pronged chocolate dipping fork underneath the coated square and lift it out of the chocolate. Tilt the fork slightly so that the center slips about an eighth of the way off the end of the fork. Level the fork and gently tap the bottom of the fork in a forward circular motion, barely touching the surface of the chocolate. Tap several times until very little chocolate is being pulled from the bottom of the square.

3. Lift the fork away from the surface of the chocolate and lightly touch the edge of the bowl with the bottom of the fork. Hold the fork at slight angle and follow the curve of the bowl with it to remove any excess chocolate that is left on the bottom of the fork.

4. Place the coated square on the upper right-hand corner of the baking mat and pull the fork away with a quick but gentle motion. Coat the sides of remaining the squares in the same manner, setting them on the baking mat in straight rows.

Decorate the tops of the Viennese Walnut Squares

1. Make a small paper cone with a tiny opening at the tip. Fill the cone with some of the tempered milk chocolate. Pipe a small dot of chocolate on the top center of each Viennese Walnut Square and affix a walnut half. Let the Viennese Walnut Squares set at room temperature for at least 1 hour, or until they can be lifted easily from the mats and the undersides are glossy.

2. Spread the remaining tempered milk chocolate into a even layer onto a waxed paper-lined baking sheet and refrigerate for 10 to 15 minutes, until hardened. Let the chocolate stand at room temperature for 30 minutes. Break into pieces and store in a zip-lock bag.

3. Store the Viennese Walnut Squares in an airtight container for up to 5 days at room temperature, or in the refrigerator for up to 2 weeks. Allow the chocolates to come to room temperature in the storage container before serving.

Toffee Pecan Madeleines

*One of the most popular holiday flavor combinations—crunchy butter rum toffee
with roasted pecans and milk chocolate—is presented in a graceful, traditional form, classically
associated with French tea cookies. Lindt Swiss milk chocolate in the 13-ounce size provides
the creamy texture necessary to this recipe. To make it easy to work, cocoa butter is added
to the milk chocolate during tempering.*

• ◆ •

YIELD: 24 MADELEINES

Preparation: 2½ hours, plus cooling, setting, and chilling times

*Special Equipment (see mail order sources on page 302): Flat metal cake spatula;
heavy 2-quart nonstick saucepan; candy thermometer; digital thermometer; heating pad
with temperature control dial (such as the type used for backaches); 2 metal madeleine
molds, each containing twelve 3⅛-by-1¾-inch fluted shell-shaped cavities; flexible
straight-edged steel baker's scraper; 8-inch offset metal cake spatula; cotton gloves.*

Butter Rum Toffee
• ◆ •
¾ cup sifted granulated sugar
½ cup (1 stick) unsalted butter, cut into tablespoons
⅓ cup dark rum, such as Myers'
½ teaspoon lecithin*
⅛ teaspoon salt

Madeleines
• ◆ •
2 ounces cocoa butter, finely chopped (see mail order sources)
1½ pounds Swiss milk chocolate, such as Lindt
1½ cups pecan halves, lightly roasted (see page 41)

**Note: When making toffee, lecithin is used as an emulsifier. It prevents
the butter from separating during the cooking process. See a mail order source
for lecithin on page 305.*

Make the butter rum toffee

1. Thoroughly oil a heavy, flat, baking sheet and both sides of a an 8-inch metal cake spatula.

2. In a heavy 2-quart non-stick saucepan, combine the sugar, butter, rum, lecithin, and salt. Cook over medium-low heat, stirring constantly with a wooden spoon, until the butter melts and the sugar dissolves completely.

3. Dip a clean pastry brush in warm water and wash down the side of the pan to remove any sugar crystals clinging to the side of the pan. Raise the heat to medium-high and bring the mixture to a boil. As soon as the froth subsides, insert a candy thermometer into the candy mixture but do not let it touch the bottom of the pan. (If using a thermometer that is mounted on a metal frame, do not worry about the base of the frame touching the bottom of the pan.) Without stirring, cook the toffee mixture for 12 to 18 minutes, until the thermometer registers 290°F (hard crack stage). Remove the pan from the heat and immediately pour the toffee onto the prepared baking sheet. Do not scrape out the toffee that sticks to the bottom of the pan.

4. Using the oiled metal cake spatula, carefully loosen the underside of the toffee rectangle to prevent it from sticking to the baking sheet as the toffee hardens. When the toffee is no longer pliable, slide the blade of the oiled spatula under the toffee to release it from the baking sheet and using your fingers, carefully flip it over onto a piece of baking parchment. Lift the baking parchment with the toffee rectangle and place it back on the baking sheet. Cool the toffee completely. Coarsely chop into ¼-inch pieces and transfer to a bowl.

Make the madeleines

1. Put the cocoa butter in a 1 cup microwave-safe glass measuring cup. Microwave at medium (50 percent) power for 2 to 5 minutes, until completely melted. Temper the milk chocolate, adding the melted cocoa butter to the unmelted milk chocolate chunks. (Refer to the tempering instructions on page 27.)

2. Wipe the insides of the twelve shell-shaped cavities in each of the two madeleine molds with a lint-free cloth or a cotton ball, until each cavity is shiny.

3. Stir the chopped pecans and ¾ cup of the chopped butter rum toffee into the tempered milk chocolate. Carefully spoon the chocolate mixture into the madeleine mold cavities. Do not over-fill. As you fill each mold cavity, gently tap the mold on the work surface to remove air pockets. Wipe up any chocolate spills that may have splashed on to the mold.

4. Refrigerate the molds for 3 hours, or until the chocolate contracts slightly from the sides of the shell cavities.

Unmold the madeleines

1. Pad a work surface with a folded kitchen towel or a double thickness of paper towels. Carefully invert the molds, one at time over the padded surface, and if necessary gently tap each mold on the work surface to release the madeleines. If they do not release from the molds after a gentle tap, it could be one of two reasons: the chocolate has not set sufficiently or the chocolate was not properly tempered. Return the molds to the refrigerator for another 30 minutes.

2. If the madeleines are still not releasing from the mold, this is an indication that the chocolate was not in temper when you filled the mold cavities with the chocolate mixture. If this should happen, do not attempt to scrape the chocolate from the molds. Simply heat the chocolate in each mold cavity with a portable hair dryer until it melts and wipe the entire mold clean. You will have to start over with newly tempered chocolate.

3. Let the unmolded madeleines come to room temperature for 30 minutes. If desired, wrap the madeleines individually in cellophane or gold confectioners' foil and store in an airtight container at cool room temperature for up to 6 weeks.

Desserts

For dessert makers at home, semisweet and bittersweet are the chocolates of choice. They contain at least 35% chocolate liquor (more than twice the chocolate essence contained in most milk chocolates), so they convey deep, multifaceted chocolate flavor with a lingering, pleasing finish. Purists prefer semisweet or bittersweet when the chocolate must fly solo in a cake, tart, cookie, or brownie; even if it is paired with a strong flavor like raspberry or lemon, the voluptuous taste of chocolate will still emerge. Semisweet and bittersweet are commonly referred to as dark chocolates, but in recent years manufacturers have begun to offer chocolates with 44%, 66%, 74%, and even 94% chocolate liquor. Some of these superdark chocolates are marvelous—a small amount will satisfy even a supernatural chocolate craving, whether eaten raw or incorporated into a dessert. But they are not to be substituted for the recipes found here unless one is specifically called for.

Black Forest Cake

This cake is named for the Black Forest region in Germany, where the finest kirschwasser is made. For those fond of the combination of cherry and chocolate, this is the classic, forevermore. A cherry filling and cherry chocolate buttercream reinforce the kirsch-soaked splendor of the cake.

•◆•

YIELD: 14 SERVINGS

Preparation: 3 hours, plus baking and cooling times
Special Equipment: Acetate sheets; wood-grain tool

Chocolate Cake
•◆•
1 cup unsweetened alkalized cocoa powder
2½ cups cake flour (not self-rising)
1 tablespoon plus 1½ teaspoons baking powder
1 teaspoon baking soda
½ teaspoon salt
¾ cup (1½ sticks) unsalted butter, at room temperature
1½ cups granulated sugar
1 cup firmly packed light brown sugar
3 large eggs, at room temperature
1 tablespoon vanilla extract
1 tablespoon unsulphered (mild) molasses
2¼ cups milk, at room temperature

Cherry Filling
•◆•
Two 15-ounce cans of tart cherries packed in water
¼ cup kirsch (cherry brandy)

Cherry Vanilla Buttercream
•◆•
¾ cup reserved juice from cherries
1¾ cups granulated sugar, divided
6 large egg yolks, at room temperature
⅔ cup half-and-half
½ vanilla bean, split and scraped
1½ cups (3 sticks) unsalted butter, at room temperature
2 tablespoons kirsch (cherry brandy)
⅛ teaspoon almond extract

Chocolate Buttercream
•◆•
4 ounces bittersweet chocolate, chopped
1 ounce unsweetened chocolate, chopped
6 large egg yolks, at room temperature
⅓ cup water
⅔ cup granulated sugar
1¼ cups (2½ sticks) unsalted butter, at room temperature
1 teaspoon vanilla extract

Meringue Mushrooms
•◆•
2 large egg whites, at room temperature
¼ cup granulated sugar
¼ teaspoon cream of tartar
1½ ounces bittersweet chocolate, chopped
Cocoa powder for dusting

Wood-Grain Chocolate Ring
•◆•
One 3-ounce bar Lindt bittersweet chocolate, chopped
Two 3-ounce bars Lindt milk chocolate, chopped

Chocolate Curls
•◆•
Two 3-ounce bars Lindt bittersweet chocolate, chopped

Make the chocolate cake layers

1. Place 2 racks, at least 4 inches apart, near the center of the oven and preheat to 350°F. Butter the bottom and sides of three 9-inch round cake pans. Dust the pans with flour and tap out the excess.

2. In a medium bowl, sift together the cocoa powder, flour, baking powder, baking soda, and salt. Set aside.

3. In the 4½-quart bowl of a heavy-duty electric mixer fitted with the paddle attachment, beat the butter at medium speed until fluffy, about 1 minute. Add the sugars and beat on medium speed for 1 to 2 minutes, or until smooth and fluffy. Add the eggs one at a time, stopping to scrape down the sides of the bowl after each addition. Add the vanilla extract and molasses and beat for 30 seconds.

4. With the mixer running at low speed, alternate the dry ingredients in 3 additions with the milk in 2 additions, beginning and ending with the dry ingredients. Scrape down the sides of the bowl between additions.

5. Divide the batter evenly between the 3 pans. Bake for 25 to 35 minutes, or until a tester inserted into the center of each cake comes out with only moist crumbs clinging to it. Cool the cakes over a wire rack for 15 minutes before removing the cakes from the pans to cool completely. Wrap tightly in plastic wrap and set aside at room temperature; the layers can be made days or even weeks ahead and frozen until needed.

Make the cherry filling

1. Drain the cherries, reserving ¾ cup of the liquid for the cherry-vanilla buttercream. Set aside ⅓ cup of the drained cherries. Place the remaining cherries in a medium bowl; stir in the kirsch. Set aside while preparing the sugar syrup for the buttercream.

2. Place the reserved ⅓ cup cherries in the bowl of a food processor fitted with the chopping blade. Pulse until the cherries are finely chopped but not puréed. Reserve.

Make the cherry vanilla buttercream

1. Place the reserved cherry juice and 1¼ cups of the sugar in a medium, heavy saucepan and bring to a boil. Cook until the temperature registers 238°F on a candy thermometer. Pour ½ cup of the hot syrup over the bowl of reserved whole cherries; cover and let the cherries steep. Store the cherries in the refrigerator until needed. Set aside the remaining syrup while preparing the buttercream.

2. Whisk the egg yolks together in a small bowl; set aside. Combine the half-and-half, vanilla bean, and remaining ½ cup of sugar in a small, heavy saucepan over medium-high heat and bring to a boil. Whisk a small amount of the hot liquid into the egg yolks, stirring constantly. Return the mixture to the pan and cook over medium heat until the mixture thickens slightly. The mixture is finished cooking when a path drawn across a sauce-coated spoon remains clear.

3. Strain the half-and-half mixture into the bowl of a 4½-quart heavy-duty mixer fitted with the whisk attachment; beat on high speed until the mixture has cooled to room temperature, about 5 to 10 minutes.

4. Once the mixture has cooled, lower the speed and gradually add the butter, 1 to 2 tablespoons at a time. The buttercream will look lumpy or curdled when half of the butter has been added, but it will smooth out at the end. Beat in the reserved syrup, kirsch, almond extract, and the reserved chopped cherries.

5. Transfer the buttercream to a clean bowl and cover with plastic. If you are planning to assemble the cake on the same day, set it aside at room temperature. The buttercream may be made a few days in advance and stored in the refrigerator, but you will have to slowly let it come to room temperature before it will be soft enough to spread.

Make the chocolate buttercream

1. Melt the chocolates according to the instructions on page 25. Set aside to cool while preparing the buttercream.

2. Place the egg yolks in the 4½-quart bowl of a heavy-duty electric mixer. Fill a wider, shallow bowl with hot water and set the bowl with the egg yolks directly over it, letting the water touch the bottom of the bowl. Stir the yolks gently for 1 minute, until warm.

3. Remove the bowl with the yolks from the water and dry the bottom. Attach the bowl to the mixer stand along with the splatter-shield and whisk attachment, and beat at medium-high speed for 5 to 7 minutes. The yolks should have tripled in volume and a ribbon falling off the beater should remain on the surface of the yolk mixture for a few seconds. While the eggs are mixing, prepare the sugar syrup.

4. In a small to medium, heavy saucepan combine the water and granulated sugar over medium-low heat. Stir with a wooden spoon to dissolve the sugar. Increase the heat to medium-high and bring the mixture to a boil. Continue to boil, unstirred, until the mixture reaches 240°F on a candy thermometer.

5. With the mixer running at medium speed, carefully pour the hot syrup down the side of the pouring spout, being sure to avoid splattering the syrup onto the whisk. Continue to beat the eggs until they have cooled to room temperature, about 5 to 10 minutes.

6. Once the mixture has cooled, lower the speed and gradually add the butter, 1 to 2 tablespoons at a time. The buttercream will look lumpy or curdled when half of the butter has been added, but it will smooth out at the end. Add the vanilla extract, then gradually beat in the melted chocolate.

7. Transfer the buttercream to a clean bowl and cover with plastic. If you are planning to assemble the cake on the same day, set it aside at room temperature. The buttercream may be made a few days in advance and stored in the refrigerator, but you will have to slowly let it come to room temperature before it will be soft enough to spread.

Make the meringue mushrooms

1. Preheat the oven to 250°F; line a baking sheet with parchment paper. Combine the egg whites and sugar in a medium mixing bowl. Place the bowl over a larger bowl filled with hot water. Stir the mixture until the sugar begins to dissolve. Remove the bowl with the egg whites from the water and dry the bottom. Using a handheld electric mixer, beat the egg whites on high speed until foamy. Add the cream of tartar. Continue to beat the mixture until it holds stiff but not dry peaks.

2. Place the meringue mixture into a pastry bag fitted with a medium plain tip (such as Ateco #5). Pipe ten 1¼-inch button-shaped circles for the mushroom caps onto the prepared baking sheet. Pipe ten ¾-inch kiss-shaped mounds for the stems. Bake for 1 hour or until hard to the touch. Cool completely and store in an airtight container until ready to use.

3. To assemble the mushrooms, melt the chocolate according to the instructions on page 25. Place a ½-inch dollop of chocolate on the flat side (the bottom) of each mushroom cap. Refrigerate the mushroom caps for one minute, until the chocolate just begins to set. Invert the mushroom caps onto stems and allow the chocolate to set completely. Dust with cocoa powder and set aside until ready to assemble cake.

Assemble the cake

1. Arrange 1 layer of chocolate cake on a serving plate. Place the cherry-vanilla buttercream in a pastry bag fitted with a medium plain tip (such as Ateco #5). Beginning at the outside edge of the cake, pipe concentric circles ¼ inch apart over the cake. Fill the spaces between the buttercream with cherries. Top with a second layer of cake and repeat process. Top with the remaining cake layer and coat the side of the cake with a thin layer of the cherry-vanilla buttercream.

2. Set aside 1 cup of the chocolate buttercream; reserve. Use the remaining buttercream to frost the cake.

Make the chocolate wood-grain ring

1. Cut a strip of acetate to fit the around the side of the cake, approximately 4-by-29 inches. Place the acetate on a clean, flat work surface so that a 4-inch side faces you. If the cake is chilled, let it stand at room temperature until the buttercream is cool but not cold. If the cake is at room temperature, chill it in the refrigerator for 15 minutes.

2. Temper the bittersweet chocolate according to the instructions on page 27. Pour the chocolate along a 4-inch edge of the acetate. Using a wood grain tool, pull the chocolate down towards the opposite edge, gently rocking the tool back and forth as you go. Allow the chocolate to set.

3. Temper the milk chocolate according to the instructions on page 27. Using an offset metal spatula, spread the milk chocolate evenly over the bittersweet chocolate pattern. When the chocolate begins to set, wrap the acetate around the cake and press gently to adhere the chocolate to the side of the cake as it sets. Once the chocolate has completely set, peel off the acetate.

Make the chocolate curls

1. Place a sheet of acetate on a flat work surface. Temper the chocolate according to the instructions on page 27. Using an offset metal spatula, spread a thin layer of chocolate on the acetate. Allow the chocolate to begin to set. Hold a bench scraper or putty knife at a 45-degree angle and push the blade diagonally against the chocolate to form curls.

Garnish the cake

1. Spread the reserved chocolate buttercream over the top of the cake. Arrange meringue mushrooms and chocolate curls on top. Store the cake in the refrigerator, but serve it at room temperature or the buttercream will be hard.

Chocolate Almond Meringue Cake with Rich Chocolate Filling

Almond and chocolate go together like kids and candy bars, and this simple dessert is a celebration of the pairing. Chocolate meringue layers studded with almonds host a super-rich chocolate filling. A glass of milk is the perfect accompaniment.

•◆•

YIELD: 6 TO 8 SERVINGS

Preparation: 1 hour, plus baking and cooling times

Rich Chocolate Filling
•◆•

7 ounces bittersweet chocolate, finely chopped
¾ cup heavy cream
3 tablespoons dark brown sugar
3 tablespoons unsalted butter

Chocolate Almond Meringue Cake
•◆•

4 tablespoons unsweetened nonalkalized cocoa powder
⅓ cup hot water
1 cup all-purpose flour
¼ cup ground almonds
1 teaspoon baking powder
¼ teaspoon baking soda
¼ teaspoon salt
½ cup (1 stick) unsalted butter, softened
¾ cup plus 2 teaspoons granulated sugar, divided
⅔ cup dark brown sugar, divided
4 large eggs, separated
½ teaspoon vanilla extract
¼ teaspoon almond extract
¼ cup sliced almonds

Make the rich chocolate filling

1. Place the chopped chocolate in a medium heatproof bowl.

2. Place the heavy cream, brown sugar, and butter in a small saucepan and cook over low heat, stirring constantly, until the sugar completely dissolves and the butter melts. Increase the heat to medium and cook until the mixture comes to a gentle boil. Remove the pan from the heat and pour the hot cream over the chopped chocolate. Let stand for 3 minutes to melt the chocolate.

3. Stir gently until the mixture is well blended and smooth. Place plastic wrap directly on the surface of the filling and set it aside at room temperature to cool for several hours until it has the consistency of frosting (don't be tempted to refrigerate the filling to speed up the process).

Make the chocolate almond meringue cake

1. Position a rack in the bottom third of the oven and preheat to 350°F. Lightly butter the bottom of two 9-inch round baking pans. Line the bottoms with parchment rounds. Butter and flour the parchment, tapping out the excess flour.

2. In a small bowl, whisk together the cocoa powder and hot water until smooth. Set aside to cool.

3. In a medium bowl, using a wire whisk, stir together the flour, ground almonds, baking powder, baking soda, and salt until well blended.

4. In the 4½-quart bowl of a heavy-duty electric mixer, fitted with the paddle attachment, beat the butter, ¼ cup granulated sugar, and ⅓ cup of the dark brown sugar at medium speed for about 4 to 5 minutes, until the mixture is light and fluffy. Scrape down the sides of the bowl with a rubber spatula as necessary. Add the egg yolks, one at a time, beating well after each addition. Beat in the vanilla and almond extracts.

5. Reduce the speed to low and add the dry ingredients one-half at a time, alternating them with the cocoa mixture. Divide the batter evenly between the prepared baking pans.

6. In a clean, grease-free 4½-quart bowl of a heavy-duty electric mixer, fitted with the whisk attachment, beat the egg whites and the remaining ⅓ cup of dark brown sugar at medium speed until the mixture looks creamy and soft peaks are beginning to form, about 2 to 3 minutes. Increase the speed to medium-high and add ½ cup of the granulated sugar one tablespoon at a time. Continue beating until the egg white mixture forms a stiff, shiny meringue. It should take about 2 to 3 minutes from the time the granulated sugar is added.

7. Using a small offset metal statula, swirl the meringue over the cake batter in the pans, making sure that the meringue completely covers the batter and extends to the sides of the pans. Evenly distribute the sliced almonds over the meringue, then sprinkle over the remaining two teaspoons of granulated sugar.

8. Bake the cakes until the meringue is puffed up and lightly browned, about 25 to 30 minutes. Run the tip of a sharp knife between the edge of the meringue and the sides of the cake pans to loosen the cakes. Transfer the cake pans to a wire rack and allow the cakes to completely cool in their pans.

Assemble the cake

1. When the cakes are completely cooled, run a small offset spatula around the sides of the cakes to loosen them. Invert one of the cakes onto a plate or baking sheet. Carefully peel off the parchment paper from the bottom of the cake and immediately invert the cake onto a serving platter; the meringue side will be facing up. Spoon the chocolate filling on top of the meringue. Spread it out evenly.

2. Follow the above procedure to remove the second cake from its pan and place the cake (meringue side up) on top of the chocolate filling. The cake should be eaten the same day it's made and may be assembled several hours before serving.

Chocolate Phyllo Pockets with Raspberry and Pineapple Compote and Chocolate Rum Ganache

Buttery phyllo encloses rich pound cake layered with chocolate rum ganache, and the warm pocket is served with cool fruit compote and whipped cream. A sophisticated dessert with dark rum blending the rich chocolate flavor, the light, sweet pineapple and raspberry compote, it is perfect for an elegant dinner party.

•◆•

YIELD: 8 SERVINGS

Preparation: 1 hour, 30 minutes, plus baking and cooling times

Pound Cake
•◆•

1 cup all-purpose flour

½ cup unsweetened alkalized cocoa powder

½ teaspoon salt

¼ teaspoon baking powder

¼ teaspoon baking soda

¾ cup (1½ sticks) unsalted butter, softened

1½ cups granulated sugar

3 large eggs

1 teaspoon vanilla extract

½ cup sour cream

Chocolate Rum Ganache
•◆•

8 ounces bittersweet chocolate, finely chopped

1 cup heavy cream

1 tablespoon dark rum

Raspberry and Pineapple Compote
•◆•

2 cups raspberries

1 cup chopped fresh pineapple

1 teaspoon dark rum

Chocolate Phyllo Pockets
•◆•

8 sheets phyllo dough (each sheet measuring 12-by-17 inches)

½ cup (1 stick) unsalted butter, melted

Garnish
•◆•

Whipped cream

Make the pound cake

1. Position a rack in the center of the oven and preheat to 350°F. Butter and flour the bottom and sides of a 9-by-5-inch loaf pan, or coat it with nonstick cooking spray. Set aside.

2. Sift together the flour, cocoa powder, salt, baking powder, and baking soda. In the 4½-quart bowl of a heavy-duty electric mixer, using the paddle attachment, beat the butter for 2 minutes at medium speed, or until creamy. Add the sugar and continue beating for 2 minutes, or until the mixture is light in texture and color. Beat in the eggs, one at a time, beating for 30 to 40 seconds after each egg is added. Scrape down the sides of the bowl frequently with a rubber spatula to keep the batter even-textured. Blend in the vanilla extract.

3. On low speed, alternately add the sifted mixture in 3 additions with the sour cream in 2 additions, beginning and ending with the sifted mixture.

4. Scrape the batter into the prepared pan. Smooth over the top with a rubber spatula. Bake the cake for about 1 hour and 15 minutes, or until the top of the cake springs back when lightly pressed with a finger. Cool the cake in the pan on a rack for 10 minutes, then invert onto another cooling rack.

Make the chocolate rum ganache

1. Place the chopped chocolate in a heat-resistant bowl.

2. In a small saucepan, bring the heavy cream to a boil over medium-high heat. As soon as the cream boils, pour it over the chopped chocolate and let the mixture stand for 30 seconds. Add the rum and stir the mixture until the chocolate is melted and the mixture is smooth. Put the ganache in the refrigerator to thicken and cool, stirring occasionally, for at least 15 minutes and up to 1 hour.

Make the raspberry and pineapple compote

1. In a medium bowl, combine the raspberries, pineapple, and rum. Mix well.

Make the chocolate phyllo packets

1. Preheat the oven to 450° F. Butter a baking sheet.

2. Cut eight ½-inch slices from the chocolate pound cake.

3. Take 1 phyllo sheet and lay it on the work surface so that the short side forms the bottom edge. Lay the remaining phyllo sheets between waxed paper and cover with a damp towel to prevent them from drying out. Brush the lower half of the phyllo sheet with melted butter, and fold the top half of the sheet over the bottom half. Brush the top with melted butter.

4. Place a piece of chocolate cake in the middle of the phyllo sheet. Spread a small amount of ganache over the cake (about 2 tablespoons), and arrange about ¼ cup of the raspberry and pineapple compote over the ganache.

5. Fold the top half of the phyllo sheet over the cake, them the bottom half. Fold the left, then the right side of the phyllo dough over the cake to complete the pocket. Place the phyllo pocket on the prepared baking sheet and brush lightly with melted butter. Repeat the process with the remaining phyllo sheets.

6. Bake the phyllo pockets for about 10 minutes, or until they are golden on top and crisp around the edges.

7. Serve warm with the whipped cream, the remaining ganache, and the raspberry and pineapple compote.

Dark Chocolate Madeleines with Mint Chocolate Glaze

The beautiful and graceful madeleine is a welcome sight on any plate or service. Light and flavorful all on its own, this version is glazed with chocolate with a hint of mint, and would be the perfect accompaniment to a tea and coffee hour, or glittering under your finest crystal after an elegant evening meal.

•◆•

YIELD: 24 MADELEINES

Preparation: 45 minutes, plus baking time

Special Equipment: Two 12-mold madeleine pans

Dark Chocolate Madeleines
•◆•

6 tablespoons unsalted butter, cut into tablespoons
2 tablespoons unsweetened alkalized cocoa powder
4 ounces bittersweet chocolate, coarsely chopped
¾ cup cake flour
½ teaspoon baking powder
¼ teaspoon salt
2 large eggs, at room temperature
1 large egg yolk, at room temperature
½ cup granulated sugar
1 teaspoon vanilla extract
2 large egg whites, at room temperature

Mint Chocolate Glaze
•◆•

4 ounces bittersweet chocolate, coarsely chopped
½ cup heavy cream
½ teaspoon mint extract

Make the dark chocolate madeleines

1. In a small, heavy saucepan, heat the butter over medium heat until light golden brown and fragrant, about 5 minutes. Remove from the heat and stir in the cocoa powder. Strain the mixture and let cool until tepid.

2. Meanwhile, melt the chocolate according to the directions on page 25. Allow to cool slightly.

3. Sift the flour, baking powder, and salt together into a small bowl. Set aside.

4. Place the eggs, egg yolk, and the granulated sugar into a 4½-quart bowl of a heavy-duty electric mixer. Place the bowl with the eggs over a bowl of hot water to warm them, stirring frequently until the sugar begins to dissolve. Remove the bowl with the eggs from the water and dry off the bottom. Attach the bowl to the mixer and beat the egg mixture using the whisk attachment on medium-high speed until the mixture forms soft peaks when the beater is lifted. Beat in the vanilla extract.

5. In a clean, grease-free bowl using a handheld electric mixer, beat the egg whites on high speed until they form stiff but not dry peaks.

6. Fold the dry ingredients into the egg mixture. Fold in the melted butter and chocolate. Finally, fold in the egg whites. Place the madeleine batter in the refrigerator to chill for 15 minutes.

7. Place 2 racks in the lower half of the oven and preheat to 375°F. Butter and flour two 12-mold madeleine pans. Chill the pans briefly. Remove the pans and the batter from the refrigerator. Place a dollop of batter in each mold and smooth with an offset palette knife or spatula. Bake for 15 minutes, or until the center springs back when lightly touched. Do not overbake. Remove the madeleines from the molds and cool on a wire rack.

Make the mint chocolate glaze

1. Place the chopped chocolate into a heat-resistant bowl. In a small saucepan, bring the heavy cream to a boil. Immediately pour the cream over the chocolate and let stand 1 minute before stirring. Stir gently until the chocolate is melted and combined. Stir in the mint extract.

2. Using a pastry brush, generously glaze half of the shell side of each madeleine. Allow the glaze to set before wrapping in plastic or storing in an airtight container. Madeleines are best when served the day they are made.

Flourless Bittersweet Chocolate Cake with Milk Chocolate Drizzle

Prepare this cake, and you can promise your guests the ultimate chocolate experience; they will not be disappointed. A simple but straightforward exercise in sweet surrender, this flourless cake is glazed with dark chocolate and further drizzled with milk chocolate. The raspberry jam and kiss of cognac add intriguing flavor notes.

• ◆ •

YIELD: 12 SERVINGS

Preparation: 50 minutes, plus baking and chilling times

Flourless Chocolate Cake
• ◆ •
8 ounces bittersweet chocolate, coarsely chopped
½ cup (1 stick) unsalted butter, cut into 1-inch pieces
2 tablespoons cognac
6 large eggs, separated, at room temperature
½ cup plus 2 tablespoons granulated sugar, divided

Chocolate Glaze
• ◆ •
4 ounces bittersweet chocolate, coarsely chopped
⅓ cup heavy cream
2 tablespoons honey

Assembly
• ◆ •
⅓ cup seedless raspberry preserves

Garnish
• ◆ •
3 ounces milk chocolate, melted

Make the flourless chocolate cake

1. Position a rack in the center of the oven and preheat to 350°F. Butter the bottom and sides of a 9-inch springform pan. Line the bottom of the pan with a round of parchment or waxed paper; butter the paper.

2. In a medium saucepan, combine the chocolate and butter. Cook over low heat, stirring constantly with a wooden spoon, until the chocolate and butter are melted. Gently whisk until smooth. Remove from heat and stir in the cognac. Let cool.

3. In a medium bowl, whisk together the egg yolks and ½ cup of the sugar until well blended. Stir in the melted chocolate mixture.

4. In the 4½-quart bowl of a heavy-duty electric mixer, using the wire whip attachment, beat the egg whites at medium speed until frothy. Increase the speed to medium-high and beat the egg whites until soft peaks start to form. One tablespoon at a time, beat in the remaining 2 tablespoons of sugar. Continue beating until the egg whites are stiff but not dry.

5. Using a large rubber spatula, gently fold the beaten egg whites into the chocolate mixture in 3 additions. Do not overmix.

6. Pour the batter into the prepared pan. Bake until the cake is puffed and a tester inserted into the center comes out with moist crumbs attached, about 30 minutes. Transfer the pan to a wire rack and cool for 10 minutes. Using a small sharp knife, cut around the sides of the cake to loosen it. Release the pan side. Invert the cake onto a wire rack. Peel off the parchment paper and cool the cake completely. Wrap in plastic and refrigerate overnight.

Make the chocolate glaze

1. Place the chocolate in a medium bowl. In a small saucepan, bring the heavy cream to a gentle boil. Using a wire whisk, stir in the honey. Pour the hot cream mixture over the chocolate and let the mixture stand for 30 seconds to melt the chocolate. Whisk the mixture until smooth. Cover the surface of the glaze with plastic wrap and set aside at room temperature for 30 minutes or until slightly thickened.

Assemble the cake

1. Remove the cake from the refrigerator and remove the plastic wrap from the cake. Place the cake on a wire rack set over a baking sheet. Using a metal spatula, spread the raspberry preserves evenly over the top and sides of the cake. Pour the chocolate glaze over the cake, covering it completely; spread evenly with a metal spatula. Drizzle the top of the glazed cake with the melted milk chocolate. Serve the cake immediately, or refrigerate. Bring the cake to room temperature before serving.

Individual Baked Alaskas

This American classic—a favorite of white tablecloth restaurants and cruise ships—is making a comeback in our retro-conscious age. The meringue insulates the ice cream during the browning, creating an intriguing interplay of flavors and temperatures.

•◆•

YIELD: 6 SERVINGS

Preparation: 2 hours, plus chilling, freezing, and baking times

Special Equipment: Ice cream machine; 4-inch round biscuit cutter

Caramel Nut Ice Cream
•◆•
6 large egg yolks
1 cup granulated sugar, divided
Pinch of salt
2 cups half-and-half
1 cup heavy cream
2 teaspoons lemon juice
2 teaspoons vanilla extract
½ cup toasted almonds (see page 41), coarsely chopped

Chocolate Fudge Cake
•◆•
1 cup sifted cake flour (not self-rising)
1 teaspoon baking soda
¼ teaspoon salt
2 cups packed light brown sugar
¾ cup (1½ sticks) unsalted butter, cut into tablespoons
¼ cup water
6 ounces unsweetened chocolate, coarsely chopped
3 large eggs, at room temperature
2 teaspoons vanilla extract

Chocolate Sauce
•◆•
1 cup unsweetened alkalized cocoa powder, sifted
½ ounce bittersweet chocolate, finely chopped
½ cup (1 stick) unsalted butter
1 cup plus 2 tablespoons granulated sugar
1 cup heavy cream
1 cup water
1 tablespoon light corn syrup

Meringue
•◆•
6 large egg whites
1 cup granulated sugar
½ cup light brown sugar

Make the caramel nut ice cream

1. In a medium bowl, whisk together the egg yolks, 1 tablespoon of the sugar, and the salt until blended.

2. In a medium saucepan, bring the half-and-half and heavy cream to a gentle boil. Remove the pan from the heat.

3. In a large, heavy saucepan, using a wooden spoon, stir together the remaining sugar and lemon juice. Over medium heat, cook the sugar mixture for 3 to 5 minutes, stirring frequently, until it liquefies and then turns to an amber-colored caramel. Remove the pan from the heat and stir in the half-and-half mixture. Return the pan to the heat and cook, stirring constantly, to help dissolve any caramel that may have hardened. Bring the caramel mixture to a gentle boil and remove the pan from the heat.

4. Gradually whisk about 1 cup of the hot caramel mixture into the beaten egg yolks until blended. Return this mixture to the saucepan. Continue cooking over medium-low heat, stirring constantly with a wooden spoon for 2 to 4 minutes, or until the custard has thickened slightly. It is done when you can run your finger down the back of the custard-coated spoon and a path remains. Do not let the custard boil.

5. Remove the pan from the heat and immediately strain the custard through a sieve into a stainless steel bowl. Place the bowl over a larger bowl of ice water and stir the custard for 5 to 10 minutes, or until cool. Stir in the vanilla extract. Remove the bowl of custard from the bowl of ice water. Cover the surface of the custard with plastic wrap and refrigerate for at least 6 hours, or overnight, until very cold.

6. Scrape the chilled custard into the container of an ice cream maker and freeze according to the manufacturer's instructions, adding the chopped almonds for the last 2 minutes of freezing. Transfer the ice cream to a bowl. Cover the surface of the ice cream with plastic wrap and cover the bowl tightly with aluminum foil. Freeze the ice cream overnight.

Make the chocolate fudge cake

1. Position a rack in the center of the oven and preheat to 350°F. Lightly butter a 15½-by-10½-inch jelly roll pan. Line the bottom of the pan with parchment or waxed paper. Lightly butter the paper and dust the pan with flour, shaking off the excess flour. Set aside.

2. In a medium bowl, using a wire whisk, stir together the flour, baking soda, and salt until thoroughly blended. Sift the flour mixture onto a piece of waxed paper.

3. In a large saucepan, combine the sugar, butter, and water. Cook, stirring occasionally over medium heat until smooth. Continue cooking until the sugar mixture comes to a boil. Remove the pan from the heat. Add the chocolate to the saucepan. Let the mixture stand for 30 seconds to melt the chocolate. Stir until smooth. Transfer the chocolate mixture to a large bowl and cool for 10 to 15 minutes, until tepid.

4. Using a wire whisk, stir in the eggs one at a time, until smooth. Stir in the vanilla extract. Using a rubber spatula, fold in the flour until combined.

5. Scrape the batter into the prepared pan, and using an offset spatula, spread the batter evenly. Bake the cake for 15 to 20 minutes, until the cake springs back when touched in the center and pulls away from the sides of the pan.

6. Cool the cake set on a wire rack for 15 minutes. Run a thin-bladed knife around the edges of the cake pan to loosen it. Invert the cake onto a wire rack. Peel off the paper and let the cake cool completely.

7. Using a 4-inch biscuit cutter, cut 6 circles from the chocolate cake. Slide a metal spatula under the cake rounds and transfer them to a baking sheet. Reserve the remaining cake for snacking. Place a large rounded scoop of ice cream on top of each cake round. Freeze uncovered for up to 8 hours.

Make the chocolate sauce

1. Place the sifted cocoa powder and chocolate in a medium bowl. In a medium saucepan, combine the butter, sugar, heavy cream, water, and corn syrup and bring to a boil. Pour the boiling liquid over the cocoa mixture and allow to stand for 3 to 4 minutes. Using a wire whisk, stir the mixture until smooth. Strain the chocolate sauce through a fine sieve into a medium bowl; let cool. Cover the surface of the chocolate sauce with plastic wrap and keep at room temperature.

Make the meringue

1. In the 4½-quart bowl of a heavy-duty electric mixer with the wire whip attachment, beat the egg whites at medium speed until soft peaks form. Gradually add the granulated and brown sugar, and beat on high speed until stiff peaks form and the mixture is glossy. Spoon the meringue into a pastry bag fitted with a medium star tip (such as Ateco #6). Pipe the meringue in overlaping shells over the ice cream, covering it completely but leaving the cake visible. Freeze until ready to bake (can be prepared 1 day ahead).

Assemble the desserts

1. Preheat oven to 500°F. Bake the desserts until the meringue is light brown, about 2 minutes. Using a spatula, transfer each baked Alaska to a plate. Spoon some sauce onto the plates and serve immediately.

Pain au Chocolat

*The French classic, presented in the classic manner. Buttery croissant dough conceals a filling of
dark chocolate. Serve at room temperature for a chewier texture, or slightly warm if you prefer.
The chocolate sticks, which are similar to the ones many professionals use, make
these a painless experience to prepare.*

•◆•

YIELD: 16 ROLLS

Preparation: 1 hour, plus rising, chilling, and baking times

Croissant Dough
•◆•
½ cup warm water (110°F to 115°F), divided
2 tablespoons plus 1 teaspoon granulated sugar, divided
2 teaspoons dry yeast
3½ cups plus 2 tablespoons all-purpose flour, divided
1½ teaspoons salt
1 cup warm milk (110°F to 115° F)
1 cup (2 sticks) unsalted butter, chilled

Chocolate Filling
•◆•
48 pain au chocolat sticks (see sources, page 302), *or*
three 3-ounce bars Lindt Swiss dark chocolate, cut into 16 pieces,
each about 1-by-3 inches

Egg Glaze
•◆•
1 large egg
1 teaspoon water

Chocolate Drizzle Garnish
•◆•
1 ounce bittersweet chocolate, melted

Make the croissant dough

1. In a small bowl, combine ¼ cup of the warm water with 1 teaspoon of the sugar. Sprinkle the yeast over the water and set the mixture aside for 10 minutes, until foamy. If the mixture is not foamy, the yeast may be inactive and should not be used.

2. In a large bowl, using a wire whisk, stir together 3½ cups of the flour, the remaining 2 tablespoons sugar, and salt. Make a well in the center of the bowl. Add the yeast mixture, the remaining ¼ cup of water, and the warm milk to the well. Using a rubber spatula, stir the liquid mixture together, gradually drawing in the flour mixture and stirring the mixture until it forms a smooth dough. Transfer the dough to a buttered bowl. Cover the bowl with a tea towel and let the dough rise in a warm, draft-free place for 1 hour.

3. Place the butter on a lightly floured work surface. Sprinkle the remaining 2 tablespoons flour over the butter and, using a rolling pin, pound the butter several times to flatten it. Fold the butter in half and continue to pound it with the rolling pin, until it is somewhat malleable. Shape the butter into a 5-inch square.

4. Roll the croissant dough on a lightly floured surface into a 9-inch square. Place the square of butter in the center of the dough on the diagonal. Fold the corners of the dough over the butter, so that they meet in the center of the square. Pinch the flaps of dough together, sealing the butter like a package. Wrap the dough well in plastic wrap and refrigerate for exactly 30 minutes.

5. Place the dough on a floured surface, seam-side-up. Roll the dough into a 14-by-8-inch rectangle. Using a pastry brush, gently brush off any flour from the surface of the dough. Fold the dough in thirds, as if it were a business letter. Rotate the dough so that a closed side is to your left. Roll the dough again into a 14-by-8-inch rectangle. Fold the dough again like a business letter. The dough has now been turned twice. Wrap the dough in plastic wrap and refrigerate for another 30 minutes.

6. Repeat the rolling, folding, and turning process two more times, so that the dough has been "turned" 4 times. Wrap the dough well in plastic wrap and refrigerate for at least 6 hours, or overnight.

7. Remove the dough from the refrigerator, and place it on a lightly floured work surface. Give the dough 2 more turns. Divide the dough into two. Roll each piece into a 12-by-8-inch rectangle. Cut each rectangle in half lengthwise to form four 12-by-4-inch strips. Cut each strip into 4 equal pieces, to form sixteen 4-by-3-inch pieces.

Fill the rolls with chocolate

1. Place 3 pain au chocolate sticks or a piece of the Lindt chocolate on each piece of dough, with the long side of the chocolate parallel to the longer side of the dough. Roll the chocolate up in the dough jelly-roll style, sealing the edges with a small dab of water.

2. Butter 2 baking sheets. Place 8 rolls on each baking sheet, seam side down, leaving at least 2 inches between rolls. Cover the rolls with the tea towel, and allow them to rise at room temperature for 1 hour.

Glaze the rolls

1. Position a rack in the center of the oven and preheat to 425°F. In a small bowl, whisk together the egg and the water until blended. Using a pastry brush, glaze each pain au chocolat evenly with the egg glaze. Bake one sheet of rolls at a time, for 18 to 20 minutes, until golden brown. Remove the pains au chocolat to a wire rack immediately and cool to desired temperature.

Garnish the rolls

1. Spoon the melted chocolate into a small parchment cone. Cut a very small hole at the tip of the cone and lightly drizzle the chocolate over the rolls. Serve immediately.

White and Dark Chocolate Ganache Sandwiches

Feathery angel food cake is given the chocolate once-over with red raspberry jam and layers of white chocolate spiked with chocolate liqueur and coffee. The dessert is then covered with dark chocolate ganache. It's a sandwich, coffee, and sweet treat all rolled into one.

•◆•

YIELD: 10 SERVINGS

Preparation: 2 hours, plus baking, chilling, and setting times

White Chocolate Coffee Ganache
•◆•
1 tablespoon chocolate-flavored liqueur, such as Godiva
1 tablespoon hot water
1 teaspoon instant espresso powder
1 teaspoon vanilla extract
6 ounces white chocolate, coarsely chopped
⅔ cup heavy cream

Angel Food Cake
•◆•
½ cup plus 2 tablespoons confectioners' sugar
½ cup cake flour (not self-rising)
7 large egg whites
¾ teaspoon cream of tartar
½ teaspoon vanilla extract
⅛ teaspoon salt
⅛ teaspoon almond extract
½ cup superfine granulated sugar

Assembly
•◆•
6 tablespoons seedless red raspberry preserves

Dark Chocolate Ganache
•◆•
10 ounces bittersweet chocolate, finely chopped
¾ cup heavy cream
3 tablespoons unsalted butter, softened and cut into tablespoons
1 teaspoon vanilla extract

Garnish
•◆•
½ pint fresh raspberries

Make the white chocolate coffee ganache

1. In a small cup, combine the liqueur, hot water, espresso powder, and vanilla extract. Stir until smooth.

2. Put the white chocolate in a small bowl. In a small saucepan over medium heat, bring the heavy cream to a gentle boil. Pour the hot cream over the chocolate and let the mixture stand for 30 seconds to melt the chocolate. Whisk until smooth and stir in the liqueur mixture. Cover the surface of the white chocolate coffee ganache with plastic wrap and refrigerate for 8 hours or overnight.

Make the angel food cake

1. Position a rack in the center of the oven and preheat to 325°F. Wash a 9-by-5-by-3-inch loaf pan and dry it thoroughly (any trace of grease will prevent the cake from rising properly).

2. In a small bowl, using a wire whisk, stir together the confectioners' sugar and cake flour. Sift the sugar-flour mixture onto a piece of waxed paper.

3. In a grease-free 4½-quart bowl of a heavy-duty electric mixer using the wire whip attachment, beat the egg whites, cream of tartar, vanilla extract, salt, and almond extract until frothy. Gradually increase the speed to high and sprinkle in the granulated sugar 2 tablespoons at a time. Continue beating the whites until stiff peaks form.

4. In 3 additions, sift the flour-sugar mixture over the batter. Using a large rubber spatula, gently fold each addition into the egg whites until fully incorporated. Scrape the batter into the prepared pan and spread it evenly with a spatula. Using a spatula, cut through the batter to break any large air bubbles.

5. Bake the angel food cake 35 to 40 minutes, or until the top is golden brown and a cake tester inserted into the center comes out clean. Invert the cake onto a wire rack and allow it to cool completely.

6. To remove the cake from the pan, run a knife around the sides of the pan several times to make sure the cake is loosened. Turn the pan upside down and rap it sharply several times against the table. Slowly lift the pan, shaking gently; the cake should ease out without sticking. Wrap the cake in plastic wrap until ready to assemble.

Assemble the cake

1. In a 4½-quart bowl of a heavy-duty electric mixer, using the wire whip attachment, beat the white chocolate coffee ganache on medium speed for 1 minute, or until it begins to form soft peaks. Cover and refrigerate the ganache until ready to use.

2. Preheat the broiler. Using a long serrated knife, cut the cake horizontally into 3 equal layers. Place the layers on a baking sheet and toast each side to a golden brown.

3. Place 1 cake layer on a metal rack. Using a small metal spatula, spread 2 tablespoons of seedless red raspberry preserves over the cake layer. Using a small offset metal spatula, smooth half of the white chocolate coffee ganache over the raspberry preserves. Place a second cake layer on top of the ganache. Repeat the preceding layering process, top the cake with the final layer, and spread it with raspberry preserves. Place the wire rack with the cake on it in the refrigerator for 1 hour to set.

Make the dark chocolate ganache

1. Put the chopped chocolate in a medium bowl. In a small saucepan, heat the heavy cream until it comes to a boil. Pour the hot cream mixture over the chocolate and let the mixture stand for 30 seconds to melt the chocolate. Whisk the mixture until smooth. Stir in the butter and vanilla extract. Let the ganache cool for 15 minutes or until slightly thickened.

Frost the cake

1. Remove the cake and the rack from the refrigerator and place it on a baking sheet. Using a metal cake spatula, spread the ganache over the top and the sides of the cake. Refrigerate the cake for 10 minutes, or until the ganache has set.

2. Using a long, sharp knife cut the cake into 10 slices, wiping the blade clean before cutting each slice. Garnish with fresh raspberries if desired.

Black Satin Chocolate Raspberry Cake

Raspberry is the fruit voted best supporting actor for chocolate, and this cake shows why. The moist sour cream cake is generously frosted and filled with dark chocolate raspberry frosting, for a rich, chocolaty, and fruity experience.

•◆•

YIELD: 10 SERVINGS

Preparation: 2 hours, plus baking, cooling, and chilling times

Sour Cream Chocolate Cake
•◆•
5 ounces unsweetened chocolate, coarsely chopped
2 cups sifted cake flour (not self-rising)
1½ teaspoons baking soda
¼ teaspoon salt
½ cup (1 stick) unsalted butter, slightly softened
⅓ cup solid vegetable shortening
½ cup packed light brown sugar
1¼ cups granulated sugar, divided
1 tablespoon vanilla extract
2 large whole eggs plus 2 large eggs, separated, at room temperature
¾ cup sour cream, at room temperature
1 cup milk, at room temperature

Raspberry Sauce
•◆•
One 12-ounce bag frozen unsweetened raspberries
⅔ cup granulated sugar
2 teaspoons arrowroot
1 tablespoon water
1 to 2 tablespoons black raspberry liqueur, such as Chambord

Dark Chocolate Shavings
•◆•
6-ounce chunk dark chocolate, about ¾-inch thick

Black Satin Raspberry Frosting
•◆•
20 ounces semisweet chocolate, coarsely chopped
1¼ cups evaporated milk
6 tablespoons unsalted butter, softened
¼ cup black raspberry liqueur, such as Chambord
4 teaspoons vanilla extract

Assembly
•◆•
6 tablespoons seedless raspberry preserves
Fresh raspberries, for garnish

Make the sour cream chocolate cake

1. Position a rack in the center of the oven and preheat to 350°F. Lightly butter the bottom and sides of three 9-inch round cake pans. Line the bottoms of the pans with parchment paper. Dust the sides of the pans with flour and tap out the excess.

2. Melt the chocolate according to the directions on page 25. Let the chocolate cool for 10 to 15 minutes, until tepid.

3. In a medium bowl, using a wire whisk, stir together the flour, baking soda, and salt until thoroughly blended. Sift the flour mixture onto a piece of waxed paper.

4. In a 4½-quart bowl of a heavy-duty electric mixer using the paddle attachment, beat the butter and shortening at medium speed for 45 to 60 seconds, until creamy. Add the brown sugar and while continuing to beat, gradually add 1 cup of the granulated sugar, 2 tablespoons at a time over a 6-minute period. Using a rubber spatula, scrape down the sides of the bowl and continue beating for 1 to 2 minutes longer, until the mixture is light in texture and off-white in color. Beat in the vanilla extract.

5. Break the 2 whole eggs into a measuring cup and add the 2 separated egg yolks. Beat with a fork until frothy. At medium speed while continuing to beat, slowly add the beaten eggs to the batter. Add the sour cream and beat until smooth. Beat in the melted chocolate until blended.

6. At low speed, one-third at a time, beat in the flour mixture, alternating it with the milk. Mix briefly, just until each addition is barely incorporated into the batter. Scrape down the sides and bottom of the bowl with a rubber spatula. Mix the batter for 10 more seconds.

7. In a grease-free 4½-quart bowl of a heavy-duty electric mixer, using the wire whip attachment, beat the 2 egg whites at low speed until frothy. Gradually increase the speed to medium-high and beat the whites until soft peaks start to form. One teaspoon at a time, add the remaining ¼ cup of sugar and continue beating the whites until stiff, shiny peaks form.

8. Using a large rubber spatula, fold the beaten egg whites into the batter to lighten it. Divide the batter evenly between the prepared pans and smooth it with the back of a soup spoon. Bake the cake layers for 15 minutes. Reposition the cake pans so that the pans at the back of the oven rack are placed in the front. Continue to bake for 5 to 10 minutes longer, until the edge of each cake layer has pulled away slightly from the side of the pan and the center springs back when gently pressed with a finger.

9. Cool the cake layers in the pans set on wire racks for 5 minutes. Run a thin-bladed knife around the edges of the cake layers to loosen them. Invert the cake layers onto wire racks. Peel off the paper circles and leave them loosely attached to the bottom of the cake layers. Reinvert the layers onto other racks so that they are right side up. Cool the cake layers completely.

Make the raspberry sauce

1. In a noncorrosive medium saucepan, combine the frozen raspberries and sugar. Cook over medium heat, stirring constantly until the sugar dissolves and the raspberries start to soften. Continue to cook at a gentle simmer for 3 to 5 minutes, until the raspberries are completely softened.

2. Press the raspberry mixture through a fine-meshed sieve into a 1-quart measuring cup, reserving 1 cup of the purée. Discard the seeds. Pour the raspberry purée into a clean noncorrosive medium saucepan.

3. Put the arrowroot in a small cup. Slowly stir in the water until the mixture is completely smooth. Scrape the arrowroot mixture into the raspberry purée and stir until blended.

4. Cook the raspberry purée over medium heat, stirring constantly with a wooden spoon, until the mixture comes to a boil. Boil for 30 to 60 seconds, until the sauce is transluscent. Do not boil for longer than 1 minute, or the sauce will become watery. Remove the pan from the heat.

5. Cool the sauce to room temperature and stir in the liqueur to taste. Transfer the sauce to a bowl; cover and refrigerate.

Make the dark chocolate shavings

1. Warm the 6-ounce chunk of dark chocolate by placing it on a piece of waxed paper. Microwave on medium (50%) power for 10-second intervals, until the chocolate starts to soften slightly.

2. Line a baking sheet with waxed paper. Grip the chocolate chunk with a folded paper towel so that your hand does not melt the chocolate. Using a sharp vegetable peeler, scrape one of the edges of the chocolate chunk in a downward motion, forming loose shavings. As you form the shavings, let them fall onto the waxed paper. Continue making shavings until most of the chocolate has been used. Refrigerate the dark chocolate shavings on the baking sheet until ready to decorate the cake.

Make the black satin raspberry frosting

1. Melt the chocolate according to the directions on page 25.

2. Put the evaporated milk, butter, black raspberry liqueur, and vanilla extract in a food processor fitted with the metal chopping blade. Add the melted chocolate. Process for 20 to 30 seconds, until the frosting is thick and creamy. Use the frosting immediately. Reserve 1 cup of the frosting for piping on top of the cake. Use the remaining frosting to fill and frost the cake.

Assemble and frost the cake

1. Remove the paper circles from the bottoms of the cake layers. If necessary, trim the tops of the cake layers with a long serrated knife so that they are level. Place 1 of the cake layers on a 9-inch cardboard cake circle. Using a small offset metal spatula, spread 3 tablespoons of the raspberry jam over the top of the cake layer. Spread ¼ cup of the black satin raspberry frosting in an even layer over the raspberry jam. Put the second cake layer on top of the frosting. Spread the remaining 3 tablespoons of the raspberry jam over the cake layer. Cover the raspberry jam with ⅔ cup of the frosting. Put the third cake layer on top of the frosting.

2. Lift up the cake, supporting the bottom in one hand. With the other hand, using a metal cake spatula, frost the top of the cake with some of the frosting. Spread more of the frosting around the side of the cake, filling in the space between the edge of the cardboard and the side of the cake. Finish the top by holding the metal cake spatula at a slight angle and with several strokes, smooth the raised lip of frosting around the upper edge toward the center of the cake until the cake is smooth.

Decorate the cake

1. Remove the tray of dark chocolate shavings from the refrigerator. Lift up the cake on the cardboard, supporting the bottom of the cake with one hand. Hold the cake over the tray of chocolate shavings. Using a baker's scraper or metal spatula, scoop up some of the shavings and gently press them against the side of the cake. Continue until the side of the cake is evenly covered with shavings.

2. Set the cake down on a work surface. Fill a pastry bag fitted with a medium closed tip (such as Ateco #5) with the reserved frosting. Pipe a reversed shell border around the top edge of the cake. Store the cake under a cake dome at room temperature for up to 3 days.

3. To serve, decorate a dessert plate with some of the raspberry sauce. Lay a slice of cake on top of the sauce. Garnish with fresh raspberries.

Death by Chocolate

Our version of this attention-getting recipe title is a sundae, but not one for the faint of heart. Dark chocolate ice cream, white chocolate coffee hazelnut whipped cream, and fudge sauce are combined into a sundae so extravagant you will be convinced you've sighed and gone to heaven.

•◆•

YIELD: 4 ICE CREAM SUNDAES

Preparation: 1½ hours, plus chilling, freezing, and cooling times

Special Equipment: Ice cream machine

Chocolate Velvet Ice Cream
•◆•
5 large egg yolks

½ cup granulated sugar, divided

⅛ teaspoon salt

1¼ cups heavy cream

1 cup milk

6 ounces semisweet chocolate, coarsely chopped

4 teaspoons vanilla extract

Hazelnut Coffee Cream
•◆•
8 ounces white chocolate, finely chopped

2½ cups heavy cream

¾ cup fresh roasted hazelnut-flavored coffee beans

1 tablespoon Italian hazelnut liqueur, such as Frangelico

1 teaspoon vanilla extract

Chocolate Fudge Sauce
•◆•
2 ounces semisweet chocolate, finely chopped

⅓ cup unsweetened alkalized cocoa powder

⅓ cup granulated sugar

⅓ cup evaporated milk

⅓ cup light corn syrup

2 teaspoons vanilla extract

Assembly
•◆•
Fresh brewed coffee, to thin sauce

4 to 8 cigarette cookies

Make the chocolate velvet ice cream

1. In a medium bowl, using a wire whisk, stir the egg yolks, 2 tablespoons of the sugar, and salt until blended.

2. In a heavy, medium, noncorrosive saucepan, bring the remaining sugar, heavy cream, and milk to a gentle boil. Remove the pan from the heat. Gradually whisk about 1 cup of the hot cream mixture into the beaten egg yolks until blended. Return this mixture to the saucepan.

3. Continue cooking over medium heat, stirring constantly with a flat-edged wooden spoon for 3 to 5 minutes, until the custard has thickened slightly. It is done when you can run your finger down the back of the coated spoon and the path remains in the custard. The custard will register 175°F on an instant-read thermometer. Remove the pan from the heat.

4. As soon as the custard is ready, add the chocolate to it. Let the custard stand for 30 seconds and then whisk until smooth. Strain the chocolate custard into a large, noncorrosive metal bowl. Set the bowl over a larger bowl containing ice water for 5 to 10 minutes, stirring frequently, until the custard is cool. Remove the bowl from the ice water bath and stir in the vanilla extract.

5. Cover the surface of the custard with plastic wrap and refrigerate 1 to 2 hours, stirring occasionally, until very thick and cold.

6. Scrape the custard into an ice cream maker and freeze according to manufacturer's instructions. Pack the churned ice cream into a 1-quart container. Cover and freeze for a few hours or overnight.

Make the hazelnut coffee cream

1. Put the white chocolate into a medium bowl. In a saucepan, bring the heavy cream and coffee beans to a gentle boil. Remove the pan from the heat, cover, and steep for 10 minutes.

2. Return the saucepan to the heat and bring the cream mixture back to a gentle boil. Remove the pan from the heat. Ladle about 1 cup of the hot cream over the white chocolate. Let the mixture stand for 30 seconds to melt chocolate. Whisk until smooth. Pour the remaining cream mixture (including the coffee beans) over the chocolate and stir until blended. Stir in the hazelnut liqueur and the vanilla extract. Cover the surface of the hazelnut coffee cream with plastic wrap and refrigerate for at least 6 hours or overnight.

Make the chocolate fudge sauce

1. Put the chocolate in a small bowl. In a heavy, medium saucepan, stir together the cocoa powder and sugar. Slowly whisk in the evaporated milk to make a smooth paste. Stir in the corn syrup.

2. Cook over medium heat, stirring constantly with a wooden spoon for 4 to 6 minutes and gradually bring the mixture to a gentle boil. Remove the pan from the heat. Pour the hot mixture over the chocolate. Let the mixture stand for 30 seconds to melt the chocolate. Whisk until smooth. Stir in the vanilla extract. Cool to room temperature, cover and refrigerate.

Assembly

1. Put four 10-ounce pilsner glasses in the freezer to chill.

2. Remove the bowl of chocolate fudge sauce from the refrigerator. Gently stir 3 tablespoons of fresh brewed coffee into the sauce to thin to a sauce-like consistency.

3. Dip one end of each cigarette cookie into the sauce. Place the dipped cookies onto a plate.

4. Strain the chilled hazelnut coffee cream into a large bowl. Discard the coffee beans. Using a hand-held electric mixer set at high speed, beat the cream for 1 to 2 minutes, until it starts to form stiff peaks. Do not overbeat or the hazelnut cream will become grainy. Reserve half the hazelnut cream for decorating the tops of the sundaes.

5. Put 1 small scoop of the chocolate velvet ice cream into the bottom of each chilled pilsner glass, and top each one with a dollop of hazelnut coffee cream. Drizzle about 1½ tablespoons of the chocolate fudge sauce over each serving. Repeat the layering process with the remaining ice cream, hazelnut cream, and sauce, finishing with a large scoop of ice cream drizzled with chocolate sauce.

6. Fill a pastry bag fitted with a large, closed star tip (such as Ateco #9) with the remaining hazelnut cream. Decorate the top of each sundae with hazelnut coffee cream. Garnish each sundae with one or two chocolate-dipped cigarette cookies. Serve immediately.

Chocolate Glazed Peanut Doughnuts

A show-stopping treat at a picnic or backyard barbecue, this "designer doughnut" will be more than any child or adult can resist. Roasted peanuts are buried in the dough and studded over the surface, clinging to a luxurious Swiss chocolate glaze.

• ◆ •

YIELD: APPROXIMATELY 14 DOUGHNUTS
AND DOUGHNUT HOLES

Preparation: 1½ hours, plus chilling, resting, frying, and cooling times

Special Equipment: One 2¾-inch round cookie cutter; one 1-inch cookie cutter;

deep-fry thermometer

Peanut Doughnuts
• ◆ •
3½ cups cake flour (not self-rising), divided
1 cup unsalted, dry roasted peanuts
1 cup granulated sugar
2 teaspoons baking powder
1½ teaspoons salt
¾ cup milk, at room temperature
1 large egg, at room temperature
3 tablespoons vegetable oil
2 teaspoons vanilla extract
Vegetable oil for frying

Chocolate Glaze
• ◆ •
18 ounces Swiss dark chocolate, coarsely chopped
¾ cup plus 2 tablespoons water
¼ cup granulated sugar
2 tablespoons light corn syrup
½ teaspoon vanilla extract
Chopped peanuts, for garnish

Make the peanut doughnuts

1. In a food processor fitted with the metal chopping blade, combine ½ cup of the flour with the peanuts. Process for 20 to 30 seconds, until coarsely chopped.

2. In a large bowl, using a wire whisk, stir together the remaining 3 cups of flour, chopped peanut mixture, sugar, baking powder, and salt, until thoroughly blended.

3. In a medium bowl, whisk together the milk, egg, oil, and vanilla extract until blended. Make a well in the center of the flour mixture and pour the milk mixture into it. Using a rubber spatula, stir the mixture until it forms a soft, moist dough. Dust a work surface with flour. Scrape the dough onto the work surface and lightly sprinkle the top of the dough with flour. Gather the dough into a ball and knead it gently 5 to 6 times, until smooth (do not over-handle).

4. Dust a large baking sheet with flour. Transfer the dough to the baking sheet. Dust your hands with flour and pat the dough into a circle that is about 11 inches in diameter and ½-inch thick. Cover the dough with plastic wrap and place the baking sheet with the dough on it in the freezer for 15 to 20 minutes, until firm.

5. Using a floured 2¾-inch round cookie cutter, cut 12 rounds from the circle of dough. With a floured 1-inch round cookie cutter, cut a hole from the center of each doughnut. Using a floured pancake spatula, transfer the doughnuts and the doughnut holes to a waxed paper-lined baking sheet.

6. Gather the scraps of dough together, wrap in plastic wrap, and refrigerate for 15 minutes. Pat the scraps into a circle ½-inch thick and make more doughnuts as above. Cover the doughnuts and refrigerate for up to 6 hours, until ready to fry them. Let the chilled doughnuts stand at room temperature for 15 minutes before frying.

Fry the doughnuts

1. Pour enough oil in a deep-fat fryer or 10-inch, high-sided skillet to come up a depth of 3 inches. Heat the oil to 375°F. Dip a pancake spatula into the hot oil and use it to transfer the doughnuts from the baking pan to the hot oil. This will prevent them from losing their shape. Three at a time, fry the doughnuts for 1 minute on each side, until golden brown. Using a slotted spoon, remove the doughnuts from the hot oil and transfer them to paper towels to drain. Set the doughnuts on a wire rack to cool. Six at a time, fry the doughnut holes in the same manner.

Make the chocolate glaze

1. In the top of a double boiler over hot but not simmering water, melt 8 ounces of the chocolate. Gradually add the remaining 10 ounces of chocolate, stirring frequently until smooth. Remove the pan from the heat.

2. In a small saucepan, combine the water, sugar, and corn syrup. Cook over medium heat, stirring with a wooden spoon until the sugar dissolves completely. Do not let the mixture boil. Remove the pan from the heat.

3. Pour the sugar syrup into a medium bowl. Whisk the melted chocolate into the sugar syrup until smooth. Stir in the vanilla extract. Keep the glaze warm by setting the bowl over a pot of warm water. (The water must touch the bottom of the bowl.) Tilt the bowl on the edge of the pot to create a deep pool of glaze for dipping.

4. Gently drop a doughnut onto the surface of the glaze. Using a fork, turn the doughnut over so that it is fully coated in chocolate. Lift the doughnut out of the glaze, scraping off the excess glaze onto the bowl's edge. Place the doughnut on a wire rack set over a baking sheet, and carefully remove the fork. Sprinkle the doughnut with chopped peanuts before the glaze sets.

5. Coat the remaining doughnuts and the doughnut holes in the same manner. Sprinkle the doughnuts with chopped peanuts, if desired, before the glaze sets. Refrigerate the doughnuts for 5 minutes to harden the glaze. Store the doughnuts in an airtight container at room temperature. The doughnuts should be served the same day they are prepared.

Le Marigny

This cake was created by Pierre Hermé, who is widely considered to be the finest pastry chef in the world; he named it in honor of a famous Paris theater. For many years, this was the best-selling cake at the famous Parisian patisserie, Fauchon. On a base of chocolate sponge are layers of chocolate sabayon mousse and thin, chewy almond macaroon. The top is glazed in chocolate, and the cake is surrounded by striped rectangles of chocolate.

• • •

YIELD: 16 SERVINGS

Preparation: allow 2 days to make this cake

Special Equipment: One 10-inch cardboard cake circle; one 9½-by-2⅜ cake ring or one 9½-by-2½-inch springform cake pan; chocolate thermometer; 2 heating pads (normally used for backaches) to keep the tempered white and dark chocolate couvertures warm; four 16-by-2⅜-inch food-grade acetate strips; icing comb; 1 closed star tip (such as Ateco #4).

Chocolate Almond Macaroon
• • •
¾ cup whole almonds
2¼ cups sifted confectioners' sugar, divided
¼ cup sifted unsweetened alkalized cocoa powder
Pinch of salt
3 large egg whites, at room temperature
2 teaspoons vanilla extract

Chocolate Almond Sponge Cake
• • •
½ cup sifted cake flour (not self-rising)
½ cup plus 1 tablespoon sifted unsweetened alkalized cocoa powder
¼ cup plus 1 tablespoon granulated sugar, divided
⅛ teaspoon baking powder
Pinch of salt
½ cup canned almond paste, crumbled into small chunks
1 large egg plus 5 large eggs, separated, at room temperature
1 cup sifted confectioners' sugar, divided
2 teaspoons vanilla extract
3 tablespoons unsalted butter, melted and cooled slightly until tepid

Cocoa Punch
• • •
¼ cup water
3 tablespoons granulated sugar
1½ tablespoons sifted unsweetened alkalized cocoa powder
½ teaspoon vanilla extract

Chocolate Sabayon
•◆•

12 ounces Valrhona Guanaja chocolate couverture, coarsely chopped*
2 large eggs plus 6 large egg yolks, at room temperature
⅔ cup granulated sugar
½ cup water
1 tablespoon vanilla extract
2 cups heavy cream

Chocolate Chantilly
•◆•

3 ounces Valrhona Guanaja chocolate couverture, finely chopped
1 cup plus 3 tablespoons heavy cream
3 tablespoons granulated sugar
1 teaspoon vanilla extract

Striped Chocolate Rectangles
•◆•

1½ pounds Valrhona Guanaja chocolate couverture, finely chopped*
1½ pounds Valrhona white chocolate couverture*

Chocolate Glaze
•◆•

4 ounces Valrhona Guanaja chocolate couverture, finely chopped*
½ cup plus 2 tablespoons heavy cream
¼ cup light corn syrup
1 teaspoon vanilla extract

Decoration
•◆•

3½-feet-by-½-inch gold ribbon

see sources, page 302

THE DAY BEFORE:

Make the chocolate almond macaroon

1. Position a rack in the center of the oven and preheat to 350°F. Line a large, heavy baking sheet with a piece of baking parchment. Trace a 10-inch circle in the center of the baking parchment; turn the piece of paper over so that the ink tracing is facing down onto the surface of the pan.

2. In a food processor fitted with a metal chopping blade, combine the almonds and ¼ cup of the sugar. Process for 45 to 60 seconds, until the mixture becomes a powder. Add the remaining 1½ cups of sugar, cocoa powder, and salt. Pulse the mixture 6 to 8 times, until the mixture is evenly blended. Transfer the cocoa-almond mixture to a piece of waxed paper.

3. In a grease-free bowl of a 4½-quart bowl of a heavy-duty electric mixer with the wire whisk attachment, beat the egg whites at low speed until frothy. Gradually increase the speed to medium-high and continue beating the egg whites until they start to form stiff peaks when the wire whisk is lifted.

4. Using a large rubber spatula, fold half of the almond-cocoa mixture into the egg whites until evenly mixed. Fold in the remaining almond-cocoa mixture. Fold in the vanilla extract.

5. Scrape the macaroon batter into the center of the 10-inch traced circle on the paper-lined pan. Using an offset metal cake spatula, evenly spread the batter within the circle.

6. Bake the chocolate macaroon for 15 to 20 minutes, or until the top of the macaroon is shiny and a cake tester or wooden toothpick inserted into the center of the macaroon comes out clean (the macaroon will be soft). Cool the macaroon on the baking sheet on a wire rack.

Make the chocolate almond sponge cake

1. Position a rack in the center of the oven and preheat to 350°F. Butter the bottom and side of a 10-by-2-inch round cake pan. Line the bottom of the cake pan with a circle of parchment or waxed paper. Lightly dust the side of the pan with flour and tap out the excess.

2. In a small bowl, using a wire whisk, stir together the flour, cocoa powder, 1 tablespoon of granulated sugar, baking powder, and salt. Sift the flour mixture onto a piece of waxed paper.

3. In the 4½-quart bowl of a heavy-duty electric mixer with the paddle attachment, beat the almond paste with the whole egg and ¼ cup confectioners' sugar at medium speed. Slowly add the remaining ¼ cup confectioners' sugar and continue beating for 30 to 60 seconds, until creamy. Remove the paddle and change to the wire whip attachment. While continuing to beat at medium speed, add the 5 egg yolks one at a time, beating well after each addition. Continue beating for 8 to 10 minutes, or until the mixture is pale yellow and forms a thick ribbon when the wire whisk is lifted. Beat in the vanilla extract.

4. In a grease-free bowl of a 4½-quart heavy-duty electric mixer with the wire whisk attachment, beat the egg whites at low speed until frothy. Gradually increase the speed to medium-high and continue beating the egg whites until they start to form stiff peaks. While continuing to beat, add the remaining ¼ cup of sugar, 1 teaspoon at a time. Beat the whites until they form stiff, shiny peaks when the wire whisk is lifted.

5. Using a large rubber spatula, fold one-third of the beaten egg whites into the egg yolk mixture. Scrape half of the remaining egg whites over the almond-egg yolk mixture. Resift half of the flour mixture over the egg whites. Gently fold the egg whites and flour mixture into the beaten almond-egg yolks. Fold in the remaining egg whites with the resifted flour mixture. Fold in the melted butter. Scrape the batter into the prepared pan and spread it evenly with a spatula.

6. Bake the chocolate almond sponge cake for 25 to 30 minutes, or until the edge of the cake has pulled away slightly from the side of the pan and the center of the cake springs bake when gently pressed. Run a small knife or metal spatula around the edge of the pan to loosen the cake from the side of the pan. Immediately invert the sponge cake onto a wire rack and remove the pan. Carefully peel the paper and leave it loosely attached to the bottom of the cake. Reinvert the cake so that it is right side up. Cool the sponge cake completely.

Make the cocoa punch

1. In a small saucepan, combine the water and sugar. Cook over medium heat, stirring constantly with a wooden spoon until the sugar dissolves. Increase the heat to medium-high and bring the syrup to a boil. Remove the pan from the heat and whisk in the cocoa powder, stirring until smooth. Stir in the vanilla extract. Transfer the cocoa punch to a small cup and cool to room temperature.

Make the chocolate sabayon

1. In the top of a double boiler over hot but not simmering water, melt the chocolate, stirring frequently, until smooth. Remove the double boiler from the heat, but leave the chocolate over the hot water to keep warm until ready to use.

2. In the 4½-quart bowl of a heavy-duty electric mixer, with the wire whisk attachment, on medium-high speed, beat the eggs and egg yolks for 6 to 8 minutes, until they are pale yellow and form a thick ribbon when the wire whisk is lifted.

3. Meanwhile, in a small saucepan combine the sugar and water. Cook over medium heat, stirring with a wooden spoon, until the sugar has dissolved. Increase the heat to medium-high and bring the sugar syrup to a boil. Cook the syrup for 5 to 8 minutes, until it registers 238°F on a candy thermometer (soft ball stage). Reduce the mixer to medium speed and in a slow, steady stream, pour the hot sugar syrup down the side of the bowl into the beating egg and yolks. Increase the speed to medium-high and continue beating for 6 to 8 minutes, until the mixture is tepid, pale yellow, and forms a thick ribbon when the wire whisk is lifted. Beat in the vanilla extract. At low speed, beat in the melted chocolate until blended.

4. In a chilled 4½-quart bowl of a heavy-duty electric mixer with the wire whip attachment, at medium-high speed, beat the heavy cream until it forms slightly stiff peaks. Using a large rubber spatula, fold one-third of the whipped cream into the chocolate mixture to lighten it. Fold in the remaining whipped cream.

Assembly

1. Remove the paper from the bottom of the chocolate almond sponge cake. Using a long serrated knife, trim the top off the cake, making sure that it's level. Horizontally slice the cake into 2 layers of equal thickness (each layer should be about ¼-inch thick). Wrap 1 of the layers in plastic and then in aluminum foil. Freeze for up to 1 month to use again.

2. Put the remaining cake layer on a flat cutting surface and place a 9½-by-2⅜-inch cake ring on top of it, making sure that the cake is centered. Press down on the cake ring, cutting out a 9½-inch circle of cake. Remove the cake ring.

3. In order to remove the macaroon from the baking parchment, set the baking parchment side onto a damp kitchen towel. Let sit for a few minutes and then carefully peel the off the dampened parchment from the bottom of the macaroon. Transfer the macaroon to a 10-inch cardboard cake circle. Put the cake ring on top of the macaroon, making sure that it is centered. Press down the cake ring to cut out a 9½-inch circle from the macaroon. Do not remove the cake ring.

4. Scrape half of the chocolate sabayon into the lined cake ring and spread it evenly with a small offset metal cake spatula. Put the layer of chocolate almond sponge cake on top of the chocolate sabayon and press it gently into place. Prick the top of the sponge cake in several spots with the tines of a fork. Brush the sponge cake with all of the cocoa punch. Cover the moistened sponge cake with the remaining chocolate sabayon, filling the ring to the brim. Holding a long metal cake spatula at a slight angle, sweep across the top of the cake ring to remove the excess chocolate sabayon. Cover the surface of the chocolate sabayon with plastic wrap and freeze the assembled cake overnight. (If desired, the cake may be frozen at this stage for up to 2 weeks before glazing the top and decorating.)

Make the chocolate chantilly

1. Put the chocolate in a small metal bowl. In a saucepan combine the heavy cream and sugar. Cook over medium-low heat, stirring constantly with a wooden spoon until the sugar dissolves. Raise the heat to medium-high and bring the mixture to a boil. Remove the pan from the heat and pour the hot cream over the chocolate. Let the mixture stand for 30 to 60 seconds to melt the chocolate. Gently whisk until smooth and then stir in the vanilla extract. Cover the surface of the chocolate mixture with plastic wrap and refrigerate overnight.

THE NEXT DAY:

Make the striped chocolate rectangles

1. Temper the Guanaja and white chocolate couvertures. (See tempering instructions on page 27).

2. Vertically position one of the 16-by-2⅜-inch acetate strips on a clean marble work surface. Affix the 4 corners of the strip to the marble, making sure that the strip is perfectly flat.

3. Pour about ⅓ cup of the tempered Guanaja chocolate couverture vertically down the center of the plastic strip. Using an offset metal cake spatula, spread the chocolate into a thin, even layer completely covering the plastic strip. (The chocolate will spread onto the marble as well.) Continue moving the spatula back and forth over the chocolate strip for 20 to 60 seconds, until the chocolate begins to feel tacky and loses its shine.

4. Immediately, before the chocolate becomes too stiff, center the icing comb at the top of the chocolate-covered strip. Draw the comb down the chocolate covered strip, pressing firmly into the chocolate, forming straight vertical lines that will enable you to see through the chocolate to the plastic strip. Remove the comb and wipe off any chocolate clinging to it. Let the chocolate set for 1 to 3 minutes or until firm.

5. Pour a scant ½ cup of the tempered white chocolate vertically down the center of the dark chocolate strip. Using a clean metal offset spatula, quickly spread the white chocolate into a thin, even layer, completely covering the dark chocolate strip and filling the hollow straight lines created by the icing comb. Let the white chocolate stand for 2 to 4 minutes, or until it is no longer shiny and starts to set, but is still pliable.

6. With a small, sharp knife, cut the 2 ends of the striped chocolate strip, releasing the strip from the marble. Slide a long metal cake spatula underneath the striped chocolate-covered strip and turn it so that it is lying horizontally in front of you. With a ruler and a small sharp knife, score the strip into 1¼-inch wide sections. Without cutting through the plastic strip, cut the striped chocolate strip score lines into 1¼-inch wide rectangles. Leave the chocolate rectangles adhered to the plastic strip for at least 1 hour to set the chocolate.

7. Using the 3 other acetate strips, prepare the remaining striped chocolate rectangles in the same manner. After cutting you should have about 40 striped chocolate rectangles. (The striped chocolate rectangles may be prepared up to 2 weeks in advance, and stored in an airtight container at cool, room temperature, about 65°F–70°F. The chocolate rectangles will be less likely to chip if they are left adhered to the acetate until ready to use.)

8. Pour any leftover tempered chocolate onto foil-lined baking sheets and refrigerate for 10 minutes, until firm. Let the chocolate set completely for 30 minutes at room temperature before breaking it up for storage. The chocolate may be used again for baking or candy making.

Make the chocolate glaze

1. Put the chocolate in a small metal bowl. In a small saucepan, combine the heavy cream and corn syrup. Cook over medium heat, stirring briefly with a wooden spoon until the mixture comes to a boil. Remove the pan from the heat and pour the hot cream over the chocolate. Let the mixture stand for 30 seconds to melt the chocolate. Gently whisk until smooth and then stir in the vanilla extract. Try not to create air bubbles as you stir the glaze.

Glaze the cake

1. Take the frozen cake out of the freezer and remove the plastic wrap. The chocolate sabayon will have contracted slightly from being frozen, leaving a space for the chocolate glaze. Place the cake on a revolving cake decorating stand. Pour the chocolate glaze over the top of the cake and using a long metal cake spatula, quickly spread the chocolate glaze over the top, sweeping off any excess glaze. (The glaze will set on contact with the frozen chocolate sabayon.)

Unmold the cake

1. Using a blow dryer, propane torch, or damp (not wet), very hot towel, carefully heat the outside of the cake ring until the edge of the frozen chocolate sabayon melts slightly. With a slight twisting motion, carefully lift up the cake ring to remove it from around the cake.

Decorate the cake

1. Scrape the chocolate chantilly into a chilled bowl of a 4½-quart heavy-duty electric mixer. With the whisk attachment, set at medium-high speed, beat the chocolate chantilly cream for 30 to 60 seconds, or until it forms stiff peaks. (Be careful not to over-whip or the chocolate chantilly will become grainy.) Quickly scrape the chocolate chantilly into a pastry bag fitted with a closed star tip (such as Ateco #4). Pipe a shell border around the top edge of the glazed cake.

2. Carefully remove the striped chocolate rectangles from the acetate strips. Using the leftover chocolate chantilly, smear a small amount on the back of each striped chocolate rectangle and adhere them shingle fashion to the side of the cake. If desired, wrap the outside of the cake with a piece of gold ribbon and tie it into a bow. Keep refrigerated until 1 hour before serving.

Chocolate Hazelnut Mousse Slices

This rich, moist, and flavorful cake represents the ultimate showcase for chocolate and hazelnut: the flavor pairing is found in the mousse, the glaze, and in the cocoa sponge cake, which is brushed with hazelnut syrup. Serve with vanilla ice cream, and the world's ills will never touch you.

•◆•

YIELD: 32 SERVINGS

Preparation: 2½ hours, plus baking, cooling, chilling, and freezing times

Cocoa Sponge Cake
•◆•

⅓ cup sifted cake flour (not self-rising)

¼ cup sifted unsweetened alkalized cocoa powder

⅓ cup plus 2 tablespoons granulated sugar, divided

¼ teaspoon baking powder

Pinch of salt

2 large eggs, separated, plus 2 large egg yolks

1 tablespoon vegetable oil

2 teaspoons warm water

1 teaspoon vanilla extract

Hazelnut Praline Powder
•◆•

¼ cup granulated sugar

⅛ teaspoon lemon juice

¼ cup roasted hazelnuts (see page 41)

Chocolate Hazelnut Mousse
•◆•

12 ounces semisweet chocolate, coarsely chopped

½ cup praline paste

½ cup plus 2 tablespoons milk

2 tablespoons Italian hazelnut liqueur, such as Frangelico

2 tablespoons vanilla extract

1¼ cups heavy cream

Hazelnut Syrup
•◆•

3 tablespoons water

1½ tablespoons granulated sugar

2 tablespoons Italian hazelnut liqueur, such as Frangelico

1 tablespoon dark rum

¼ teaspoon vanilla extract

Assembly
•◆•

2 ounces semisweet chocolate, finely chopped

1 teaspoon vegetable oil

Chocolate Glaze
•◆•
8 ounces semisweet chocolate, finely chopped
¾ cup plus 2 tablespoons heavy cream
3 tablespoons light corn syrup
1 tablespoon Italian hazelnut liqueur, such as Frangelico
1 teaspoon vanilla extract

Decoration
•◆•
One 3½-inch square sheet of 22-karat German gold leaf

Make the cocoa sponge cake

1. Position the rack in the center of the oven and preheat to 350°F. Line the bottom of a 17½-by-11½-inch jelly roll pan with aluminum foil and leave a 2-inch overhang on the short ends. Fold the overhang underneath the pan. Lightly butter the foil and the sides of the pan. Dust the bottom and sides with flour and tap out the excess.

2. In a small bowl, using a wire whisk, stir together the flour, cocoa powder, 1 teaspoon of the sugar, baking powder, and salt until thoroughly blended. Sift the mixture onto a piece of waxed paper.

3. In the 4½-quart bowl of a heavy-duty electric mixer, using the wire whisk attachment, beat the whole eggs at medium-high speed. Add ⅓ cup of the remaining sugar in a steady stream. Add the egg yolks and continue beating for 4 to 7 minutes, until the batter is pale yellow and forms a thick ribbon. Lower the speed to medium and beat in the oil, water, and vanilla extract.

4. In a grease-free 4½-quart bowl of a heavy-duty electric mixer, using a clean wire whisk attachment, beat the egg whites until frothy. Gradually increase the speed to medium-high and continue beating the whites until they start to form soft peaks. One teaspoon at a time, add the remaining 5 teaspoons of sugar and continue to beat the whites until they form stiff, shiny peaks.

5. Scrape one-third of the egg whites on top of the beaten egg yolks. Resift one-third of the flour mixture over the whites and, using a balloon whisk or a large rubber spatula, fold the flour mixture and the egg whites into the yolk mixture, making sure to bring the whisk near the bottom of the bowl to free any flour that may be clinging to the bowl. One-third at a time, gently fold in the remaining whites with one-third of the resifted flour mixture. Do not over-fold the batter. Scrape the batter into the prepared pan and spread it into a thin, even layer with an offset spatula.

6. Bake the sponge cake for 8 to 12 minutes, until the edge of the cake has pulled away slightly from the side of the pan and the center springs back when gently pressed. (The sponge cake will only be about ⅜-inch thick.) Cool the sponge cake in the pan on a wire rack.

Make the hazelnut praline powder

1. Lightly oil the bottom of a 9-inch cake pan. In a heavy, nonstick skillet, using a wooden spoon, stir together the sugar and lemon juice until thoroughly blended. Over medium heat, cook the sugar mixture for 4 to 6 minutes, stirring frequently until it liquefies and then turns to a dark amber color. Remove the pan from the heat and stir in the hazelnuts. Quickly spread the hazelnut praline into the prepared pan and cool for 20 to 30 minutes, until firm.

2. Transfer the praline to a cutting board, coarsely chop the praline with a large knife, and then put it in the food processor fitted with the metal chopping blade. Process for 30 to 45 seconds, until finely ground. Transfer the praline powder to a small bowl and reserve for the chocolate hazelnut mousse.

Make the chocolate hazelnut mousse

1. Put the chocolate in the food processor fitted with the metal chopping blade. Process for 30 to 45 seconds, until finely chopped. Add the praline paste and process for 5 to 10 seconds, until fully blended.

2. In a small saucepan, set over medium heat, bring the milk to a gentle boil. With the motor of the food processor running, pour the hot milk through the feed tube. Process for 15 to 20 seconds, until the chocolate mixture has completely melted. Scrape down the sides of the work bowl. Add the hazelnut liqueur and the vanilla to the chocolate mixture. Process for 15 to 20 seconds, until the mixture is smooth and creamy. Scrape the chocolate mixture into a large bowl and let stand for a few minutes, until tepid.

3. In a chilled 4½-quart bowl of a heavy-duty electric mixer, using the wire whisk attachment, whip the heavy cream at medium-high speed, until soft mounds start to form. Do not over-whip the cream.

4. Using a large rubber spatula, gently fold one-third of the whipped cream into the chocolate mixture to lighten it. Fold in the remaining whipped cream and the reserved praline powder. Do not over-fold the mousse. Cover the surface of the mousse with plastic wrap and refrigerate to set, about 1 hour.

Make the hazelnut syrup

1. In a small saucepan combine the water and sugar. Cook over medium heat, stirring with a wooden spoon until the sugar dissolves. Stop stirring; raise the heat to medium-high and bring the syrup to a boil. Remove the pan from the heat and let the syrup cool to room temperature. Stir in the hazelnut liqueur, rum, and vanilla extract.

Assembly

1. Melt the chocolate according to the directions on page 25. Stir the oil into the melted chocolate until smooth.

2. Cover the sponge cake with a piece of waxed paper and a baking sheet. Invert the jelly roll pan onto the baking sheet and carefully peel off the aluminum foil from the top of the sponge cake.

3. Using a long serrated knife, carefully cut the sponge cake in half crosswise so that you have 2 pieces of sponge cake that measure approximately 10-by-8-inches each.

4. Using an offset metal cake spatula, spread the melted chocolate into a thin, even layer over the top of one of the sponge cake layers. Cover the other cake with plastic wrap to prevent it from drying out. Refrigerate the baking sheet with the cake layers for 5 to 10 minutes, until the chocolate coating is firm.

5. Remove the chocolate hazelnut mousse and the cake layers from the refrigerator. Turn the chocolate-coated sponge cake layer over so that the chocolate-coated side is lying against the surface of the baking sheet. (The thin chocolate coating will make it easier to handle the chocolate hazelnut mousse slices.)

6. Using a pastry brush, moisten the top of the chocolate-coated sponge cake layer with half of the hazelnut syrup. Using an offset metal cake spatula, spread half of the mousse evenly over the moistened cake layer. Top the mousse with the other piece of sponge cake. Moisten the cake with the remaining syrup. Spread the remaining mousse in a smooth, even layer over the cake. Cover the mousse with a piece of waxed paper and then cover the assembled cake with plastic wrap. Freeze the cake for 8 hours or overnight. (If desired, the cake may be wrapped in aluminum foil and frozen for up to 1 month.)

Make the chocolate glaze

1. Put the chocolate in a small bowl. In a small saucepan, set over medium heat, bring the heavy cream and corn syrup to a gentle boil. Pour the hot cream over the chocolate and let the mixture stand for 30 seconds. Gently whisk until smooth, being careful not to create too many air bubbles. Stir in the hazelnut liqueur and the vanilla extract.

2. Take the cake out of the refrigerator and remove the plastic wrap and waxed paper. Pour three-quarters of the warm glaze over the top of the cake. Using a large metal cake spatula, quickly spread the glaze into an even layer over the surface of the mousse. Refrigerate the cake for 5 minutes, until the glaze is firm. Pour the remaining glaze into a small parchment cone.

3. Drizzle most of the remaining glaze over the surface of the chilled glaze. Use the remaining glaze to garnish the dessert plates.

Cut the hazelnut mousse slices

1. With 2 long metal cake spatulas, transfer the glazed cake to a cutting surface. Using a long, thin-bladed knife, cut the cake in 2-inch wide strips. Between each cut, rinse the knife under hot water and wipe the blade dry before cutting the next strip. Cut each strip into 2-inch rectangles.

Decorate the chocolate hazelnut mousse slices

1. Using the tip of a cotton swab, pick up a small dab of gold leaf and very gently affix it to the center of a chocolate hazelnut mousse slice. Decorate the remaining slices in the same manner. To serve, drizzle a little glaze on a dessert plate and place a chocolate hazelnut mousse slice on top. If not serving immediately, store the chocolate hazelnut slices in an airtight container in the refrigerator for up to 2 days.

Ganache-Filled Fried Wontons with Ginger Ice Cream and Chocolate Sorbet

Pleasantly pungent, ginger ice cream matches beautifully (in both temperature contrast and flavor blend) with the chocolate in the deep-fried wontons and sorbet. Serving the wontons after they have cooled will ensure the perfect, truffle-like consistency in the center. The playful fortune cookies garnishing the plate can be personalized for guests—write a fortune for each, and leave the note protruding from the cookie with the intended's initials showing.

•◆•

YIELD: 8 SERVINGS

Preparation: 2½ hours, plus chilling, freezing, baking, and frying times

Special Equipment: Ice cream machine; silicone baking mat; deep-fry thermometer

Ginger Ice Cream
•◆•
Eight ¼-inch slices (about 1 inch in diameter) fresh ginger, peeled

⅓ cup water

¾ cup granulated sugar

6 large egg yolks

⅛ teaspoon salt

1¾ cups milk

1½ cups heavy cream

Chocolate Sorbet
•◆•
⅔ cup unsweetened alkalized cocoa powder

3 cups water

1 cup granulated sugar

3 tablespoons light corn syrup

3 tablespoons dark, flavorful honey, such as wildflower honey

¼ teaspoon salt

2 teaspoons vanilla extract

Cinnamon Sugar
•◆•
1 cup granulated sugar

1 tablespoon ground cinnamon

Asian-Spiced Dipping Sauce
•◆•
Two ¼-inch slices (about 1 inch in diameter) peeled fresh ginger

1⅓ cups water, divided

¾ cup granulated sugar

2 whole pieces star anise

One 2-inch long cinnamon stick, broken

5 whole cloves

½ vanilla bean, split lengthwise and scraped

3 tablespoons honey (same type as for sorbet)

3 tablespoons cognac or brandy

Chocolate Fortune Cookies
•◆•
8 fortunes

2 large egg whites

1 teaspoon water

½ teaspoon vanilla extract

4 tablespoons unsalted butter, at room temperature

2 tablespoons honey (same type as for sorbet)

⅛ teaspoon salt

⅔ cup confectioners' sugar

¼ cup unsweetened alkalized cocoa powder, sifted

¼ cup all-purpose flour

Ganache Filling
•◆•
7 ounces bittersweet chocolate, such as Valrhona Le Noir (see sources on page 302)

½ cup heavy cream

1 tablespoon cognac or brandy

Ganache-Filled Fried Wontons
•◆•
Twenty-four 3-inch square wonton wrappers

1 large egg

Oil for deep-frying

Make the ginger ice cream

1. Lightly crush the slices of ginger with the side of a chef's knife or cleaver. In a small saucepan, combine the crushed ginger, water, and sugar. Cook over medium heat, stirring constantly, until the sugar dissolves. Increase the heat to medium-high and bring to a gentle boil; boil for 1 minute, stirring occasionally. Remove the pan from the heat and allow to steep for 30 minutes. Strain the ginger syrup through a fine-meshed sieve into a small bowl.

2. In a large heatproof bowl, beat the yolks and salt until just blended.

3. In a large heavy saucepan, combine the milk, heavy cream, and ginger syrup. Cook over medium-high heat and bring the mixture to a gentle boil, stirring occasionally. Gradually whisk about three-quarters of the hot cream mixture into the beaten egg yolks until blended. Return this mixture to the saucepan.

4. Cook over low heat, stirring constantly with a flat-edged wooden spoon, for 2 to 4 minutes or until the custard has thickened slightly. Do not let the custard come to a boil. The custard is done when you can run your finger down the back of the custard-coated spoon and a path remains in the custard for several seconds.

5. Remove the pan from the heat and immediately strain the hot custard into a stainless steel bowl. Set the bowl over a larger bowl containing ice water for 5 to 10 minutes, stirring occasionally, until the custard is cool.

6. Remove the bowl of custard from the bowl holding the ice water and press a sheet of plastic wrap onto the surface of the custard to prevent a skin from forming. Refrigerate the custard until thickened and cold, at least 3 hours, but preferably overnight, to allow the flavors to develop.

7. Pour the chilled custard into the container of an ice cream maker and freeze according to the manufacturer's directions. Scrape the churned ginger ice cream into a freezer container. Cover and freeze for a few hours or overnight.

Make the chocolate sorbet

1. Place the cocoa powder in a medium-sized heatproof bowl.

2. In a large heavy saucepan, combine the water, sugar, corn syrup, honey, and salt. Cook over medium heat, stirring constantly, until the sugar dissolves. Increase the heat to medium-high and bring the syrup to a gentle boil; boil for 1 minute, stirring occasionally. Remove the pan from the heat.

3. Whisk about 1 cup of the hot syrup into the cocoa powder until the cocoa is melted and the mixture is smooth. Add the cocoa mixture to the pan of hot syrup, whisking until well-blended. Return the pan to the heat; bring the mixture to a boil and boil for one minute, stirring occasionally. Remove from the heat and stir in the vanilla extract.

4. Strain the mixture into a large heatproof bowl and allow to cool to room temperature. Cover the bowl and refrigerate until cold, at least 4 hours.

5. Whisk the chilled sorbet mixture if it has separated. Pour the mixture into the container of an ice cream maker and freeze according to the manufacturer's directions. Scrape the churned chocolate sorbet into a freezer container. Cover and freeze for a few hours or overnight.

Make the cinnamon sugar

1. Pour the sugar into a mixing bowl. Add the cinnamon and stir until the spice is evenly dispersed in the sugar. (The cinnamon sugar may be made a few days ahead and stored in a tightly covered container at room temperature.)

Make the Asian-spiced dipping sauce

1. Lightly crush the slices of ginger with the side of a chef's knife or cleaver. Set aside.

2. In a medium-sized heavy saucepan, combine ⅓ cup of the water and the sugar. Cook over medium heat, stirring constantly with a wooden spoon, until the sugar dissolves. Increase the heat to medium-high and continue to cook, without stirring, for 4 to 6 minutes, until the syrup begins to brown. Lower the heat to medium-low and continue to cook, swirling the pan, until the syrup turns a light amber color. Remove the pan from the heat and slowly add the remaining water to the caramel (be careful as the mixture will bubble up). Return the pan to medium heat and stir until any bits of hardened caramel are completely melted and the caramelized syrup is smooth. Add the crushed ginger, star anise, cinnamon stick, cloves, and the vanilla bean seeds and pod. Bring to a gentle boil; boil for 2 minutes, stirring occasionally.

3. Remove the pan from the heat and immediately whisk the honey and cognac into the hot syrup. Allow the mixture to steep until it comes to room temperature; then strain the sauce into a container. Cover and refrigerate until cold. (The sauce can be made up to 3 days ahead and stored in the refrigerator.)

Make the chocolate fortune cookies

1. To make the fortunes: Cut out eight ½-inch-by-5-inch strips of paper. Write a message on each strip. To customize, write the initial of the designated person on one end of the strip, making sure that the initial is exposed when forming the cookie.

2. In a small mixing bowl, whisk together the egg whites, water, and vanilla extract.

3. In a large mixing bowl, using a hand-held electric mixer set at medium speed, beat the butter, honey, and salt until blended. On low speed, gradually add the confectioners' sugar and beat until absorbed. Continuing to beat at low speed, add the cocoa powder and then the egg white mixture, beating in each addition until absorbed. Scrape down the bowl with a rubber spatula as necessary. Using the rubber spatula, stir in the flour, mixing until the batter is thoroughly blended and forms a smooth paste.

4. Scrape the cookie batter into a small container. Cover the surface of the batter with plastic wrap and refrigerate for at least 1 day. (The batter will keep, refrigerated, for up to 3 days.)

5. Position a rack in the center of the oven and preheat to 325°F. Have ready a baking sheet, the silicone mat, and a standard size muffin tin. Make a template: Using the rim of a bowl as a guide, draw two 4-inch diameter circles, spaced well apart, on a sheet of parchment paper the same size as the silicone mat.

6. On a work surface, place the silicone mat over the parchment template. Using a small offset metal spatula, spread a thin layer of batter to make 1 round. Repeat to make another round. You will need 2 to 3 teaspoons of batter for each cookie. Transfer the mat to the baking sheet and bake until set, about 8 to 10 minutes.

7. Let rest for about 30 seconds. Using a metal spatula, transfer 1 of the cookies from the mat to the work surface. Place a message along the diameter. Quickly fold the cookie in half over the fortune. Shape into a fortune, cookie: bring the two ends of the semicircle toward each other so that they are almost, but not quite, touching. Place the formed cookie into the muffin tin to hold its shape while cooling. Immediately repeat this shaping with the second baked cookie. If the second cookie has cooled too much and does not bend easily, return the baking sheet to the oven for 30 seconds to soften the cookie, then shape as before.

8. Repeat steps 6 and 7 to make at least 8 fortune cookies. The batter will produce more cookies than needed, as they are fragile and one or two may break.

9. Transfer the fortune cookies to a wire rack to cool completely. (The cookies may be made up to 2 days ahead; place them in a single layer on a tray. Cover them loosely with aluminum foil and keep them at room temperature, away from humidity.)

Make the ganache filling

1. Place the chocolate on a work surface and use a chef's knife or an offset serrated knife to very finely chop the chocolate. Alternatively, the chocolate may be placed in the bowl of a food processor fitted with the metal chopping blade and pulsed until very finely chopped, making sure not to over-process and melt the chocolate. Transfer the chopped chocolate to a heatproof bowl.

2. Place the heavy cream in a small saucepan and cook over medium heat until it comes to a gentle boil. Remove the pan from the heat and pour the hot cream over the chopped chocolate. Let stand for 3 minutes to melt the chocolate.

3. Add the cognac and stir gently until the mixture is well blended and smooth. Place plastic wrap directly on the surface of the ganache and refrigerate until cold.

Assemble the ganache-filled wontons

1. Line a jelly roll pan or baking pan with waxed paper. Remove the ganache from the refrigerator. Form about 2 teaspoons of filling into a mound and place on the prepared pan. Repeat to make 24 mounds. Place the filled pan in the refrigerator until the mounds of ganache firm up, about 30 minutes.

2. Have ready another pan lined with waxed paper. For the egg wash, beat the egg in a small bowl until blended. Place a wonton wrapper on a work surface with one of the corners pointing towards you. Using a pastry brush, paint a ½-inch-wide border of egg wash along the two top adjacent edges of the wrapper. Place a mound of chilled ganache in the center of the wrapper. Picking up the corner closest to you, fold the wrapper over the filling forming a triangle with the long side at the bottom. Press down on the edges to seal, while at the same time pushing out any air. Brush a small amount of egg wash on the top of the right corner tip. Bend the tips so as to cross them, placing the egg washed-right tip over the left while pressing to seal. Place the filled wonton on the prepared pan. Repeat to form 24 wontons, placing them on the tray in a single layer.

3. Freeze the tray of ganache-filled wontons for at least 2 hours. The wontons may be fried at this point or placed in a plastic freezer storage bag and frozen for up to 3 days.

Fry the wontons

1. Pour enough oil in a deep-fat fryer or large straight-sided saucepan to come halfway up the pan. The oil should come up to a depth of 2 to 3 inches. Heat the oil between 360°F and 365°F. Line a baking sheet with paper towels.

2. Fry the frozen wontons, 4 or 5 at a time, for about 1 to 1½ minutes until golden brown on all sides. Using a spider or slotted spoon, remove the wontons from the hot oil and transfer them to the prepared baking sheet to drain for a second or two. Roll the warm wontons in the cinnamon sugar, then transfer them to a wire rack to cool.

3. The wontons may be served while still warm but are at their best when allowed to cool for a few hours or until the ganache filling has set up to a truffle-like consistency.

Assemble the dessert (Asian style)

1. Have ready 8 small chilled bowls, 8 tiny Asian-style sauce plates, and 8 large dinner plates (which may be round, oval, or oblong).

2. Spoon some of the Asian-spiced dipping sauce into each of the sauce plates.

3. Place 1 scoop of ginger ice cream (about ⅓ cup) and 1 scoop of chocolate sorbet (about ⅓ cup) in each of the small chilled bowls. Top each bowl with 3 fried wontons.

4. Arrange an assembled bowl, a chocolate fortune cookie, and a plate of dipping sauce on each dinner plate along with a pair of chopsticks and an oriental soup spoon. Serve at once.

Assemble the dessert (traditional style)

1. Have ready 8 chilled shallow soup bowls and 8 under-plates. Pour the spiced dipping sauce into a small pitcher.

2. Place a soup bowl on an under-plate. Arrange 1 scoop of ginger ice cream (about ⅓ cup), 1 scoop of chocolate sorbet (about ⅓ cup), and 3 fried wontons in each of the chilled bowls. Garnish with a chocolate fortune cookie. Serve at once and pass the Asian-spiced dipping sauce.

Individual Chocolate Banana Cakes with Two Sauces

The ultimate dessert for the sophisticated banana lover, these chocolate-banana cakes, kissed with a hint of rum, are topped with caramelized bananas, deluged in caramel-banana and chocolate sauces, then drizzled with chopped macadamia nuts.

•◆•

YIELD: 10 SERVINGS

Preparation: 2 hours, plus baking and cooling times
Special Equipment: Ten 3-by-1¼-inch-high metal ring molds; plastic squeeze bottle

Caramel Banana Purée
•◆•
4 ripe bananas (about 6 ounces each)
½ cup water, divided
1 cup granulated sugar
¼ cup dark rum

Chocolate Banana Cakes
•◆•
½ cup unsweetened nonalkalized cocoa powder
2 teaspoons vanilla extract
2 cups sifted cake flour
¾ teaspoon baking powder
½ teaspoon baking soda
¼ teaspoon salt
½ cup plus 2 tablespoons (1¼ sticks) unsalted butter, softened
1 cup granulated sugar
2 large eggs, at room temperature
½ cup sour cream, at room temperature

Caramel Banana Custard Sauce
•◆•
1¼ cups milk
1 cup heavy cream
¼ cup granulated sugar
4 large egg yolks
⅛ teaspoon salt

Macadamia Crunch
•◆•
1 cup macadamia nuts
3 tablespoons water
¾ cup granulated sugar

Chocolate Sauce
•◆•
6 ounces bittersweet chocolate, such as Lindt Excellence, finely chopped
½ cup water
½ cup granulated sugar
½ cup heavy cream
1 tablespoon unsalted butter, softened
½ teaspoon vanilla extract

Assembly
•◆•
3 ripe bananas (about 6 ounces each)
⅓ cup granulated sugar

Make the caramel banana purée

1. Peel and cut the bananas into ½-inch chunks. Place them in a bowl and set aside.

2. In a medium heavy saucepan, combine ¼ cup of the water and the sugar. Cook over medium heat, stirring constantly with a wooden spoon until the sugar dissolves. Increase the heat to medium-high and continue to cook without stirring for 4 to 6 minutes until the syrup begins to caramelize. Lower the heat to medium-low and continue to cook, swirling the pan, until the caramel turns to a rich amber color. Remove the pan from the heat and slowly add the remaining ¼ cup water and the rum (be careful as the mixture will bubble up). Return the syrup to medium heat and stir until any bits of hardened caramel are completely melted and the syrup is smooth. Add the bananas and stir for 3 minutes, separating the banana chunks and making sure that they are coated with the caramel. Remove from the heat and let cool for 5 minutes.

3. Transfer the caramel banana mixture to the bowl of a food processor fitted with the metal blade. Process for 1 minute until the banana is liquefied and the mixture is smooth. There will be about 2 cups of purée. Place 1 cup of the purée in a bowl and reserve for the chocolate banana cakes. Place the remaining purée in another bowl and reserve for the chocolate custard sauce.

Make the chocolate banana cakes

1. Position a rack in the center of the oven and preheat to 350°F. Lightly butter the bottom of a large baking sheet. Dust the sheet with flour, tapping off the excess. Butter the insides of the ring molds and arrange the buttered molds on the prepared baking sheet, making sure the ring molds are not touching each other.

2. Place the cocoa powder in a medium bowl. Slowly whisk in 1 cup of the caramel banana purée to make a smooth paste; whisk in the vanilla extract. Set aside.

3. In a medium bowl, using a wire whisk, stir together the sifted flour, baking powder, baking soda, and salt until blended.

4. In a 4½-quart bowl of a heavy-duty electric mixer, using the paddle attachment, beat the butter and sugar at medium speed for about 4 minutes until the mixture is light and fluffy. Add the eggs, one at a time, beating well after each addition. On low speed, beat in the cooled cocoa banana mixture until absorbed. Scrape down the sides of the bowl with a rubber spatula as necessary.

5. Beat half of the flour mixture into the butter mixture. Beat in the sour cream, then beat in the remaining flour mixture, mixing only until each addition is incorporated.

6. Divide the batter evenly among the assembled ring molds, smoothing the tops with the bottom of a small spoon. Bake for 18 to 22 minutes, or until a tester inserted into the center of one of the cakes comes out clean. Place the baking pan containing the cakes on a wire rack and allow to cool for 10 minutes.

7. Run the tip of a sharp knife between the cake and the top edge of each ring mold to loosen. Lift the molds off the cakes and use a metal spatula to transfer each cake to a wire rack to cool. If the molds are too hot to handle, use tongs or a kitchen towel to remove them. When the cakes are completely cool, wrap each one individually with plastic wrap. (The wrapped cakes may be kept at room temperature for up to 1 day.)

Make the caramel banana custard sauce

1. In a medium heavy saucepan, combine the milk, heavy cream, sugar, and the remainder of the caramel banana purée. Cook over medium heat, stirring constantly, until the sugar dissolves. Increase the heat to medium-high and bring the mixture to a gentle boil.

2. Place the yolks and salt in a medium heatproof bowl and beat with a fork until blended. Gradually whisk the hot cream mixture into the beaten yolks. Return the yolk-cream mixture to the saucepan. Cook over low heat, stirring constantly with a wooden spoon for 1 to 3 minutes or until the custard has thickened slightly. It is done when you can run your finger down the back of the custard-coated spoon and a path remains in the custard for several seconds. Do not let the custard come to a boil.

3. Remove the pan from the heat and immediately strain the hot custard into a stainless steel bowl. Set the bowl over a larger bowl containing ice water and stir the sauce for 5 to 10 minutes, until cool. Cover the surface of the caramel banana custard sauce with plastic wrap and refrigerate the bowl of custard.

Make the macadamia crunch

1. Position a rack in the center of the oven and preheat to 325°F. Spread the macadamia nuts in a single layer on a jelly roll pan and place in the oven to warm, about 5 minutes. Do not let the nuts color.

2. Generously butter both a baking sheet and a metal spatula. In a medium heavy saucepan, combine the water and sugar. Cook over medium heat, stirring constantly with a wooden spoon until the sugar dissolves. Increase the heat to medium-high and continue to cook without stirring for 4 to 6 minutes until the syrup begins to caramelize. Lower the heat to medium-low and continue to cook, swirling the pan, until the syrup turns a rich amber color. Remove the pan from the heat and add the warmed macadamia nuts all at once. Stir to coat with the caramel. Quickly transfer the caramel-nut mixture to the prepared baking sheet. Using the buttered spatula, press the mixture into an even layer. Allow the mixture to stand for about 25 to 30 minutes or until cool and hardened.

3. Place the cooled caramel nut mixture onto a work surface. With a chef's knife, coarsely chop the mixture, discarding any shards of pure caramel. Transfer the macadamia crunch to a small container and keep covered in a cool, dry place until needed.

Make the chocolate sauce

1. Place the chopped chocolate in a heatproof bowl and set aside.

2. In a small saucepan, combine the water, sugar, and heavy cream and cook over medium heat, stirring constantly, until the sugar dissolves. Increase the heat to medium-high and cook the mixture until it comes to a gentle boil. Remove the pan from the heat and slowly pour the hot cream over the chopped chocolate. Let stand for 3 minutes to melt the chocolate.

3. Whisk the sauce gently until well-blended and smooth. Whisk in the butter and vanilla extract. Pour the chocolate sauce into the plastic squeeze bottle. The sauce should be used at room temperature or slightly chilled.

Assemble the dessert

1. Remove the caramel banana custard sauce from the refrigerator and whisk to blend. Place the 10 chocolate cakes on a baking sheet.

2. Peel the bananas and slice them in half lengthwise. Thinly slice the banana halves crosswise, discarding the ends (the slices should be no thicker than $\frac{1}{16}$-inch). Arrange the slices on the tops of the cakes to completely cover them.

3. To caramelize the bananas (using a broiler): Position a rack 5 to 6 inches under the source of heat and preheat the broiler. Sprinkle the banana slices evenly with a generous teaspoon of the granulated sugar. Place the cakes under the broiler for about 1 to 2 minutes, or until the sugar melts and turns to a light amber caramel. (Depending on the size of your broiler, this may be more easily done working in batches, a few cakes at a time.)

4. To caramelize the bananas (using a propane torch): Sprinkle the banana slices evenly with a generous teaspoon of the granulated sugar. Using a household propane torch, caramelize the top of each cake by heating the sugar with the flame until the sugar melts and turns into a light amber caramel.

5. Ladle some caramel banana custard sauce onto each dessert plate, tilting the plate to coat the bottom completely. Pipe chocolate sauce onto the banana sauce in a decorative pattern and place a cake in the center. Sprinkle macadamia crunch around the cake. Serve immediately.

Chocolate Espresso Triangles

Chocolate is the ideal canvas to display the hearty flavor of espresso; like rays of energy it bursts from the espresso-soaked cake, the espresso buttercream, and the chocolate glaze. It may seem like overkill, but espresso desserts actually go quite well with coffee.

•◆•

YIELD: 16 TRIANGLES

Preparation: 2 hours, plus cooling and standing times

Chocolate Genoise Cake
•◆•

½ cup cake flour (not self-rising)
¼ cup unsweetened nonalkalized cocoa powder
Pinch of salt
5 large eggs, at room temperature
½ cup granulated sugar
¼ cup (½ stick) unsalted butter, melted
2 ounces bittersweet chocolate, melted and cooled

Soaking Syrup
•◆•

¼ cup water
¼ cup granulated sugar
2 tablespoons coffee liqueur

Espresso Buttercream
•◆•

1 teaspoon instant espresso powder
1 teaspoon hot water
½ cup plus 1 tablespoon granulated sugar, divided
¼ cup cold water
2 large egg whites, at room temperature
⅛ teaspoon cream of tartar
1 cup (2 sticks) unsalter butter, softened
1 tablespoon coffee liqueur

Chocolate Glaze
•◆•

½ pound bittersweet chocolate, finely chopped
1 cup heavy cream
2 tablespoons light corn syrup
1 tablespoon coffee liqueur

Garnish
•◆•

16 chocolate-covered espresso beans

Make the chocolate genoise cake

1. Position a rack in the center of the oven and preheat to 350°F. Lightly butter an 11½-by-17½-inch jelly roll pan. Line it with parchment paper; coat the sides of the pan with nonstick spray and dust with flour, tapping out the excess.

2. Sift together the flour, cocoa powder, and salt and set aside.

3. In the 4½-quart bowl of a heavy-duty electric mixer, using the wire whip attachment, beat the eggs and sugar until well combined. Place the bowl in a pot of simmering water. The bowl must touch the water. Whisk constantly until the sugar is dissolved and the mixture begins to thicken, about 2 minutes. A candy thermometer inserted into the mixture should read 105°F.

4. Immediately remove the bowl from the water, dry off the bottom, and return the bowl to the mixer stand. Beat the mixture at medium-high speed for about 5 minutes, or until the mixture is pale yellow and forms a thick ribbon.

5. Remove ½ cup of this mixture to a medium bowl; whisk in the melted butter and chocolate.

6. With a large rubber spatula, gently but quickly fold in the flour-cocoa mixture into the egg-sugar mixture, one-quarter at a time. Fold in the chocolate mixture. Pour the batter into the prepared pan. Bake for 10 to 12 minutes, until the cake springs back when lightly touched.

Make the soaking syrup

1. In a saucepan bring the water and sugar to a boil; allow to cool. Stir in the coffee liqueur. Set aside.

2. Turn the genoise out onto a cooling rack and peel off the parchment paper. Brush the soaking syrup evenly over the top of the cake. Let cool.

Make the espresso buttercream

1. In a small bowl, dissolve the espresso powder in the hot water. Mix until smooth and set aside.

2. In a small heavy saucepan, combine ½ cup of the sugar and the cold water and heat over medium heat, stirring for 3 to 4 minutes, or until the sugar dissolves. Dip a clean pastry brush in warm water and wash down the sides of the pan to remove any sugar crystals. Raise the heat to medium-high and bring the mixture to a boil. Cook, without stirring, until the syrup registers 240°F on a candy thermometer, about 5 to 8 minutes. When the syrup reaches 230°F, start preparing the egg whites.

3. In the grease-free 4½-quart bowl of a heavy-duty electric mixer, using the wire whip attachment, beat the egg whites at low speed until frothy. Add the cream of tartar and increase the speed to medium-high, beating until soft peaks start to form. Gradually beat in the remaining tablespoon of sugar and beat until stiff peaks start to form.

4. At this point the sugar syrup should register 240°F on the candy thermometer. While beating at medium-low speed, gradually pour the sugar syrup in a slow, steady stream near the side of the bowl onto the beaten whites. Increase the speed to medium-high and beat for 5 to 8 minutes, or until the mixture is completely cool and stiff, and glossy peaks form when the wire whip is lifted.

5. One tablespoon at a time, beat in the softened butter. (If the mixture looks curdled at any point, increase the speed to high and beat until smooth, then reduce the speed to medium-high and continue to beat in the butter.) Beat in the dissolved espresso mixture and the coffee liqueur. (The buttercream can be covered and stored at room temperature for up to 4 hours before assembling the cakes.)

Assemble the cakes

1. Cut the genoise cake crosswise into quarters (each piece will measure about 11½-by-4½ inches). Spread a quarter of the buttercream on top of one piece of cake, top with another piece of cake, and continue layering buttercream and cake until all is used (you should end with the buttercream). Refrigerate until the buttercream is firm, at least 1 hour.

2. Remove the cake from the refrigerator and cut it into 16 small triangle-shaped cakes: cut the cake in half lengthwise, and then into quarters crosswise. Cut each quarter twice diagonally to form a total of 16 triangles. Place the cakes on a wire rack and return to the refrigerator while preparing the glaze.

Make the chocolate glaze

1. Place the chocolate in a heatproof bowl. In a medium saucepan, bring the cream and corn syrup to a gentle boil. Pour the hot cream mixture over the chocolate and let the mixture stand for 30 seconds to melt the chocolate. Whisk the mixture until smooth. Whisk in the coffee liqueur. Let cool until thickened but still pourable, about 20 to 25 minutes.

Glaze and garnish the cakes

1. Remove the cakes from the refrigerator and place them, still on the wire rack, on a baking sheet. Pour the glaze over the cakes, covering them completely. If necessary, use a metal icing spatula to smooth the glaze over the sides of the cakes, but do not use the spatula on the tops of the cakes, or the glaze will not be shiny and smooth. Carefully place a chocolate-covered espresso bean on top of each cake. Let the glaze set. Store the triangles in an airtight container in the refrigerator until 1 hour before serving.

Dipped Bittersweet Chocolate Scones with Rum-Macerated Dried Cherries

These provocative and full-flavored scones will be as welcome as they are unexpected after any meal or coffee hour. A luxurious vanilla dough catches a dense shower of chopped bittersweet chocolate and dried cherries. The pairing of fruit and chocolate—together sweet-tart and rich—makes an unforgettable quick bread.

• ◆ •

YIELD: 12 SCONES

Preparation: 30 minutes, plus baking and cooling times

Macerated Dried Cherries

• ◆ •

1 cup dried sweet cherries

2 tablespoons rum

Scone Dough

• ◆ •

4 cups bleached all-purpose flour

5¼ teaspoons baking powder

¼ teaspoon cream of tartar

1 teaspoon salt

¾ cup (1½ sticks) unsalted butter, chilled and cut into small pieces

1 cup confectioners' sugar

1 cup heavy cream

4 large eggs

1 tablespoon vanilla extract

Five 3.5-ounce bars bittersweet chocolate, such as Lindt Excellence 70% Cocoa Extra Fine Dark Chocolate, hand-cut into chunks

Dipping Chocolate

• ◆ •

8 to 10 ounces bittersweet chocolate, melted and cooled to tepid

Make the macerated dried cherries

1. Place the cherries in a nonreactive bowl with the rum. Stir and let stand, uncovered, for 2 hours. Thoroughly pat dry the cherries on sheets of paper toweling; set aside.

2. Preheat the oven to 400°F. Set out 2 cookie sheets or rimmed baking sheets.

Make the scone dough

1. In a large bowl, thoroughly whisk together the flour, baking powder, cream of tartar, and salt. Scatter over the cubes of butter and, using a pastry blender (or two round-bladed table knives), cut the fat into the flour mixture until reduced to small, pearl-size bits. Stir in the sugar. In a medium-size bowl, whisk together the heavy cream, eggs, and vanilla extract. Pour the whisked mixture over the dry ingredients, add the cherries and chocolate, and stir to form a dough. The dough will be lightly sticky to the touch. Divide the dough in half.

2. Turn the dough onto a floured work surface and knead briefly 6 to 8 times. If the dough is very sticky, sprinkle the work surface with extra flour as you are kneading it; the dough, however, should remain moist.

3. Form each piece of dough into a 7½-inch round disc. Cut each round into 6 pie-shaped wedges. Transfer the scones to the baking sheet using a wide metal spatula; space the triangles of dough about 3 inches apart.

4. Bake the scones for 18 minutes or until set; the exterior of each will be firm, golden, and slightly springy to the touch. Cool the scones on the baking sheets for 1 minute, then transfer them to cooling racks. Cool completely.

Dip the scones

1. Dip one triangular corner of each scone into the melted chocolate to coat. Place the chocolate-coated scones on sheets of waxed paper. Let the scones stand until the chocolate has set. Serve the scones the same day they are made.

Saronno Truffles

Close your eyes, you're in Italy: A bellezza blend of dark and milk chocolates, espresso, and amaretto form the velvety, mousse-like center, coated in a crisp shell of bittersweet chocolate and crushed amaretti cookies.

•◆•

YIELD: 60 TRUFFLES

Preparation: 3 hours, plus infusing, freezing, chilling, and setting times

Special Equipment: (see mail order sources on page 302): ½-inch plain decorating tip (such as Ateco #6); disposable pastry bags; digital thermometer; heating pad with temperature control dial (such as the type used for backaches); 2 silicone baking mats; cotton gloves.

Amaretto Espresso Ganache
•◆•

1 vanilla bean, split in half lengthwise
1 cup heavy cream
3 tablespoons freshly roasted espresso coffee beans, coarsely ground
10 ounces Swiss dark chocolate, such as Lindt*
2 ounces Swiss milk chocolate, such Lindt*
2 teaspoons invert sugar, such as Nulomoline**
1 tablespoon unsalted butter, at room temperature
3 tablespoons Amaretto di Saronno liqueur
Confectioners' sugar, for rolling truffle centers

Dark Chocolate Amaretti Coating
•◆•

1 pound bittersweet chocolate couverture, such as Valrhona Caraque
(see mail order sources on page 302)
1 cup crushed Amaretti di Saronno cookies (about 20 cookies)

*Note: Use 3-ounce Lindt Swiss dark and Lindt Swiss milk chocolate bars for preparing the ganache. These particular chocolates contains just the right proportion of cocoa solids and cocoa butter to enable the espresso ganache to set up properly.

**Note: Invert sugar acts as a softener and helps to prolong the freshness of the ganache filling. See a mail order source for Nulomoline on page 305.

Prepare the amaretto espresso ganache

1. Using the sharp tip of a small knife, scrape the paste of tiny black seeds from inside the split vanilla bean. Put the vanilla bean paste in a small bowl; cover with plastic wrap and reserve. In a small, heavy saucepan, combine the scraped vanilla pods and cream. Over medium heat, stir the cream mixture, until scalding hot. Remove the pan from the heat, cover with a lid so that it is slightly ajar, and allow the mixture to infuse for 30 minutes.

2. Add the ground coffee to the infused vanilla cream mixture and again heat the mixture until it is scalding hot. Remove the pan from the heat and partially cover with a lid. Allow the vanilla-coffee cream mixture to infuse for 10 minutes.

3. Meanwhile, coarsely chop the dark and milk chocolates. Put the chocolate in a food processor fitted with the metal chopping blade. Process for 15 to 20 seconds, until finely chopped. Remove the lid of the food processor and leave the chocolate in the work bowl.

4. Add the invert sugar to the infused vanilla-coffee mixture. Bring the mixture to a gentle boil over medium heat, while stirring constantly.

5. Pour the hot cream mixture through a fine-meshed sieve over the chopped chocolate. Press down on the coffee grounds to extract as much of the cream mixture as possible. Using a clean spatula, press down on the chocolate so that it is completely submerged in the hot cream. Add the reserved vanilla seed paste to the chocolate cream mixture. Let the mixture stand for 30 seconds. Replace the lid of the food processor and pulse 6 to 8 times, until the mixture is creamy. Scrape down the sides of the work bowl, and add the butter and amaretto. Pulse 4 to 6 more times, until smooth. Scrape the ganache onto a baking sheet, letting it spread into a thin layer. Cover the surface with plastic wrap and freeze for at least 1 hour, until firm.

Whip the ganache

1. Cut the pointed end off a disposable pastry bag and insert a ½-inch plain decorating tip (such as Ateco #6). Twist the portion of the pastry bag that is just above the wider opening of the tip. Tuck this twisted portion of the bag into the wider opening of the tip. (This will prevent the whipped ganache from leaking out the end of the tip before you are ready to pipe.) Place the bag into a 2-cup glass measuring cup. Turn down the top 2 to 3 inches of the pastry bag, forming a cuff around the outside of the measuring cup. (The cup will support the bag as you fill it with the whipped ganache.)

2. Remove the plastic wrap from the chilled ganache. Gently warm the bottom of the baking sheet by passing it back and forth a few times over a gas flame or electric range top set on medium. Heat the

pan only until the ganache starts to melt slightly, making it easy to remove it from the surface of the pan. Using a rubber spatula, scrape half (about 1 cup plus 2 tablespoons) of the ganache into the bowl of a heavy-duty electric mixer.

3. Set the bowl over another bowl of hot, not simmering water (the water must touch the bottom of the bowl) for 30 seconds to 2 minutes, stirring constantly with a rubber spatula until the ganache reads 65°F on an instant-read thermometer and has softened to the consistency of handmade mayonnaise. Be careful not to overheat the ganache. If the ganache becomes warmer than 65°F, place the bowl over a bowl of ice water for 2 to 4 seconds. Stir the ganache with a rubber spatula, just until it starts to thicken. Remove the bowl from the ice water.

4. Using the wire whip attachment, whip the softened ganache at medium speed for 30 seconds to 2 minutes, or until it lightens in color and forms soft peaks. It should have the texture of a fluffy chocolate buttercream frosting. (If the whipped ganache becomes too firm and appears grainy, replace the bowl over the hot water for 2 to 4 seconds and stir gently until it softens enough to be rewhipped. Conversely, if the ganache is too soft and will not form soft peaks, place it over the bowl of ice water and stir for 2 to 4 seconds, until it just starts to thicken. Continue whipping until the ganache reaches the proper consistency.)

Pipe the truffle centers

1. Immediately scrape the ganache into the prepared pastry bag. Work quickly as the ganache will start to set up shortly after it is whipped. Hold the bag in a perpendicular position and pipe ⅞-inch mounds with pointed peaks on a clean baking sheet. If the ganache is the correct consistency, it will pipe easily and hold its shape. Quickly finish piping the ganache mounds.

2. Using the remaining chilled ganache, repeat steps 3 and 4 of whipping the ganache, and step 1 of piping the truffle centers. Loosely cover the piped truffle centers with plastic wrap and refrigerate for 10 to 20 minutes, until firm enough to roll. Do not overchill the truffle centers or they will become too stiff to form into rounds.

Roll the truffle centers

1. Sift a light dusting of confectioners' sugar over the chilled centers. Using a small, metal cake spatula, remove the truffle centers from the surface of the baking sheet. Lightly coat the palm of your hands with confectioners' sugar. With your fingertips, pinch a truffle center into a round, then roll it between the palms of your hands into a ⅞-inch ball. Place the rolled center on a waxed paper-lined baking sheet. Roll the remaining truffle centers in the same manner. Let the centers set at room temperature for 45 to 60 minutes to form a thin, dry crust.

Seal-coat the truffle centers

1. Temper the dark chocolate using one of the tempering methods on page 27. Put the tempered chocolate into a 1-quart glass bowl and set it on a heating pad set to low to maintain the correct coating temperature. Line a baking sheet with a silicone baking mat with the textured side facing up. Arrange your work area so that the baking sheet with the uncoated truffle centers is on the left side of the bowl of tempered chocolate and the baking mat-covered baking sheet is on the right side of the tempered chocolate. Reverse the positions if you are left-handed.

2. Remove a dab (about 1 tablespoon) of tempered dark chocolate with the fingers of one hand and put it on the palm of the other hand. Touch the 2 palms together a couple of times so that there is a thin layer of dark chocolate on both palms. Pick up a truffle center and gently roll it between both palms until it is coated with an almost tissue-thin, even layer of dark chocolate. Using your forefinger and second finger of one hand, place the coated center on the baking mat-lined baking sheet, withdrawing your last finger with a twisting motion. Pick up another truffle center and coat it with dark chocolate in the same manner; place the coated truffle on the prepared baking sheet. Dab the palm of one hand with more dark chocolate, touch the palms together a couple of times, and one at a time, coat two more truffle centers. Continue to seal-coat the remaining truffle centers in the same manner. Allow the coating to set for 15 minutes. Disregard any small cracks that may appear on the surface of some of the truffles; these cracks will be completely covered by a second coating of dark chocolate that is textured with crushed amaretti cookies.

Dip the seal-coated truffles

1. Meanwhile, line a second baking sheet with a silicone baking mat with the textured side facing up. Monitor the temperature and check the temper of the dark chocolate.

2. Stir ¾ cup of the amaretti cookies into the tempered chocolate. With your left hand, pick up a seal-coated truffle center and gently drop it on the surface of the tempered amaretti chocolate mixture. With the forefinger and second finger of your right hand, dip the center into the chocolate. (If you are left-handed, reverse the procedure.) Roll the center gently between your fingers on the surface of the chocolate to get an even coating that is textured with bits of the crushed amaretti. Lift up the coated center; move your fingers in a scissor-type motion to release any drips and gently scrape your fingertips along 1 edge of the bowl. Place the coated center onto the second silicone baking mat-lined baking sheet, withdrawing your last finger with a twisting motion. Make sure that the small flat bottom created by setting down the truffle with the first coating of chocolate is also the base when you set it down after the second coating of chocolate; otherwise your truffles will be oddly shaped.

3. As you continue to coat the truffles, gradually add the remaining ¼ cup of amaretti crumbs to maintain a nicely textured coating. When all the truffles have been dipped, let them set at room temperature for about 1 hour, or until they can be lifted from the baking mat easily and the undersides of the truffles are glossy.

4. Spread the remaining tempered dark chocolate into a even layer onto a waxed paper-lined baking sheet and refrigerate for 10 to 15 minutes, until hardened. Let the chocolate stand at room temperature for 1 hour and then break into pieces. Store in an airtight container for up to 1 month.

5. Store the Saronno Truffles in an airtight container for up to 5 days at cool room temperature, or in the refrigerator for up to 2 weeks. Allow the chocolates to come to room temperature in the storage container before serving.

Raspberry Jewels

The essence of real raspberries and raspberry eau de vie form the teasingly tart, welcome classic combination with dark chocolate. Inside the glistening jewel of dark chocolate is this tantalizing, satiny ganache.

•◆•

YIELD: 80 CHOCOLATES

Preparation: 3 hours, plus setting, infusing, and chilling times

Special Equipment (see mail order sources on page 302): Digital thermometer; heating pad with temperature control dial (such as the type used for backaches); 2 clear, rigid polycarbonate chocolate molds, each containing 40 geodesic dome-shaped mold cavities; ¾-inch natural-bristle flat pastry brush; flexible straight-edged steel baker's scraper; 8-inch offset metal cake spatula; cotton gloves.

Hollow Dark Chocolate Jewels
•◆•

2 pounds bittersweet chocolate couverture, such as Valrhona Caraque or Caraibe (see mail order sources on page 302)

Raspberry Essence
•◆•

1 cup unsweetened frozen raspberries
¼ cup plus 2 tablespoons granulated sugar

Raspberry Ganache
•◆•

½ vanilla bean, split in half lengthwise
⅔ cup plus 2 tablespoons heavy cream
10 ounces Swiss dark chocolate, such as Lindt*
2 teaspoons invert sugar, such as Nulomoline**
2 tablespoons unsalted butter
2 tablespoons raspberry eau de vie (clear raspberry brandy)

*Note: Use 3-ounce Lindt Swiss dark chocolate bars for preparing the ganache. This particular chocolate contains just the right proportion of cocoa solids and cocoa butter to enable the ganache filling to set up properly.

**Note: Invert sugar acts as a softener and helps to prolong the freshness of the ganache filling. See a mail order source for Nulomoline on page 305.

Prepare the hollow dark chocolate jewels

1. Temper the bittersweet chocolate. (Refer to the tempering instructions on page 27.)

2. Thoroughly clean the inside of each dome-shaped cavity in the 2 chocolate molds with a lint-free cloth or a cotton ball.

3. With a ¼-inch flat, dry pastry brush, using a quick dabbing brush stroke, paint the inside of each mold cavity with a thin, even layer of tempered chocolate. Try to work quickly and avoid creating air bubbles.

4. Using a flexible straight-edged steel baker's scraper, level the edges of the chocolate-lined cavities by scraping the surface of the chocolate mold. Hold the scraper at a slight angle and run the scraper over the length of mold. Let the chocolate set at room temperature for 3 to 10 minutes, until the chocolate starts to harden but is still slightly tacky. Leave the brush on the heating pad so the chocolate will not harden on the bristles.

5. Brush the inside of each mold cavity with a second thin layer of chocolate and level the edges with the baker's scraper. Allow the hollow chocolate jewels to harden at room temperature while preparing the ganache filling. Keep the tempered chocolate warm, stirring occasionally and monitoring the temperature with a digital thermometer. Do not let the chocolate get too hot (above 92°F), or it will go out of temper.

Prepare the raspberry essence

1. In a small, heavy saucepan, combine the frozen raspberries and sugar. Cook over medium-low heat, stirring constantly with a wooden spoon for 5 minutes, until the sugar is completely dissolved and the berries are soft. Raise the heat to medium and continue cooking for 5 minutes longer, or until the mixture becomes thick and syrupy.

2. Press the raspberry mixture through a fine sieve and discard the seeds. There should be ¼ cup of raspberry essence. (If the volume is less than ¼ cup, make up the difference by stirring in a little raspberry eau de vie.)

Make the raspberry ganache

1. Using the sharp tip of a small knife, scrape the paste of tiny black seeds from inside the split vanilla bean. Combine the vanilla bean paste, scraped vanilla pods, and heavy cream in a small, heavy saucepan. Bring the mixture to a gentle boil over medium heat. Remove from the heat; cover the pan and let the mixture infuse for 20 minutes.

2. Meanwhile, coarsely chop the chocolate and put it in a food processor fitted with the metal chopping blade. Process the chocolate for 15 to 20 seconds, until finely chopped. Remove the lid of the food processor and leave the chocolate in the work bowl.

3. Add the raspberry essence and the invert sugar to the cream mixture and reheat until it comes to a gentle boil. Take the pan off the heat. Using tongs, remove the vanilla bean pods and discard. Pour the hot cream over the chopped chocolate. Using a rubber spatula, press down on the chocolate so that it is completely submerged in the hot cream. Let the mixture stand for 1 minute.

4. Add the butter and replace the lid of the food processor. Pulse 4 to 6 times, until the mixture is creamy and smooth. Scrape down the sides of the work bowl, and add the raspberry eau de vie. Pulse 2 to 3 times until blended.

5. Scrape the raspberry ganache into a bowl. Check the temperature of the ganache; it should read between 80°F to 84°F. If it is warmer than 84°F, allow the ganache to cool before filling the chocolate jewels.

Fill the hollow dark chocolate jewels

1. Spoon half of the raspberry ganache on top of one end of one of the chocolate-lined molds. Using an 8-inch offset metal cake spatula, carefully spread the ganache over the surface of the mold and press a portion of it into each of the mold cavities. Try to avoid creating air pockets. Holding the spatula at a 90-degree angle, scrape the excess filling off the surface of the mold.

2. Fill the second chocolate mold with the remaining raspberry ganache. Refrigerate the filled molds for 15 to 25 minutes, until the ganache is firm. Then let the molds sit at room temperature for 15 minutes before sealing with tempered chocolate.

Seal the bottoms of the filled jewels

1. Check the temperature and fluidity of the tempered bittersweet chocolate. It needs to be between 89°F and 91°F, a little warmer than usual so that it is easy to seal the bottoms of the filled jewels with a thin covering of chocolate.

2. Rest one end of a jewel mold on the edge of the bowl of tempered chocolate. Pour about ⅓ cup of tempered chocolate over the top half of the mold. Using an 8-inch offset metal cake spatula and holding it at a slight angle, spread the chocolate in a thin, even layer over the filled jewels. Still holding the spatula at a slight angle, scrape the excess chocolate back into the bowl, leaving behind a thin layer of chocolate capping each jewel. Turn the mold around and seal the remaining jewels with chocolate. Repeat the process with the second jewel mold. Refrigerate the jewel molds for 1½ hours.

3. Pour the remaining tempered chocolate onto a waxed paper-lined baking sheet and refrigerate for 10 to 15 minutes, until firm. Let the chocolate stand at room temperature for 30 minutes. Break into pieces and store in a zip-lock bag.

Unmold the jewels

1. Pad a work surface with a folded kitchen towel or a double thickness of paper towels. Remove the jewel molds from the refrigerator. Holding a mold upright, check underneath the mold to see if the surface of the chocolate that is against the surface of each jewel cavity is uniformly frosty. If there are any clear spots, return the molds to the refrigerator and check again in about 30 minutes.

2. Carefully invert the molds one at time over the padded surface, and if necessary, gently tap each mold on the work surface to release the jewels. (If they do not release from the molds after a gentle tap, it could be one of three reasons: the chocolate has not set sufficiently; there is excess chocolate around the mold cavities; or the chocolate was not properly tempered. If the problem is excess chocolate, it will be obvious. You will see a layer of chocolate on the surface of the mold surrounding the jewel cavities. Tap the pan firmly on the work surface until the jewels release from the mold. If the jewels are still not releasing from the mold, this is an indication that the chocolate was not in temper when you brushed the mold cavities with chocolate to form the hollow chocolate jewels. If this should happen, do not attempt to scrape the chocolate from the molds. Simply heat the chocolate in each mold cavity with a portable hair dryer until it melts and wipe the entire mold clean. You will have to start over with newly tempered chocolate couverture.) Let the unmolded jewels stand at room temperature for 30 minutes.

3. Sometimes the unmolded jewels need to be trimmed, especially if there was excess chocolate on the mold during the unmolding process. Wearing cotton gloves and using a small, sharp knife, carefully trim around the base of each jewel. Store the Raspberry Jewels in an airtight container at cool room temperature for up to 5 days, or in the refrigerator for up to 2 weeks. Allow the chocolates to come to room temperature in the storage container before serving.

Pistachio Pyramids

Cherry brandy adds a fruity undernote to this combination of dark chocolate and pistachios; the creamy filling is encased in a sleek, dark chocolate pyramid. The dramatic shape is sure to add an intriguing visual flair to any candy tray. Use a pastry bag to fill the hollow chocolate pyramids to ensure that there are no air pockets.

• ◆ •

YIELD: 36 LARGE CHOCOLATES

Preparation: 3½ hours, plus infusing, chilling, freezing, and setting times

Special Equipment: (see mail order sources on page 302): Digital thermometer; heating pad with temperature control dial (such as the type used for backaches); 2 clear, rigid polycarbonate chocolate molds, each containing 18 ridged pyramid-shaped mold cavities; ¾-inch natural-bristle flat pastry brush; flexible straight-edged steel baker's scraper; 2 disposable pastry bags; ½-inch plain decorating tip (such as Ateco #6); 8-inch offset metal cake spatula; cotton gloves.

Pistachio Ganache
• ◆ •
1 vanilla bean, split in half lengthwise
1 cup plus 2 tablespoons heavy cream
⅓ cup plus 2 tablespoons pistachio paste (see mail sources on page 302)
12 ounces Swiss dark chocolate, such as Lindt*
2 teaspoons invert sugar, such as Nulomoline**
3 tablespoons kirsch
⅔ cup chopped, shelled, unsalted pistachio nuts

Hollow Dark Chocolate Pyramids
• ◆ •
2¼ pounds bittersweet chocolate couverture, such as Valrhona Caraque
or Caraibe (see mail order sources on page 302)

*Note: Use 3-ounce Lindt Swiss dark chocolate bars for preparing the ganache. This particular chocolate contains just the right proportion of cocoa solids and cocoa butter to enable the ganache filling to set up properly.

**Note: Invert sugar acts as a softener and helps to prolong the freshness of the ganache filling. See a mail order source for Nulomoline on page 305.

Make the pistachio ganache

1. Using the sharp tip of a small knife, scrape the paste of tiny black seeds from inside the split vanilla bean. Combine the vanilla bean paste, heavy cream, and pistachio paste in a small, heavy saucepan. Add the scraped pods to the cream. While stirring constantly, slowly heat the mixture over medium heat, until the pistachio paste is completely dissolved and the mixture comes to a gentle boil. Remove from the heat. Cover with a lid and allow the mixture to infuse for 30 minutes.

2. Meanwhile, coarsely chop the chocolate and put it in a food processor fitted with the metal chopping blade. Process for 15 to 20 seconds, until finely chopped. Remove the lid of the food processor and leave the chocolate in the work bowl.

3. Add the invert sugar to the pistachio-cream mixture. Heat the mixture until it comes to a gentle boil. Using tongs, remove the vanilla bean pods and discard. Pour the hot cream over the chopped chocolate. Using a rubber spatula, press down on the chocolate so that it is completely submerged in the hot cream. Let the mixture stand for 1 minute.

4. Replace the lid of the food processor. Pulse 4 to 6 times, until the mixture is creamy and smooth. Scrape down the sides of the work bowl, and add the kirsch. Pulse 2 to 3 times until blended.

5. Scrape the ganache onto a baking sheet, letting it spread into a thin layer. Cover the surface with plastic wrap and freeze for at least 1 hour, until firm.

Prepare the hollow dark chocolate pyramids

1. Temper the bittersweet chocolate. (Refer to the tempering instructions on page 27.)

2. Thoroughly clean the inside of each pyramid cavity in the 2 chocolate molds with a lint-free cloth or a cotton ball.

3. With a ¼-inch flat, dry pastry brush, using a quick, dabbing brush stroke, paint the inside of each mold cavity with a thin, even layer of tempered chocolate. Try to work quickly and avoid creating any air bubbles.

4. Using a flexible straight-edged steel baker's scraper, level the edges of the chocolate-lined cavities by scraping the surface of the chocolate mold. Hold the scraper at a slight angle and run the scraper over the length of mold. Let the chocolate set at room temperature for 3 to 10 minutes, until the chocolate starts to harden but is still slightly tacky. Leave the brush on the heating pad so that the chocolate will not harden on the bristles.

5. Brush the inside of each pyramid cavity with a second thin layer of chocolate and level the edges with the baker's scraper. Allow the hollow chocolate shells to harden at room temperature while preparing the ganache filling. Keep the tempered chocolate warm, stirring occasionally and monitoring the temperature with a thermometer. Do not let the chocolate get too hot (above 92°F), or it will go out of temper.

Whip the pistachio ganache

1. Cut the pointed end off a disposable pastry bag and insert a ½-inch plain decorating tip (such as Ateco #6). Twist the portion of the pastry bag that is just above the wider opening of the decorating tip. Tuck this twisted portion of the bag into the wider opening of the tip. (This will prevent the whipped ganache from leaking out the end of the tip before you are ready to pipe.) Place the bag into a 2-cup glass measuring cup. Turn down the top 2 to 3 inches of the pastry bag, forming a cuff around the outside of the measuring cup. (The cup will support the bag as you fill it with the whipped ganache.)

2. Remove the plastic wrap from the chilled ganache. Gently warm the bottom of the baking sheet by passing it back and forth a few times over a gas flame or electric range top set on medium. Heat the pan only until the ganache starts to melt slightly so that it can be easily removed from the pan. Using a rubber spatula, scrape half (about 1 cup) of the ganache into the bowl of a heavy-duty electric mixer.

3. Set the bowl over another bowl of hot, not simmering water (the water must touch the bottom of the bowl) for 30 seconds to 2 minutes, stirring constantly with a rubber spatula until the ganache reads 65°F on a digital thermometer and has softened to the consistency of handmade mayonnaise. Be careful not to overheat the ganache. If the ganache becomes warmer than 65°F, place the bowl over a bowl of ice water for 2 to 4 seconds. Stir the ganache with a rubber spatula, just until it starts to thicken. Remove the bowl from the ice water.

4. Using the wire whip attachment, whip the softened ganache at medium speed for 30 seconds to 2 minutes, or until it lightens in color and forms soft peaks. It should have the texture of a fluffy chocolate buttercream frosting. (If the whipped ganache becomes too firm and appears grainy, replace the bowl over the hot water for 2 to 4 seconds, and stir gently until it softens enough to be rewhipped. Conversely, if the ganache is too soft and will not form soft peaks, place it over the bowl of ice water and stir for 2 to 4 seconds, until it just starts to thicken. Continue whipping until the ganache reaches the proper consistency.) Quickly fold in ⅓ cup of the chopped pistachio nuts.

Fill the hollow chocolate pyramids

1. Immediately scrape the ganache into the prepared pastry bag. Work quickly as the ganache will start to set up shortly after it is whipped. Insert the tip of the pastry bag into a hollow chocolate pyramid and pipe the ganache until it is almost overflowing the top of the mold cavity. Fill the remaining chocolate pyramids in the same manner.

2. Using an 8-inch offset metal cake spatula, carefully spread the ganache over the surface of the mold so that the ganache is level with the top of each mold cavity. Holding the spatula at a 90-degree angle, scrape the excess filling off the surface of the mold.

3. Using the remaining chilled ganache, repeat step 4 of whipping the pistachio ganache and steps 1 and 2 of filling the hollow chocolate pyramids, filling the second chocolate mold. (Stir the excess ganache from the first batch of filling into the second batch of softened ganache before whipping.) Refrigerate the filled molds for 15 to 25 minutes, until the ganache is firm. Then let the molds sit at room temperature for 15 minutes before sealing with tempered chocolate.

Seal the bottoms of the filled pyramids

1. Check the temperature and fluidity of the tempered bittersweet chocolate. It needs to be between 89°F and 91°F—a little warmer than usual—so that it is easy to seal the bottoms of the filled mold cavities with a thin covering of chocolate.

2. Rest one end of a chocolate mold on the edge of the bowl of tempered chocolate. Pour about ⅓ cup of tempered chocolate over the top half of the mold. Using an 8-inch offset metal cake spatula and holding it at a slight angle, spread the chocolate in a thin, even layer over the filled chocolate shells. Still holding the spatula at a slight angle, scrape the excess chocolate back into the bowl, leaving behind a thin layer of chocolate capping each mold cavity. Turn the mold around and seal the remaining chocolate shells with tempered chocolate. Repeat the process with the second chocolate mold. Refrigerate the chocolate molds for 2 hours.

3. Pour the remaining tempered chocolate onto a waxed paper-lined baking sheet and refrigerate for 10 to 15 minutes, until firm. Let the chocolate stand at room temperature for 30 minutes. Break into pieces and store in a zip-lock bag.

Unmold the chocolates

1. Pad a work surface with a folded kitchen towel or a double thickness of paper towels. Remove the chocolate molds from the refrigerator. Holding a mold upright, check underneath the mold to see if the surface of the chocolate that is against the surface of each pyramid mold cavity is uniformly frosty. If there are any clear spots, return the chocolate molds to the refrigerator and check again in about 30 minutes.

2. Carefully invert the molds, one at time over the padded surface, and if necessary gently tap each mold on the work surface to release the pyramids. (If they do not release from the molds after a gentle tap, it could be one of three reasons: the chocolate has not set sufficiently; there is excess chocolate around the mold cavities; or the chocolate was not properly tempered. If the problem is excess chocolate, it will be obvious. You will see a layer of chocolate on the surface of the mold surrounding the pyramid cavities. Tap the pan firmly on the work surface until the pyramids release from the mold. If the pyramids are still not releasing from the mold, this is an indication that the chocolate was not in temper when you brushed the mold cavities with chocolate to form the hollow chocolate pyramids. If this should happen, do not attempt to scrape the chocolate from the molds. Simply heat the chocolate in each mold cavity with a portable hair dryer until it melts and wipe the entire mold clean. You will have to start over with newly tempered chocolate couverture.) Let the unmolded pyramids come to room temperature for 30 minutes.

3. Sometimes the unmolded chocolates need to be trimmed, especially if there was excess chocolate on the mold during the unmolding process. Wearing cotton gloves and using a small, sharp knife, carefully trim around the base of each pyramid. Store the Pistachio Pyramids in an airtight container at cool room temperature for up to 5 days, or in the refrigerator for up to 2 weeks. Allow the chocolates to come to room temperature in the storage container before serving.

Cherry Vanilla Hearts

Vanilla is the perfect flavor canvas on which to paint fruit highlights, as evidenced by this cherry vanilla masterwork. Inside a dark chocolate heart lies a creamy ganache flavored with tart dried cherries that have been soaked in Kijafa, a Danish cherry wine, and the essence of Tahitian vanilla.

•◆•

YIELD: 42 HEARTS

Preparation: 3 hours, plus soaking, infusing, chilling, and setting times. Allow time for the macerated cherries to soak overnight.

Special Equipment: (see mail order sources on page 302): Digital thermometer; heating pad with temperature control dial (such as the type used for backaches); 2 clear, rigid polycarbonate chocolate molds, each containing 21 heart-shaped mold cavities; ¾-inch natural-bristle flat pastry brush; flexible straight-edged steel baker's scraper; 8-inch offset metal cake spatula; cotton gloves.

Macerated Cherries
•◆•
½ cup dried tart cherries
½ cup Kijafa (Danish cherry wine)

Hollow Dark Chocolate Hearts
•◆•
1¾ pounds bittersweet chocolate couverture, such as Valrhona Caraque or Caraibe (see mail order sources on page 302)

Cherry Vanilla Ganache
•◆•
1 vanilla bean, split in half lengthwise
¾ cup heavy cream
10 ounces Swiss dark chocolate, such as Lindt*
1½ teaspoons invert sugar, such as Nulomoline**
1 tablespoon unsalted butter, softened

Decoration
•◆•
One 3⅛-inch sheet of 23-karat edible patent gold leaf
(see mail order sources on page 302)

*Note: Use 3-ounce Lindt Swiss dark chocolate bars for preparing the ganache. This particular chocolate contains just the right proportion of cocoa solids and cocoa butter to enable the ganache filling to set up properly.

**Note: Invert sugar acts as a softener and helps to prolong the freshness of the ganache filling. See a mail order source for Nulomoline on page 305.

THE NIGHT BEFORE

Macerate the cherries

1. Combine the dried cherries and cherry wine in a small saucepan and bring to a gentle simmer over low heat. Cover the pan and remove from the heat. Let the cherries infuse in the wine overnight at room temperature.

THE NEXT DAY

Prepare the hollow dark chocolate hearts

1. Temper the bittersweet chocolate. (Refer to the tempering instructions on page 27.)

2. Thoroughly clean the inside of each heart-shaped cavity in the 2 chocolate molds with a lint-free cloth or a cotton ball.

3. With a ¾-inch flat, dry pastry brush, using a quick dabbing brush stroke, paint the inside of each mold cavity with a thin, even layer of tempered chocolate. Try to work quickly and avoid creating air bubbles.

4. Using a flexible straight-edged steel baker's scraper, level the edges of the chocolate-lined cavities by scraping the surface of the chocolate mold. Hold the scraper at a slight angle and run it over the length of mold. Let the chocolate set at room temperature for 3 to 10 minutes, until the chocolate starts to harden but is still tacky. Leave the brush on the heating pad so that the chocolate will not harden on the bristles.

5. Brush the inside of each heart-shaped cavity with a second thin layer of chocolate and level the edges with the baker's scraper. Allow the hollow chocolate hearts to harden at room temperature while preparing the ganache filling. Keep the tempered chocolate warm, stirring occasionally and monitoring the temperature with a digital thermometer. Do not let the chocolate get too hot (above 92°F), or it will go out of temper.

Make the cherry vanilla ganache

1. Using the sharp tip of a small knife, scrape the paste of tiny black seeds from inside the split vanilla bean. Combine the vanilla bean paste and heavy cream in a small, heavy saucepan. Add the scraped pods to the cream. Bring the mixture to a gentle boil over medium heat. Remove from the heat; cover the pan and let the mixture infuse for 30 minutes.

2. Meanwhile, coarsely chop the chocolate and put it in a food processor fitted with the metal chopping blade. Process the chocolate for 30 to 40 seconds, until finely chopped. Remove the lid of the food processor and leave the chocolate in the work bowl.

3. Add the invert sugar to the cream mixture and reheat until it comes to a gentle boil. Take the pan off the heat. Using tongs, remove the vanilla bean pods and discard. Pour the hot cream over the chopped chocolate. Using a rubber spatula, press down on the chocolate so that it is completely submerged in the hot cream. Let the mixture stand for 1 minute.

4. Add the butter and replace the lid of the food processor. Pulse 4 to 6 times, until the mixture is creamy and smooth. Scrape down the sides of the work bowl, and add the macerated tart cherries along with any remaining cherry wine not soaked up by the cherries. Pulse the mixture 2 to 4 times, just until the cherries are coarsely chopped and the mixture is blended.

5. Scrape the ganache into a bowl. Check the temperature of the ganache; it should read between 80°F to 84°F. If it is warmer than 84°F, allow the ganache to cool before filling the chocolate hearts.

Fill the hollow dark chocolate hearts

1. Spoon half of the cherry vanilla ganache on top of one end of one of the chocolate-lined molds. Using an 8-inch offset metal cake spatula, carefully spread the ganache over the surface of the mold and press a portion of it into each of the mold cavities. Try to avoid creating air pockets. Holding the spatula at a 90-degree angle, scrape the excess filling off the surface of the mold. Press any stray bits of cherry back into place.

2. Fill the second chocolate mold with the remaining cherry vanilla ganache. Refrigerate the filled molds for 15 to 25 minutes, until the ganache is firm. Then let the molds sit at room temperature for 15 minutes before sealing with tempered chocolate.

Seal the bottoms of the filled hearts

1. Check the temperature and fluidity of the tempered bittersweet chocolate. It needs to be between 89°F and 91°F—a little warmer than usual—so that it is easy to seal the bottoms of the heart molds with a thin covering of chocolate.

2. Rest one end of a heart mold on the edge of the bowl of tempered chocolate. Pour about ⅓ cup of tempered chocolate over the top half of the mold. Using an 8-inch offset metal cake spatula and holding it at a slight angle, spread the chocolate in a thin, even layer over the filled hearts. Still holding the spatula at a slight angle, scrape the excess chocolate back into the bowl, leaving behind a thin layer of chocolate capping each heart. Turn the mold around and seal the remaining hearts with chocolate. Repeat the process with the second heart mold. Refrigerate the heart molds for about 1 hour.

3. Pour the remaining tempered chocolate onto a waxed paper-lined baking sheet and refrigerate for 10 to 15 minutes, until firm. Let the chocolate stand at room temperature for 30 minutes. Break into pieces and store in a zip-lock bag.

Unmold the hearts

1. Pad a work surface with a folded kitchen towel or a double thickness of paper towels. Remove one of the heart molds from the refrigerator. Holding a mold upright, check underneath the mold to see if the surface of the chocolate that is against the surface of each heart cavity is uniformly frosty. If there are any clear spots return the molds to the refrigerator and check again in about 30 minutes.

2. Carefully invert the molds, one at a time over the padded surface, and if necessary, gently tap each mold on the work surface to release the hearts. (If they do not release from the molds after a gentle tap, it could be one of three reasons: the chocolate has not set sufficiently; there is excess chocolate around the mold cavities; or the chocolate was not properly tempered. If the problem is excess chocolate, it will be obvious. You will see a layer of chocolate on the surface of the mold surrounding the heart mold cavities. Tap the pan firmly on the work surface until the hearts release from the mold. If the hearts are still not releasing from the mold, this is an indication that the chocolate was not in temper when you brushed the mold cavities with chocolate to form the hollow chocolate hearts. If this should happen, do not attempt to scrape the chocolate from the molds. Simply heat the chocolate in each mold cavity with a portable hair dryer until it melts and wipe the entire mold clean. You will have to start over with newly tempered chocolate couverture.) Let the unmolded hearts come to room temperature for 30 minutes.

3. Sometimes the unmolded hearts need to be trimmed, especially if there was excess chocolate on the mold during the unmolding process. Wearing cotton gloves and using a small, sharp knife, carefully trim around the base of each heart.

Decorate the hearts

1. Using the tip of a cotton swab, gently rub the paper side of the gold sheet pressing a small amount of gold leaf onto the top center of each heart. Store the Cherry Vanilla Hearts in an airtight container at cool room temperature for up to 5 days, or in the refrigerator for up to 2 weeks. Allow the chocolates to come to room temperature in the storage container before serving.

Caramel Rum Kisses

We bring a hint of island flavor to an elegant European candy: A whipped mousse ganache filling flavored with caramel and rum is piped into kiss shapes, sitting on bittersweet chocolate bases. The kiss is coated in a dark chocolate sheath and decorated with a dot of milk chocolate. The whipped mousse ganache is piped onto the bases so that the dipping fork will have a more solid purchase during the chocolate coating process—the fork will stick if applied to the ganache.

•◆•

YIELD: ABOUT 60 KISSES

Preparation: 4 hours, plus cooling, infusing, freezing, chilling, and setting times.

Special Equipment: (see mail order sources page 302): Flat metal cake spatula; heating pad with temperature control dial (such as the type used for backaches); digital thermometer; closed star decorating tip (such as Ateco #2); ⅜-inch plain decorating tip (such as Ateco #8); 2 silicone baking mats; disposable pastry bags; 3-pronged chocolate dipping fork; cotton gloves.

Caramel Rum Mousse Ganache
•◆•

½ cup sifted granulated sugar
¼ teaspoon lemon juice
1 vanilla bean, split in half lengthwise
¾ cup plus 2 tablespoons heavy cream
10 ounces Swiss dark chocolate, such as Lindt*
2 teaspoons invert sugar, such as Nulomoline**
2 tablespoons unsalted butter, softened
2 tablespoons dark rum, such as Myers'

Round Chocolate Bases
•◆•

3 ounces bittersweet chocolate couverture, such as Valrhona Caraque
or Caraibe (see mail order sources on page 302)

Dark Chocolate Coating
•◆•

1¼ pounds bittersweet chocolate couverture, such as Valrhona Caraque
or Caraibe (see mail order sources on page 302)

Decoration
•◆•

4 ounces milk chocolate couverture, such as Valrhona Lactée
(see mail order sources on page 302)

**Note: Use 3-ounce Lindt Swiss dark chocolate bars for preparing the ganache.
This particular chocolate contains just the right proportion of cocoa solids and
cocoa butter to enable the whipped ganache to set up properly.*

***Note: Invert sugar acts as a softener and helps to prolong the freshness of the
ganache filling. See a mail order source for Nulomoline on page 305.*

Prepare the caramel rum mousse ganache

1. Lightly oil a heavy baking sheet and a flat metal cake spatula.

2. In a small, nonstick saucepan or skillet, combine the sugar and lemon juice. Stir with a wooden spoon until the sugar is evenly moistened. Cook over medium heat, swirling the pan frequently, until the mixture liquefies and turns to an amber-colored caramel.

3. Pour the hot caramel onto the prepared baking sheet. Set the baking sheet on a cooling rack and allow the caramel to cool for 3 minutes.

4. Using the oiled cake spatula, carefully loosen the undersides of the caramel to prevent it from sticking to the baking sheet. Let the caramel cool until it hardens completely.

5. Coarsely chop the caramel and put it into a food processor fitted with the metal chopping blade. Process for 15 to 20 seconds, until it is finely ground. Scrape the caramel powder into a small, heavy saucepan.

6. Using the tip of a small knife, remove the paste of tiny black seeds from inside the split vanilla bean. Add the scraped vanilla pod and seeds to the saucepan. Add the heavy cream and stir with a wooden spoon until blended. Cook over medium heat, stirring frequently until the caramel powder is completely dissolved and the mixture is scalding hot. Remove the pan from the heat and allow the mixture to infuse for 30 minutes.

7. Meanwhile, coarsely chop the dark chocolate. Put the chocolate in the food processor with the metal chopping blade. Process for 15 to 20 seconds, until finely chopped. Remove the lid of the food processor and leave the chocolate in the work bowl.

8. Add the invert sugar to the caramel-cream mixture and reheat, stirring frequently until the mixture comes to a gentle boil. Using tongs, remove the vanilla bean halves from the hot cream mixture. Pour the hot cream over the chopped chocolate in the food processor workbowl. With a rubber spatula, press down on the chocolate so that it is almost completely submerged in the hot cream. Let the mixture stand for 30 seconds. Replace the lid of the food processor and pulse 6 to 8 times, until the mixture is creamy. Scrape down the sides of the work bowl, and add the butter and rum. Pulse 4 to 6 more times, until smooth. Scrape the ganache onto a baking sheet, letting it spread into a thin layer. Cover the surface with plastic wrap and freeze for at least 1 hour, until firm.

Make the round chocolate bases

1. Temper the bittersweet chocolate using the instructions on page 27. The working temperature for making the chocolate bases should be 91°F to 92°F, slightly higher than the normal dipping temperature. (The process of spreading the chocolate into a thin layer will continue to temper the chocolate.)

2. Place a 12-by-16-inch rectangle of baking parchment or waxed paper on a flat Formica or wood work surface, with the long sides lying parallel in front of you. (Do not lay paper on a marble, granite, or metal countertop, as the chocolate will set up too quickly on any of these work surfaces.)

3. Pour the tempered chocolate in a thin line about 8 inches long down the center of the paper. Using an 8-inch offset metal cake spatula, quickly spread the chocolate into a paper-thin rectangle, about ⅟₃₂-inch thick, leaving about a ¼-inch border around the edge of the paper. Continue moving the spatula back and forth over the chocolate rectangle for 10 to 20 seconds, or until the chocolate starts to feel tacky and begins to lose its sheen.

4. As the chocolate starts to set, press the ⅞-inch round open end of an open star decorating tip (such as Ateco #2) into the chocolate rectangle, leaving about ⅛ inch of space between each circle. Continue using the tip as a cutter, until you have pressed 60 to 70 ⅞-inch rounds. Leave the chocolate rounds attached to the paper. Cover the rounds with a sheet of baking parchment or waxed paper and weight with a heavy baking sheet. (The weight will prevent the chocolate rounds from curling up as the chocolate contracts while it hardens.) Leave the chocolate rounds under the baking sheet until ready to pipe the centers.

Whip the caramel rum mousse ganache

1. Cut the pointed end off a disposable pastry bag and insert a ⅜-inch plain decorating tip (such as Ateco #8). Twist the portion of the pastry bag that is just above the wider opening of the decorating tip. Tuck this twisted portion of the bag into the wider opening of the tip. (This will prevent the whipped ganache from leaking out the end of the tip before you are ready to pipe.) Place the bag into a 2-cup glass measuring cup. Turn down the top 2 to 3 inches of the pastry bag forming a cuff around the outside of the measuring cup. (The cup will support the bag as you fill it with the whipped ganache.)

2. Remove the plastic wrap from the chilled ganache. Gently warm the bottom of the baking sheet by passing it back and forth a few times over a gas flame or electric range top set on medium. Heat the pan only until the ganache starts to melt slightly so that it can be easily removed from the pan. Using a rubber spatula, scrape half (about 1 cup) of the ganache into the bowl of a heavy-duty electric mixer.

3. Set the bowl over another bowl of hot, not simmering water (the water must touch the bottom of the bowl) for 30 seconds to 2 minutes, stirring constantly with a rubber spatula until the ganache reads 65°F on a digital thermometer and has softened to the consistency of homemade mayonnaise. Be careful not to overheat the ganache. If the ganache becomes warmer than 65°F, place the bowl over a bowl of ice water for 2 to 4 seconds. Stir the ganache with a rubber spatula, just until it starts to thicken. Remove the bowl from the ice water.

4. Using the wire whip attachment, whip the softened ganache at medium speed for 30 seconds to 2 minutes, or until it lightens in color and forms soft peaks. It should have the texture of a fluffy chocolate buttercream frosting with a good piping consistency. If the whipped ganache becomes too firm and appears grainy, replace the bowl over the hot water for 2 to 4 seconds, and stir gently until it softens enough to be rewhipped. Conversely, if the ganache is too soft and will not form soft peaks, place it over the bowl of ice water and stir for 2 to 4 seconds, until it just starts to thicken. Continue whipping until the ganache reaches the proper consistency.

Pipe the whipped ganache

1. Immediately scrape the ganache into the prepared pastry bag. Work quickly as the ganache will start to set up shortly after it is whipped. Remove the baking sheet and paper covering the sheet of chocolate rounds. Hold the bag in a perpendicular position, barely touching the middle of a round chocolate base. Pipe the ganache into a 1-inch mound (slightly larger than the ⅞-inch chocolate base) with a slightly rounded bottom and pointed peak. If the ganache is the correct consistency, it will pipe easily and hold its shape. Quickly finish piping the ganache onto the remaining bases.

2. Repeat steps 3 and 4 of whipping the caramel rum mousse ganache, and step 1 of piping the whipped ganache, using the remaining chilled ganache. Loosely cover the piped caramel ganache centers with plastic wrap and refrigerate for 15 to 25 minutes, until firm.

3. Individually transfer the chilled centers (still attached to their chocolate bases) to a paper-lined baking sheet. The leftover chocolate trimmings can be saved for another use. Cover the centers loosely with a sheet of waxed paper or baking parchment and let them stand at room temperature for 1 hour before coating.

Coat the kisses

1. Temper the dark chocolate using one of the tempering methods on page 27. Put the tempered chocolate into a 1-quart glass bowl and set it on a heating pad set to low to maintain the correct coating temperature. Line 2 baking sheets with 2 silicone baking mats with the textured side facing up. Arrange the work area so that the uncoated centers are to the left of the tempered chocolate, with the silicone baking mat-covered baking sheet on the right. Reverse these positions if you are left-handed.

2. Gently drop a kiss center (still attached to its chocolate base) with the pointed peak facing up, onto the surface of the melted chocolate. Slide the prongs of a 3-pronged dipping fork underneath the center and at an angle, gently submerge the center into the chocolate until it is completely coated. Lift the center out of the chocolate and tilt the fork slightly so that the center slips about an eighth of the way off the end of the fork. Level the fork and gently tap the bottom of the fork in a forward circular motion, barely touching the surface of the chocolate. Tap several times until very little chocolate is being pulled from the bottom of the center.

3. Lift the fork away from the surface of the chocolate and lightly touch the edge of the bowl with the bottom of the fork. Hold the fork at a slight angle and follow the curve of the bowl with it to remove any excess chocolate that is left on the bottom of the fork.

4. Place the coated kiss on the upper right-hand corner of the silicone baking mat and pull the fork away with a quick but gentle motion. Coat the remaining kiss centers in the same manner, setting them on the silicone baking mats in straight rows.

Decorate the kisses

1. Temper the milk chocolate using the quick tempering instructions on page 30. Make a small paper cone with a tiny opening at the tip. Fill the cone with some of the tempered milk chocolate. Decorate the pointed tip of each kiss with a tiny dot of milk chocolate. Let the kisses set for at least 1 hour before removing them from the baking mats.

2. Spread the remaining tempered dark chocolate into a even layer onto a waxed paper-lined baking sheet and refrigerate for 10 to 15 minutes, until hardened. Let the chocolate stand at room temperature for 30 minutes. Break into pieces and store in a ziplock bag.

3. Store the Caramel Rum Kisses in an airtight container for up to 5 days at room temperature, or in the refrigerator for up to two weeks. Allow the chocolates to come to room temperature in the storage container before serving.

Ginger Bites

The spicy zing of ginger creates intriguing flavor sparks when combined with dark chocolate. Here, finely chopped crystallized ginger is added to dark chocolate ganache, and ginger cream rounds out the memorable chocolate experience. Bottomless rectangular flan forms are normally used for tarts, but they are also useful tools in the candy kitchen. They are perfect for molding many types of ganache fillings and other confections, and the rectangular shape is easy to handle.

•◆•

YIELD: 60 SQUARES

Preparation: 3 hours, plus setting, infusing, and chilling times. Allow time for the fresh ginger cream to infuse overnight.

Special Equipment (see list of mail order sources on page 302): Two 4⅛-by-14¼-inch stainless steel, open-bottomed flan forms (for molding the ginger ganache); digital thermometer; heating pad with temperature control dial (such as the type used for backaches); 4½-inch offset metal cake spatula; 8-inch offset metal cake spatula; thin-bladed slicing knife; 2 silicone baking mats; 3-pronged chocolate dipping fork; cotton gloves.

Ginger Cream
•◆•
1¼ cups heavy cream
¼ cup peeled, finely chopped fresh ginger

Ginger Ganache
•◆•
9 large slices crystallized ginger
12 ounces Swiss dark chocolate, such as Lindt*
2 teaspoons invert sugar, such as Nulomoline**
2 tablespoons unsalted butter, softened

Dark Chocolate Coating
•◆•
1¾ pounds bittersweet chocolate couverture, such as Valrhona Caraque
(see mail order sources on page 302)

*Note: Use 3-ounce Lindt Swiss dark chocolate bars for preparing the ganache. This particular chocolate contains just the right proportion of cocoa solids and cocoa butter to enable the ganache to set up properly.

**Note: Invert sugar acts as a softener and helps to prolong the freshness of the ganache filling. See a mail order source for Nulomoline on page 305.

THE NIGHT BEFORE

Prepare the ginger cream

1. In a small saucepan, combine the heavy cream and ginger. Bring to a gentle boil, stirring often. Remove from the heat and pour the mixture into a glass measuring cup. Cool for 20 minutes, stirring occasionally. Cover with plastic wrap and refrigerate 12 hours or overnight.

THE NEXT DAY

Make the ginger ganache

1. Tear off a 16-inch-long piece of aluminum foil. Fold it in half lengthwise and slit it in half along the fold with a sharp knife. Line a heavy, flat baking sheet with the 2 strips of aluminum foil. Set a 4⅜-by-14¾-inch rectangular flan form on top of each of the foil strips. Create a foil bottom for each flan form by tightly folding the excess foil up to cover the 4 outer sides of each flan form.

2. Rinse the crystallized candied ginger slices under warm water to remove the sugar coating. Pat the slices dry with a paper towel and finely chop them.

3. In a food processor fitted with the metal chopping blade, process the dark chocolate until finely chopped.

4. Scrape the chilled cream mixture into a small saucepan and add the invert sugar. Bring the mixture to a gentle boil, stirring often. Immediately pour the hot cream through a fine-meshed sieve over the chopped chocolate. Using a spoon, press down on the chopped ginger to extract every bit of the infused cream. With a rubber spatula, make sure that dark chocolate is completely submerged in the hot cream. Let the mixture stand 1 minute.

5. Add the softened butter and replace the lid of the food processor. Pulse 6 to 8 times, until the mixture is creamy. Scrape down the sides of the work bowl; add the chopped crystallized ginger and pulse 2 to 3 times, just until blended.

6. Divide the ginger ganache evenly between the 2 prepared flan forms (about 1 cup plus 2 tablespoons for each form). Using a small, offset metal cake spatula, spread the ganache into an even layer. Carefully cover the surface of the ganache with plastic wrap. Using a plastic scraper, smooth the plastic wrap so that it is flush with the surface of the filling. Refrigerate for 1 hour, or until firm.

Coat the ganache rectangles

1. Temper the bittersweet chocolate using one of the tempering methods on page 27. Put the tempered chocolate into a 1-quart glass bowl and set it on a heating pad set to low to maintain the correct coating temperature.

2. Remove the baking sheet with the ganache rectangles from the refrigerator and peel off the plastic wrap. Heat the blade of a small, sharp knife over a gas flame or under hot running water (wipe the blade dry) and quickly cut around the inside edges of one of the flan forms to loosen the ganache filling. Fold down the foil and remove the flan form. With the tip of the knife, trim the excess foil around the base of the ganache rectangle and discard. Trim the slight ridge on the top edge of the ganache rectangle so that the surface of the rectangle is level. Repeat the unmolding and trimming process with the second flan form.

3. Cut 4 pieces of cardboard that measure the size of the unmolded ganache rectangles and cover with aluminum foil. Slip a long metal cake spatula underneath one of the ganache rectangles (the foil is still attached to the bottom of the rectangle) and transfer it to one of the foil-covered pieces of cardboard. Repeat with the second ganache rectangle.

4. Check the temperature and fluidity of the tempered dark chocolate. It needs to be between 90°F and 92°F—a little warmer than usual—so that it is very fluid, making it easy to cover the surface of the ganache rectangles with a thin layer of chocolate. Carefully adjust the temperature of the tempered bittersweet chocolate if necessary.

5. Lift up one of the ganache rectangles (still on the cardboard) and holding the bottom with the palm of one hand, rest one end of the rectangle on the edge of the bowl of tempered chocolate. Spoon a scant ¼ cup of tempered chocolate over the top of the front half of the ganache rectangle. Using an 8-inch offset metal cake spatula and holding it at a slight angle, spread the chocolate in a tissue-thin (almost see-through), even layer over the front half of the rectangle. Still holding the spatula at a slight angle, scrape the excess chocolate back into the bowl. Turn the ganache rectangle around and cover the remaining top half with a tissue thin layer of tempered chocolate. Repeat the process with the second ganache rectangle.

6. Let the chocolate-coated rectangles set at room temperature for 3 to 5 minutes, until they are no longer wet.

7. Place the third foil-covered cardboard rectangle over the top of one of the chocolate-coated ganache rectangles and invert. Remove the foil-covered cardboard and carefully peel off the foil that is adhered to the ganache filling. (If for some reason you have trouble removing the foil because the ganache has softened, simply chill the rectangles for 5 to 10 minutes, and then try again.) Repeat with the second chocolate-coated ganache rectangle.

8. Coat the second side of each of the ganache rectangles with a tissue-thin layer of tempered chocolate using the same method as described above. Allow the chocolate to set at room temperature for 3 to 5 minutes, until no longer wet. The ganache filling is now sandwiched between 2 thin layers of bittersweet chocolate. Keep the chocolate in temper while cutting the ganache rectangles into squares.

Cut the bittersweet chocolate-covered ganache rectangles into squares

1. Using a long metal cake spatula or knife, transfer one of the rectangles to a cutting board. Heat a long, thin-bladed knife under hot running water and wipe dry. Carefully trim ⅛ inch from all 4 edges of the rectangle. Rinse the knife under hot water and wipe the knife dry between each cut. Continue to cut the trimmed rectangle into 1¼-inch strips. Cut each strip into three 1¼-inch squares. Transfer the cut squares to a baking sheet, with the flat, smooth surface of each square facing up. Trim and cut the remaining ganache rectangle into 1¼-inch squares and transfer them to the baking sheet.

Dip the ganache squares in bittersweet chocolate

1. Line 2 baking sheets with silicone baking mats with the textured side facing up. Arrange your work area so that the baking sheet of ganache squares is to the left of the tempered chocolate, with a silicone baking mat-covered baking sheet on the right. Reverse these positions if you are left-handed.

2. Pick up a ganache square with your left hand and gently drop it on the surface of the chocolate. Slide the prongs of a 3-pronged chocolate dipping fork underneath the center and at an angle, and gently submerge the center into the chocolate until it is completely coated. Tilt the fork slightly so that the center slips about an eighth of the way off the end of the fork. Level the fork and gently tap the bottom of the fork in a forward circular motion, barely touching the surface of the chocolate. Tap several times until very little chocolate is being pulled from the bottom of the square.

3. Lift the fork away from the surface of the chocolate and lightly touch the edge of the bowl with the bottom of the fork. Hold the fork at slight angle and follow the curve of the bowl with it to remove any excess chocolate that is left on the bottom of the fork.

4. Place the coated square on the upper right-hand corner of the silicone baking mat and pull the fork away with a quick but gentle motion. Dip a second ganache square into the chocolate and set it on the silicone baking mat. Mark the top of the first coated ganache square by turning the fork on its side and diagonally gently touching the top of the square with just one prong of the dipping fork. Lift the fork with a slightly forward motion and then pull it back towards you to remove the fork. This motion will create a mark or "string" line of chocolate diagonally crossing the top of the coated ganache square. Continue to alternate the dipping and the marking process until all the ganache centers have been coated. Let the squares set at room temperature for at least 1 hour, or until they can be lifted from the mats easily and the undersides are glossy.

5. Spread the remaining tempered chocolate into a even layer onto a waxed paper-lined baking sheet and refrigerate for 10 to 15 minutes, until hardened. Let the chocolate stand at room temperature for 30 minutes. Break into pieces and store in a ziplock bag.

6. Store the Ginger Bites in an airtight container for up to 5 days at room temperature, or in the refrigerator for up to 2 weeks. Allow the chocolates to come to room temperature in the storage container before serving.

CHOCOLATE

Guide

IMPORTED CHOCOLATES AND
DOMESTIC ARTISANS

Bolivar
206 E. 60th St.
New York, NY 10022
212-838-0440

Burdick Chocolates
P.O. Box 593
Walpole, NH 03608
800-229-2419 or 603-756-3701

Bernard Callebaut Chocolates
1313 First SE
Calgary, Alberta,
Canada T2G 5L1
800-661-8367

Candinas Chocolates
2435 Old P.B.
Verona, WI 53593
800-845-1554

Chocolat L'africain from Angelina in Paris
Fresh Neuhaus Chocolates
Teuscher Chocolate
De Bauve et Gallais
Imported by Chocolat of Seattle
2039 Bellevue Square
Bellevue, WA 98004
888-826-4354

Chocolates by Francois Payard
1032 Lexington Ave.
New York, NY 10021
212-717-5252 Ext. 193

Chocolats Le Français
269 S. Milwaukee Ave.
Wheeling, IL 60090
847-541-1317

Christopher Norman Chocolates
75 Bank St., Suite 2K
New York, NY 10014
212-677-3722

Cloud Nine
300 Observer Highway, 3rd Floor
Hoboken, NJ 07030
800-398-2380

Fran's
1300 East Pike
Seattle, WA 98122
800-422-FRAN

Godiva
139 Mill Rock Rd. East, Suite 2
Old Saybrook, CT 06475
800-9-GODIVA

House of Brussels
208-750 Terminal Ave.
Vancouver, British Columbia Canada V6A 2M5
800-661-1524
604-687-1524

Laderach and Carma of Switzerland
Imported by Albert Uster
9211 Gaither Rd.
Gaithersburg, MD 20877
800-231-8154

La Maison du Chocolat
1018 Madison Ave.
New York, NY 10021
212-744-7117

Le Belge
37 Commercial Boulevard, Suite 108
Novato, CA 94949
415-883-6781

Leonidas
485 Madison Ave.
New York, NY 10022
800-900-CHOC
212-980-2608

Manon (Belgium)
Louise de Bruin (Switzerland)
Marquise de Sevigny (France)
Altmann & Kuhn (Austria)
Imported by Rococoa Faerie Queene Chocolates
415 Castro St.
San Francisco, CA
415-252-5814

Martine's
Bloomingdale's
1000 3rd Ave., Sixth Floor
New York, NY 10022
212-705-2347

Neuhaus Chocolate Boutique
922 Madison Ave.
New York, NY 10021
212-861-2800

Perugina
520 Madison Ave.
New York, NY 10022
800-272-0500
212-688-2490

Richart Design et Chocolat
7 E. 55th St.
New York, NY 10022
800-RICHART

Teuscher Chocolates of Switzerland
620 Fifth Ave.
New York, NY 10020
800-554-0924 (for store information)

VARIETY CHOCOLATES, CHOCOLATE
BARS, NOVELTIES

Bridgewater Chocolates
P.O. Box 131
Bridgewater, CT 06752
800-888-8742

Brown & Haley
P.O. Box 1596
Tacoma, WA 98401
253-593-3000

Chocolations
13190 Telfair Ave.
Sylmar, CA 91342
800-808-2263
818-364-8300

Cocoa Mill Chocolate Company
115 West Nelson St.
Lexington, VA 24450
800-421-6220

Divine Delights
24 Digital Dr., Suite 10
Novato, CA 94949
800-4-HEAVEN
415-382-7585

Donnelly Chocolates
1509 Mission St.
Santa Cruz, CA 95060
831-458-4214

Ethel M
P.O. Box 98505
Las Vegas, NV 89193-8505
800-438-4356

Fannie May
1123 West Jackson Blvd.
Chicago, IL 60607
800-890-3629

Green Mountain Chocolate Company
35 Crossroads
Waterbury, VT 05676
800-686-8783
802-244-8356

Guittard Chocolate Co.
10 Guittard Rd.
Burlingame, CA 94010
800-HOT-CHOC
415-697-4427

Harbor Sweets
251 Jefferson St., Ms-4
Waldoboro, ME 04572-6011
800-243-2115

Josephine Krick Chocolates
available from:
Sugar Plum Candies
5500 Old Cheney Rd.
Lincoln, NE 68516
402-420-1900

Joseph Schmidt Confections
3489 16th St.
San Francisco, CA 94114
800-861-8682

Karl Bissinger French Confections
3983 Gratiot St.
St. Louis, MO 63110
800-325-8881

Krum's
4 Dexter Plaza
P.O. Box 1020
Pearl River, NY 10965
800-ME-CANDY or 914-735-5100

Lake Champlain Chocolates
431 Pine St.
Burlington, VT 05401
800-634-8105

Li-Lac Chocolates
120 Christopher St.
New York, NY 10014
800-624-4874

Malley's
14822 Madison Ave.
Lakewood, OH 44107
800-448-4279
216-226-8300

Moonstruck Chocolatier
6663 Beaverton Hillsdale Highway, Suite 194
Portland, OR 97225
800-557-6666

Mother Myrick's
P.O. Box 1142
Manchester Center, VT 05255
888-669-7425

Russell Stover & Whitman's Sampler
2707 Pembrooke
St. Joseph, MO 64506
800-477-8683

Sarris Candies
511 Adams Ave.
Canonsburg, PA 15317
800-255-7771

See's Candies
20600 South Alameda Blvd.
Long Beach, CA 90801
800-478-7339

Shelton-Mathews
2503 Mahoney
Youngstown, OH 44509
800-844-9497

Spiaggia
980 N. Michigan
Chicago, IL 60611
312-280-2750

Sweet Inspirations
P.O. Box 1014
Sag Harbor, NY 11963
800-772-0773
516-725-7400

Valentino
3115 Pico Blvd.
Santa Monica, CA 90405
310-829-4313

Vosges Haut-Chocolat
2105 W. Armitage
Chicago, IL
888-301-9866

CHOCOLATE NOVELTY SPECIALISTS

Chocolate Inn
7 Bixley Heath
Lynbrook, NY 11563
800-526-3437

Choco-Logo Confectionery Design
17 Elm St.
Buffalo, NY 14203
716-855-3500

Gosanko Chocolate Art
24700 Military Rd. South
Kent, WA 98032
800-584-7790
206-839-1147

Hearts & Flowers
P.O. Box 262
East Norwich, NY 11732
516-931-4239

Topographic Chocolate Co.
2601 Blake St., Suite 100
Denver, CO 80205
800-779-8985
303-292-6364

Tom & Sally's
6 Harmony Place
Brattleboro, VT 05301
800-827-0800
802-254-4200

CHOCOLATE GIFT BASKETS AND
MONTHLY DESSERT MAIL ORDER CLUBS

Desserts Monthly
1400 West and 400 North
Orem, UT 84057
800-477-6575
801-225-6575

Essentially Chocolate
15737 Crabbs Branch Way
Rockville, MD 20855
800-FYI-GIFT
310-770-5660

Fancy Foods Gourmet Club
Washington, DC
800-576-3548
808-752-7032

The Heavenly Chocolate Club
480-C Scotland Rd.
Lakemoor, IL 60050
800-800-9122
800-MAMA-MIA

COOKIES, BROWNIES, BAKED GOODS

Black Hound
111 North Tenth St.
Brooklyn, NY 11211
800-344-4417

Carlie's Brownies
63 Greene St., Suite 601
New York, NY 10012
888-4-CARLIE
212-334-3566

Catamount Cookies
P.O. Box 2354
Manchester Center, VT 05255
888-768-2883
802-297-1121

Charles and Laurel Desserts
537 Greenwich St.
New York, NY 10013
212-229-9339
888-810-CAKE

Cheryl & Co. Cookies
646 McCorkle Blvd.
Westerville, OH 43082-8708
800-443-8124

Fairytale Brownies
2724 North 68th St., Suite 1
Scottsdale, AZ 85257
800-324-7982
602-276-9643

International Brownies
Shaws Place
602 Rear Middle St.
Weymouth, MA 02189
800-230-1588

Joan & Annie's Brownies
Williston, VT
800-588-2769

Miss Beasley's & Miss Grace Cakes
16805 South Central Ave.
Carson, CA 90746
800-367-2253
800-800-2253

Mrs. Field's Cookies
321 West Landale Dr.
Salt Lake City, UT 84115
800-331-8278

Nancy's Healthy Kitchen
18320-2 Oxnard St.
Tarzana, CA 91356
800-626-2987
818-776-2670

Selma's Best of the Batch Cookies
P.O. Box 160756
Alamonte Springs, FL 32716
800-992-6654
407-884-9433

CHOCOLATE COMPANIES

ADM Cocoa
12500 W. Carmen Ave.
Milwaukee, WI 53225-6199
414-358-5700

Baker's Chocolate
800 Westchester Ave.
Rye Brook, NY 10573
800-431-1001

Barry Callebaut
1500 Suckle Highway
Pennsauken, NJ 08110
800-836-2626
609-663-2260

Belcolade
Imported by Intercontinental Resources
115 River Rd.
Edgewater, NJ 07020
201-945-3700

The Blommer Chocolate Company
Blommer Dr.
E. Greenville, PA 18041
215-679-4472

Chocolates El Rey
El Rey America, Inc.
P.O. Box 853
Fredericksburg, TX 78624
800-ELREY-99
210-997-2200

Chocovic Chocolates
Available from International Foods & Confections
914-762-9480

Guittard Chocolate Co.
10 Guittard Rd.
Burlingame, CA 94010
415-697-4427

Hawaiian Vintage Chocolate
4614 Kilauea Ave., Suite 435
Honolulu, HI 96816
800-429-6246

Hershey Foods
PO Box 810
Hershey, PA 17033-0810
717-534-4200

Lindt & Sprungli
Stratham Industrial Park
1 Fine Chocolate Plaza
Stratham, NH 03885
800-338-0839
603-778-8100

M & M Mars
High St.
Hackettstown, NJ 07840
908-852-1000

Merckens Chocolate
150 Oakland St.
Mansfield, MA 02048
800-637-2536

Nestlé Foods/Peter's Chocolates
800 N. Brand
Glendale, CA 91203
818-549-6000

Rapunzel
122 Smith Rd.
Kinderhook, NY 12106
800-207-2814
518-758-6398

8060 Valencia St.
Aptos, CA 95003
800-743-7840
408-685-9658

Scharffen Berger Chocolates
250 So. Maple Ave. E & F
So. San Francisco, CA 94080
800-930-4528
415-866-3300

Valrhona
LMC 73rd, Inc.
Valrhona Chocolates Division
1901 Avenue of the Stars, Suite 1800
Los Angeles, CA 90067
310-277-0401

Van Leer Chocolate Corporation
110 Hoboken Ave.
Jersey City, NJ 07302
201-798-8080

Wilbur's Chocolate Co.
48 N. Broad St.
Lititz, PA 17543
800-233-0139
717-626-1131

World's Finest Chocolate
4801 S. Lawndale
Chicago, IL 60632-3062
800-366-2462
773-847-4600

TEMPERING MACHINES

ACMC Table Top Temperer
3194 Lawson Blvd.
Oceanside, NY 11572
516-766-1414

The Sinsation Chocolate Maker
Chandré LLC
14 Catharine St.
Poughkeepsie, NY 12601
800-3-CHOCLA

Hilliard's Chocolate System
Hilliard's
275 East Center St.
West Bridgewater, MA 02379-1813
508-587-3666

BAKING AND CANDY-MAKING EQUIPMENT AND INGREDIENTS

ABC Emballuxe, Inc.
650 Crémanzie Est
Montréal, Quebec Canada H2P 1E9
514-381-6978
Individual pastry molds, demisphere molds, acetates, and custom transfer sheets and silkscreens

Albert Uster
9211 Gaither Road
Gaithersburg, MD 20877
800-231-8154
Swiss baking and confectionery products, transfer sheets, professional tools

Assouline & Ting
314 Brown Street
Philadelphia, PA 19123
800-521-4491
215-627-3000
Chocolate, fruit purées, extracts, nut pastes, and flours

The Baker's Catalogue
King Arthur Flour
P.O. Box 876
Norwich, VT 05055-0876
800-827-6836
Specialty flours and baking ingredients

Barry Callebaut
St. Albans Town Industrial Park
RD #2, Box 7
St. Albans, VT 05478-9126
800-556-8845
Imported and domestic chocolate couvertures, praline paste, and molds

Beryl's Cake Decorating Equipment
P.O. Box 1584
N. Springfield, VA 22151
800-488-2749
703-256-6951
Tools for wedding cakes, chocolate work, and confectionery work

Braun Brush Company
43 Albertson Avenue
Albertson, NY 11507
800-645-4111
516-741-6000
Extensive line of brushes for the baking industry; custom-made brushes

Bridge Kitchenware Corp.
214 E. 52nd Street
New York, NY 10022
800-274-3435
212-838-6746
$3 for catalogue, refundable with first purchase. Bakeware, pastry equipment, molds, cake rings

The Candy Factory
12530 Riverside Drive
N. Hollywood, CA 91607
818-766-8220
$5 for catalogue, refundable with first purchase. Candy molds, custom molds, flavoring oils, colors

The Chef's Collection
10631 Southwest 146th Place
Miami, FL 33186
800-590-CHEF
Brand-name professional cookware, cutlery, and gourmet accessories

Chocolates à la Carte
13190 Telfair Ave.
Sylmar, CA 91342
800-808-2263
818-364-6777
Chocolate forms, signature chocolates

Chocolate Tree Ltd.
1048 North Old World
Third St.
Milwaukee, WI 53203
414-271-5774
Ambrosia and other chocolates

Continental Foods
1701 East 123rd St
Olathe, KS 66061
800-345-1543
Chocolate, pastry ingredients, kitchen equipment

A Cook's Wares
211 37th Street
Beaver Falls, PA 15010
412-846-9490
Chocolate, extracts, bakeware

Creative Culinary Tools
264 SE 46th Terrace
Cape Coral, FL 33904
800-340-7278
813-549-7715
Custom silkscreens, molds, grilles,
mold-making compound

Dairy Fresh Chocolate
57 Salem St.
Boston, MA 02113
800-336-5536
617-742-2639
Callebaut, Lindt, Peter's, and Valrhona chocolates

DeChoix Specialty Foods
58-25 52nd Avenue
Woodside, NY 11377
800-834-6881
718-507-8080
Chocolate, fruit purées and pastes, nuts, and
nut products

Demarle, Inc., USA
2666-B Rte 130 N
Cranbury, NJ 08512
609-395-0219
Silpats, flexipan molds, custom flexipans,
bread mats, and forms

Easy Leaf Products
6001 Santa Monica Blvd.
Los Angeles, CA 90038
800-569-5323
213-469-0856
23-karat edible patent gold leaf

European Connection Inc.
313 Mount Vernon Place
Rockville, MD 20852-1118
301-838-0335
Transfer sheets, flavoring oils

Ferncliff House
PO Box 177
Tremont City, OH 45372
937-390-6420
Van Leer, Guittard, Merckens, Nestlé chocolates;
candy- and pastry-making supplies

Gourmail
126A Pleasant Valley, #401
Methuen, MA 01844
800-366-5900, ext. 96
Valrhona chocolate couverture; Cocoa Barry
chocolate couverture

Gourmand
2869 Towerview Road
Herndon, VA 22071
800-627-7272
703-708-0000
Chocolate, flavorings, extracts, pastes

Harry Wils and Co, Inc.
182 Duane Street
New York, NY 10013
212-431-9731
Fruit purées, quick frozen fruits, chocolate,
extracts, nuts, and nut products

Holcraft Collection
P.O. Box 792
211 El Cajon Ave.
Davis, CA 95616
916-756-3023
Chocolate molds, antique molds

Hygo
P.O. Box 267
Lyndhurst, NJ 07071
800-672-9727
201-507-0447
Disposable pastry bags for cold and hot fillings

Industrial Plastics Supply Co.
309 Canal Street
New York, NY 10013
212-226-2010
Plastic demispheres, tubing, grilles

International School of Confectionery Arts
9290 Gaither Road
Gaithersburg, MD 20877
301-963-9077
Sugar, candy, and chocolate-making
equipment, Isomalt

Istanbul Express
2434 Durant Ave.
Berkeley, CA 94704
510-848-3723
Ghirardelli, Guittard, Merckens, McLindon
chocolates, chocolate molds

J.B. Prince Company
36 E. 31st Street, 11th Floor
New York, NY 10016
212-683-3553
Flexipans, cake rings, molds, stencil grilles, silpats,
baking tools and equipment

Kerekes
7107-13th Avenue
Brooklyn, NY 11228
800-525-5556
718-232-7044
Molds, baking tools, and equipment

Kitchen Witch Gourmet Shop
127 N. El Camino Real, Suite D
Encinitas, CA 92024
760-942-3228
Cocoa Barry chocolate

La Cuisine
323 Cameron Street
Alexandria, VA 22314
800-521-1176
Bakeware, molds, cake rings, silicone sheets,
flexipans, chocolate, pastes, Tahitian vanilla beans

Maison Glass
P.O Box 317H
Scarsdale, NY 10583
914-725-1662
800-822-5564
Nut pastes

Matfer Kitchen and Bakery Supplies
16249 Stagg St.
Van Nuys, CA 91406
800-766-0799
818-782-0792
Kitchen equipment, baking ingredients

Metropolitan Cutlery, Inc.
649 Morris Turnpike
Springfield, NJ 07081
888-886-6083
201-467-4222
Professional bakeware, butane stoves

New York Cake and Baking Distributors
56 W. 22nd St.
New York, NY 10010
800-94-CAKE-9
212-675-CAKE
Airbrushes, cake decorating supplies, gum
paste supplies

Paradigm
5775 SW Jean Rd., Suite 106A
Lake Oswego, OR 97035
800-234-0250
503-636-4880
Ghirardelli, Guittard, Lindt, Merckens, and
Peter's chocolates, dessert sauces

Patisfrance
161 East Union Avenue
E. Rutherford, NJ 07073
1-800-PASTRY-1
Fruit purées, chocolate, transfer sheets, nut
products, flavoring pastes, extracts, and essences

Pearl Paint
308 Canal Street
New York, NY 10013
800-221-6845, ext. 2297
212-431-7932, ext. 2297
Acetate, custom silkscreens, airbrushes, art supplies

Previn Inc.
2044 Rittenhouse Square
Philadelphia, PA 19103
215-985-1996
Digital pocket thermometer, chocolate molds,
candy-making supplies

Rafal Spice Company
2521 Russell
Detroit, MI 48207
800-228-4276
313-259-6373
Essential oils, extracts, flavorings

**Sweet Celebrations (formerly Maid of
Scandinavia)**
7009 Washington Avenue S.
Edina, MN 55439
800-328-6722
Chocolate, cake decorating and gumpaste
supplies, chocolate and candy making supplies
(including Nulomoline and lecithin), molds,
baking supplies, and equipment

The Sweet Shop
P.O. Box 573
Ft. Worth, TX 76101
800-222-2269
817-332-7941
Peter's chocolates

Sparrow
59 Waters Ave.
Everett, MA 02149
800-783-4116
617-389-4115
Cote D'Or, Valrhona, Schokinag,
Callebaut chocolates

Swiss Connection
501 First St.
Orlando, FL 32824
800-LE-SWISS
407-857-9195
Lindt, Barry Callebaut, Braun (coating) chocolates,
molds, mixes, ingredients, and supplies

Swiss Chalet Fine Foods, Inc.
Miami (headquarters): 305-592-0008
Houston: 713-868-9505
Los Angeles: 562-946-6816
Marmalades, fruit compounds, chocolate, flavorings

Tomric Plastics
136 Broadway
Buffalo, NY 14203
716-854-6050
Chocolate molds, candy-making supplies

Tropical Nut & Fruit
P.O. Box 7507
1100 Continental Blvd.
Charlotte, NC 28273
800-438-4470
704-588-0400
Ambrosia, Baker's, Blommer, Guittard, Merckens,
Peter's, and more chocolates, dried fruits, and nuts

White Toque, Inc.
536 Fayette Street
Perth Amboy, NJ 08861
800-237-6936
Fruit purées, quick frozen wild berries, shelf-
stable fruit, and chocolate sauces

Williams-Sonoma
P.O. Box 7456
San Francisco, CA 94120-7456
800-541-2233
Chocolate, flours, baking pans, and equipment

**The Wilton School of Cake Decorating and
Confectionary Art**
2240 W. 75th St.
Woodridge, IL 60517
630-963-7100
Cake decorating supplies

Zabar's
2245 Broadway
New York, NY 10024
212-496-1234
Kitchen equipment, specialty food products

ORGANIZATIONS

American Boxed Chocolate Manufacturers
c/o Vorhaus & Co.
1700 Broadway
New York, NY 10019
212-554-7423

**Chocolate Manufacturers Association
of the U.S.A.**
7900 Westpark Dr., Suite A320
McClean, VA 22102
703-790-5011

Chocolate Lovers of America
P.O. Box 4121
Laguna Beach, CA 92652

Metric Conversion Guide

LENGTH

To convert	Multiply by
inches into millimeters	25.4
inches into centimeters	2.54
millimeters into inches	0.03937
centimeters into inches	0.3937
meters into inches	39.3701

VOLUME

To convert	Multiply by
quarts into liters	0.946
pints into liters	0.473
quarts into milliliters	946
milliliters into ounces	0.0338
liters into quarts	1.05625
milliliters into pints	0.0021125
liters into pints	2.1125
liters into ounces	33.8

WEIGHT

To convert	Multiply by
ounces into grams	28.35
grams into ounces	0.03527
kilograms into pounds	2.2046

TO CONVERT FAHRENHEIT TO CELSIUS

Subtract 32, then multiply this number by $\frac{5}{9}$

For example: $350°F - 32 = 318 \times \frac{5}{9} = 176.6°C$

TO CONVERT CELSIUS TO FAHRENHEIT

Multiply by 9, divide this number by 5, then add 32

For example: $180°C \times \frac{9}{5} = 324 + 32 = 356°F$